INCLUSIVE URBAN SCHOOLS

INCLUSIVE URBAN SCHOOLS

edited by

DOUGLAS FISHER, PH.D.
and

NANCY FREY, PH.D.
San Diego State University

Baltimore • London • Sydney

Paul H. Brookes Publishing Co.
Post Office Box 10624
Baltimore, Maryland 21285-0624

www.brookespublishing.com

Typeset by A.W. Bennett, Inc., Hartland, Vermont.
Manufactured in the United States of America by
Sheridan Books, Fredericksburg, Virginia.

The students in this book have been disguised or are based on composite
accounts. Identifying details have been changed to protect confidentiality. In
some instances, certain schools have been disguised. In other instances, real
school names have been used by consent of the schools' principals.

Library of Congress Cataloging-in-Publication Data

Inclusive urban schools / edited by Douglas Fisher and Nancy Frey.
   p.   cm.
   Includes bibliographical references and index.
   ISBN 1-55766-663-6
   1. Urban Schools—United States—Case studies.   2. Inclusive education—
United States—Case studies.   3. Children with disabilities—Education—United
States—Case studies.   I. Fisher, Douglas, 1965–   II. Frey, Nancy, 1959–
LC5131.I47 2003
371.9′046′091732—dc21

                                                  2003052481

British Library Cataloguing in Publication data are available from the British Library.

CONTENTS

About the Editors

Douglas Fisher, Ph.D., is Associate Professor in the College of Education, Department of Teacher Education, at San Diego State University, where he teaches classes in English language development and literacy. His background includes adolescent literacy and instructional strategies for diverse student needs. He often presents at local, state, and national conferences and has published numerous articles on reading/literacy, differentiated instruction, accommodations, and curriculum development. He serves as Director of Professional Development for the City Heights Educational Collaborative in San Diego, California.

Nancy Frey, Ph.D., is Assistant Professor in the College of Education, Department of Teacher Education, at San Diego State University, where she teaches classes in literacy and differentiated instruction. Her background includes early literacy, writing instruction, and instructional strategies for diverse learners. She is the author of numerous books and articles on curriculum development and modification and on reading/literacy. She serves as Professional Development Schools Coordinator for the City Heights Educational Collaborative in San Diego, California.

ABOUT THE CONTRIBUTORS

Nancy Annaromao, B.S., is teaching under a special education teacher license for her first year, having completed a post-baccalaureate special education teacher program at University of Wisconsin–Milwaukee. She teaches first grade at Congress School in Milwaukee, Wisconsin.

Jan Bloedorn, M.A., came to the field of special education later in life, as a second career. She found that it is true what they say—it is all about timing. Had she not pursued her careers as she did, she would have never had the privilege of knowing Dr. Maureen W. Keyes—the greatest advocate for children with challenges and their families that she has ever met.

Rebecca Jean Bond, M.A., is a high school teacher in San Diego, California, who supports students with disabilities in their general education classes. She also teaches at a local community college in its Disability Services Management program. Her interests include behavioral support strategies, peer tutoring, and curriculum modification.

Kerri L. Briggs, Ph.D., is Special Assistant to the Assistant Secretary for Elementary and Secondary Education at the U.S. Department of Education. In this capacity, Dr. Briggs contributes to the implementation of efforts associated with the No Child Left Behind Act of 2001 (PL 107-110). Prior to her appointment at the U.S. Department of Education, she was Director of Evaluation at the Texas Center for Reading and Language Arts, The University of Texas at Austin. She completed her doctoral degree in education policy and organizational studies at the University of Southern California.

Fredda Brown, Ph.D., is Professor in the Graduate Program in Special Education at Queens College, The City University of New York.

Leonard C. Burrello, Ed.D., is Professor of Education and Chair of Educational Leadership at Indiana University–Bloomington. He is co-author of *Stories of Leadership Transforming Schools* (manuscript submitted for publication, 2003).

Barbara E. Buswell, M.A., is Executive Director of PEAK Parent Center, a federally funded Parent Training and Information Center with two Colorado locations. She is the mother of three children, one of whom received special education services. Prior to creating PEAK Parent Center, Ms. Buswell was a secondary English teacher. Ms. Buswell has a master's degree in inclusive educational reform.

Tayotis Caldwell, M.S., was taught by his mother to always dream. Born in the projects of Milwaukee, Wisconsin, Mr. Caldwell set his goals on getting his mother out of the projects and into what life's dreams were made of—"the world." With the help of his sixth-grade teacher and the support of his family, he achieved that dream and has vowed to inspire students to dream and achieve.

Elizabeth Castagnera, M.A., is a high school teacher in San Diego, California, who supports students with disabilities in their general education classes. She also teaches at a local community college in its Disabilities Service Management program. Her interests include modifications and accommodations for inclusive high school education as well as quality of life issues for people with disabilities.

Mark W. Doyle, M.S.Ed., owns and operates Everyone is Welcome in St. Charles, Illinois. Mr. Doyle is nationally known for his work in the area of community inclusion. He is invited to speak at many workshops, state and national conferences, and local parent group meetings. Mr. Doyle teaches graduate-level special education courses as Adjunct Instructor for National-Louis University, Evanston, Illinois. He is an active member of both TASH and the Illinois TASH chapter, has served as President and Past President of the Illinois TASH Board of Governors, and has served on several International TASH committees. He also serves as President on the Board of Directors of Kane-Kendall Case Coordination Services for Kane and Kendall counties in Illinois.

Meaghan S. Edmonds, M.A., received her bachelor's degree from the University of Notre Dame in Indiana and her master's degree from The University of Texas at Austin. As a research associate, Ms. Edmonds is pursuing a doctoral degree in educational psychology and works at the Texas Center for Reading and Language Arts, The University of Texas at Austin. Her work at the Texas Center for Reading and Language Arts focuses on evaluation projects and professional development initiatives. Her research interests include policy evaluation and observation methods.

Mary Falvey, Ph.D., is Professor in the Division of Special Education at California State University, Los Angeles, where she coordinates the credential and master's degree programs in severe disabilities. She also coordinates the master's degree program in inclusive education. Dr. Falvey presents, writes, and provides technical assistance to numerous school districts and state departments of education.

Alan Gartner, Ph.D., is Director of Research at the Office of the Mayor, City of New York. Previously, Dr. Gartner served as Co-Director of the National Center on Educational Restructuring and Inclusion; Dean for Research at The Graduate Center, The City University of New York; and Executive Director at the Division of Special Education, New York City Public Schools. With Dorothy Kerzner Lipsky, he is co-author of three books and many journal articles. Dr. Gartner is author or co-author of an additional 15 books.

Bill Henderson, Ed.D., is Principal of the Patrick O'Hearn Elementary School, an inclusive school in Boston. He also is a frequent contributor at conferences.

Denyse Patel Henry, M.A., was formerly an exceptional student education instructor who supported students with disabilities in general education classrooms. She received her bachelor's degree in education—specializing in special education, varying exceptionalities—from Florida Atlantic University. She received her master's degree in curriculum and instruction, with an emphasis in reading, from San Diego State University in California. Ms. Henry is employed as a consultant for an educational software company.

Keona Jones, M.E.L., is Assistant Principal at Congress School in Milwaukee, Wisconsin. She is a former special education teacher who is now in her fifth year as a professional educator.

Craig H. Kennedy, Ph.D., is Associate Professor of Special Education and an investigator at the John F. Kennedy Center for Research on Human Development at Vanderbilt University in Nashville, Tennessee. His research interests include a variety of issues related to people with severe disabilities.

Maureen W. Keyes, Ph.D., is Associate Professor in the Department of Exceptional Education at the University of Wisconsin–Milwaukee. She taught children with disabilities for 18 years in public schools before completing her doctoral degree at the University of Wisconsin–Madison. With Dr. Colleen A. Capper and Dr. Elise Frattura, Dr. Keyes co-authored the book *Meeting the Needs of Students of All Abilities: How Leaders Go Beyond Inclusion* (Corwin Press, 2001). Her research focuses on the role of spirituality on justice in the lives of educator/leaders and what school leaders can do to transform schools for justice and equity.

Dorothy Kerzner Lipsky, Ph.D., is Director of the National Center on Educational Restructuring and Inclusion at The Graduate Center, The City University of New York. As Director, Dr. Lipsky conducts research, provides training and technical assistance, disseminates material, and develops policy concerning restructuring and inclusion. Previously, she served as a school superintendent, principal, classroom teacher, chief administrator, and school board member. Dr. Lipsky is author and co-author of many journal articles, including one cited by the federal court in *Oberti v. Board of Education of the Borough of Clementon School District* (1993), and three books, the most recent honored as an "Academic Book of the Year" by the American Library Association.

James McLeskey, Ph.D., is Professor and Chair of the Department of Special Education at the University of Florida in Gainesville. He has worked for 15 years with local schools as they have developed, implemented, and evaluated inclusive programs. He and Dr. Nancy L. Waldron co-wrote *Inclusive Schools in Action: Making Differences Ordinary* (Association for Supervision and Curriculum Development, 2000), which describes this work.

Craig A. Michaels, Ph.D., is Associate Professor of Special Education within the Department of Educational and Community Programs at Queens College, The City University of New York.

Mary Beth Minkley, M.E.L., is Assistant Superintendent for the Racine Unified School District in Racine, Wisconsin. At the direction of Dr. Thomas Hicks, this urban district has initiated the inclusive Quality District Model with Continuous Progress in reading for 2003 and in math for 2004. As former Principal of Congress School, Milwaukee, Wisconsin, Ms. Minkley redesigned Congress School to be totally inclusive for children with mild to severe disabilities. In addition, she extended the official school year to 196 student contact days. The success of these changes was evidenced by the U.S. Department of Education's designating Congress School as a Blue Ribbon School of Excellence for the 2000–2001 school year.

Beth Mount, D.P.A., has been searching for 25 years for new ways to discover, affirm, and describe the beauty and strength in the lives of people with disabilities, their families, and the people who support them. For 12 years, she has been involved with person-centered planning and community building in New York City. Living in New York City has given Dr. Mount the opportunity to deepen her understanding of the universal themes in the spirituality and artwork of world cultures. As another way to help tell people's stories, she works on fabric art (see http://www.capacityworks.com) while her son does his homework.

Connie Lyle O'Brien and **John O'Brien** work in partnership to learn about building more just and inclusive communities for people with disabilities, their families, and their allies. They use what they learn to advise people with disabilities and their families, advocacy groups, service providers, and governments and to spread the work among people interested in change by writing and through workshops. They are affiliated with the Center on Human Policy at Syracuse University in New York state (http://soeweb.syr.edu/thechp) and the Marsha Forest Centre (formerly the Centre for Integrated Education and Community; http://www.inclusion.com/C-Marsha.Forest.Centre.html) in Toronto, Canada.

Laura Owens, Ph.D., earned her master's degree in special education from the University of Wisconsin–Milwaukee and her doctoral degree from the University of Wisconsin–Madison. She is Assistant Professor in the Department of Exceptional Education at the University of Wisconsin–Milwaukee and is the Director/Founder of Creative Employment Opportunities (CEO) in Milwaukee, an employment agency for individuals with disabilities. Previously, Dr. Owens was a general and special educator.

J. Michael Peterson, Ph.D., is Professor in Teacher Education at Wayne State University in Detroit, Michigan. He has 30 years of experience in working with children and adults with disabilities. Dr. Peterson is co-author of *Inclusive Teaching: Creating Effective Schools for All Learners* (Allyn & Bacon, 2003).

Alice Leilani Quiocho, Ed.D., is Associate Professor in the College of Education at California State University–San Marcos. She has 28 years of experience in public schools as a teacher, elementary and middle school principal, and director of professional development. She still works closely with public schools. Dr. Quiocho's areas of expertise include language and literacy, English language development, and biliteracy.

Virginia Roach, Ed.D., is Deputy Executive Director of the National Association of State Boards of Education in Alexandria, Virginia. She has conducted evaluation studies, written numerous articles, and presented across the United States regarding the inclusion of students with disabilities as part of general education reform. A lifelong advocate for people with disabilities, Dr. Roach began her career as a special education teacher.

Fredda Rosen is Director of Job Path in New York City. She and her colleagues support people with developmental disabilities in their efforts to make choices about their lives. Job Path, which was established in 1978, strives to be a reflective organization in which staff thoughtfully consider the implications of their work and carefully listen to people.

Diane Lea Ryndak, Ph.D., specializes in educational services for students with significant disabilities in inclusive general education environments. In conjunction with teaching courses on this subject at the University of Florida in Gainesville, Dr. Ryndak works with several school districts to facilitate systematic sustainable reform for the benefit of all students.

Caren L. Sax, Ed.D., C.R.C., teaches in the Rehabilitation Counseling program in San Diego State University's Department of Administration, Rehabilitation, and Postsecondary Education. She coordinates the Certificate of Rehabilitation Technology program with the College of Engineering and distance-teaches coursework as part of an online master's degree program. She has directed federal- and state-funded grant projects focused on the following areas: assistive technology applications, new approaches for continuing education opportunities for community rehabilitation personnel, and systems change efforts that have improved school-to-work transition services for students with disabilities. With Dr. Colleen A. Thoma, Dr. Sax co-authored *Transition Assessment: Wise Practices for Quality Lives* (Paul H. Brookes Publishing Co., 2002).

Judy A. Schrag, Ed.D., is a national educational consultant and Co-Principal of Education and Human Services Group, Port Orchard, Washington. She is a policy consultant, project evaluator, expert legal consultant, and group facilitator. She was previously Director of the Office of Special Education Programs (OSEP) at the U.S. Department of Education. Dr. Schrag also was Washington State's Assistant State Superintendent of Public Instruction for Special Services and was Idaho State Director of Special Education.

Ron Taylor, M.F.A., is an author, filmmaker, father, and teacher in Milwaukee, Wisconsin. At Light On Communications (http://www.lightoncom .com), he and Dr. Maureen W. Keyes work on various projects to enhance the skills of those who nurture children with disabilities.

Jacqueline Thousand, Ph.D., coordinates the special education credential and master's degree programs at California State University–San Marcos. She continues her research and advocacy to promote inclusive education, collaborative teaming and learning, co-teaching, creative problem solving, and self-determination for the benefit of students with and without disabilities.

Alice Udvari-Solner, Ph.D., holds a joint appointment at the University of Wisconsin–Madison in the Department of Curriculum and Instruction and the Department of Outreach. The graduate and undergraduate courses that she teaches on accommodating diverse learners in general education environments are integral to the university's elementary, secondary, and special education teacher certification programs. Central to Dr. Udvari-Solner's teaching and research are the design of differentiated instruction, effective curricular adaptations, collaborative teamwork among general and special educators, and systems change toward inclusive education.

Richard A. Villa, Ed.D., has worked with thousands of educators and parents across North America and around the world in developing and implementing instructional support systems for educating all students within general education environments. Dr. Villa has been a classroom teacher, special education teacher, director of pupil personnel services, special education director, and director of instructional services, and he has taught graduate and undergraduate courses.

Nancy L. Waldron, Ph.D., is Associate Professor in the Department of Educational Psychology at the University of Florida in Gainesville, and serves as Director of the School Psychology program. Her teaching and research interests include academic assessment and intervention, school consultation, the inclusion of students with disabilities in general education, and preparation and credentialing issues in school psychology.

To Cheryl Liles,
Director of the Florida Inclusion Network,
for her commitment to creating a world
that is safe for every child

chapter 1

URBAN EDUCATION AND INCLUSIVE SCHOOLS

An Introduction

NANCY FREY AND DOUGLAS FISHER

> Inclusion is a part of the very culture of a school or school dis-
> trict and defines how students, teachers, administrators and oth-
> ers view the potential of children. Hence, inclusion has
> implications for how schools are organized and restructured, the
> curriculum, instruction, teacher training, and the types of mate-
> rials and instructional technology used in the school. In fact,
> many schools have become inclusive schools when they restruc-
> tured under current school reform efforts. (Roach, Ashcroft,
> Stamp, & Kysilko, 1995, p. 7)

The underlying value of inclusive education is that all children should be
welcomed members of the classroom, school, and larger community. Certainly a great deal of research has been done on supporting individual students with disabilities in general education classes (e.g., Fisher & Ryndak,
2001; McGregor & Vogelsberg, 1998). This substantial database suggests
that it is more than possible to provide access for students with disabilities
to the best available educational practice and to demonstrate positive student achievement in inclusive environments (Kennedy & Itkonen, 1994;
McLeskey & Waldron, 2000).

Unfortunately, most service delivery models have failed to make effective and inclusive practices readily available and accessible to most students
with disabilities (U.S. Department of Education, 2001). After decades of
specific federal support through the Individuals with Disabilities Education
Act (IDEA), only 27% of all students receiving special education services
between 1996 and 1998 graduated with a diploma, compared with 75% of
students without disabilities (U.S. Department of Education, 2000). Much

of this is due to the alarming dropout rates seen among students with individualized education programs (IEPs). Life beyond high school is even less hopeful. According to the National Longitudinal Transition Study (Wagner, Blackorby, Cameto, Hebbeler, & Newman, 1993), only 20% of youth with disabilities are independent in the domains of work, residential activities, and social activities 3–5 years out of school.

Schools are being held accountable not only for the achievement of students with disabilities, but also for the achievement of typical students. Data on student achievement underscore the failure to make best and emerging educational practices available to all youth (Haycock, 2001). This impact is most significant in large urban communities. Specifically, urban districts have average student dropout rates of more than 40%, and more than 70% of urban students read, write, and compute below grade level (Haycock, 2001).

Student achievement among urban youth with and without disabilities needs to become a national priority. Focusing on the achievement of *all* urban youth is logical and justified, as many youth with disabilities who are urban residents are also socioeconomically, culturally, and linguistically diverse (Bondy & Ross, 1998; Oswald, Coutinho, Best, & Singh, 1999). Educational reform is critically important, but only if it is designed and evaluated in terms of its impact on student achievement (Langer, 2001).

A great deal is known about policies and practices that are positively linked to student achievement, particularly for students with disabilities in inclusive environments. The literature substantiates, for example, the importance of active parent–school partnerships (Schaffner & Buswell, 1995), challenging and relevant curricula (Fisher, Sax, & Pumpian, 1999), individualized supports and accommodations (Fisher & Frey, 2001), positive behavior supports and strategies (Koegel, Koegel, & Dunlap, 1996), peer interactions (Cushing & Kennedy, 1997), transition planning (Sax & Thoma, 2002), and access to the full range of programs and supports available to children without disabilities (Meyer, Park, Grenot-Scheyer, Schwartz, & Harry, 1998).

Tremendous parallels exist between the problems and solutions in reforming education within urban environments and those in promoting effective inclusive education. Because a large percentage of students with disabilities are educated in urban environments, these problems and solutions cannot and should not be viewed separately; unfortunately, they are. Specific reform initiatives, and individuals involved in implementing these reforms, are too often fragmented within and across site, district, state, and national levels.

To many people, the problems and needs of urban America seem insurmountable. It is easy to conjure images of massive poverty, dilapidated private and public structures, crime, vandalism, drug and alcohol problems, child abuse and neglect, and gang fights. Urban and suburban housing and employment patterns continue to result in ethnic and racial segregation and urban unemployment. African American urban males are more likely to die of gunshot wounds than from any other cause (Centers for Disease Control and Prevention, 2001). For many, these urban realities become correlated with the facts that more than 75% of urban youth are not Caucasian, that more than 325 languages are spoken in these multiethnic communities, that 19.7% of urban children are English language learners, and that enormous disparity exists in the educational achievement curves of urban youth (Council of the Great City Schools, 2001; Hart, Atkins, & Ford, 1998; U.S. Census Bureau). To people who presume causal relationships in these correlations, urban educational reform appears pointless. People who draw such conclusions often move away from urban areas, vote for private school voucher initiatives, give up, and blame the victims.

Other people, however, are careful to look for ways of tapping the strength and resilience that exist in these urban environments. They know that children cannot be held accountable for their educational failures when little public equity exists, especially when factors such as the size, age, condition, and resources of school buildings; the amount of per-student spending; and the degree of tracking are all negatively represented in the inner cities. The fact that many urban children show no marked differences from others when they enter school but increasingly fail in comparison after each year of attendance (Feldman, 2001) turns the attention to school and community structures (i.e., policies and practices) and away from a pessimistic deficit view of and expectations for urban children.

People who believe that educational reform is possible work hard to bring resources to ideas, ideas to actions, and actions to outcomes. Whether they are involved in building new schools from the ground up with widespread community partnerships or in aggressively challenging traditional tracking, testing, curriculum, or pedagogy, they demonstrate that change is possible. The reforms that seem most successful in urban environments have a grass roots means of engaging and empowering parents and members of the community to partner with administrators, teachers, and students.

Similar to the challenges of urban education in general, the problems and needs of children with disabilities, especially those with severe disabilities, may seem insurmountable. Obvious physical disabilities, adaptive devices and equipment (e.g., gastrointestinal tubes), behavioral disruptions, and unusual verbalizations are outside the realm of experience and understanding of many people. These realities become correlated with the fact that educating children with disabilities is expensive and challenging. To people who conclude that disability is the cause of poor educational achievement, special education and including children with disabilities in general education classrooms appears to be pointless and counterproductive. People who draw such conclusions often question why teachers' time and resources are spent on these children at the expense of "normal kids who could really learn something."

Other people, however, are careful to look for ways of tapping the strength and resilience of these children and their families. They know that children cannot be held accountable for their educational failures because with effective services and supports, all children, including those with severe disabilities, can function and contribute across a wide range of educational, employment, home, and social endeavors. The failure to establish effective service delivery models and implement effective and emerging best practices is a public decision that becomes blurred when children are pitied and their parents and advocates are devalued.

People who believe inclusive education is possible work hard to bring resources to ideas, ideas to actions, and actions to outcomes. They, too, are involved in building new schools from the ground up; establishing new community partnerships; and aggressively challenging current placement, testing, curriculum, and pedagogy, thus demonstrating that change is possible. Their reforms seem to be most successful in environments where administrative leadership exists, general and special educators are partners in curriculum design and instruction, and parents and other community members are involved and empowered in the life of the school. These reforms seem to be most pervasive and best sustained when special education reform and the inclusion of students with disabilities are solidly based in general education reform efforts at all levels of educational policy and practice.

For inclusive urban schools to be successful, several changes must occur. First, the traditional paradigm for explaining student achievement must be challenged. Too often, students in urban communities—especially students with disabilities in urban communities—are not expected to achieve, and this becomes a self-fulfilling prophecy. Thus, achievement and school structures that facilitate achievement must be the focus.

Second, ways to bring the best educational research into urban schools and classrooms must be created. For example, as Briggs and Edmonds (Chapter 4) note, there is considerable evidence regarding effective literacy instruction for students with and without disabilities. The challenge is to ensure that teachers in urban schools have access to that research and are supported in implementing its findings with all the students in their classrooms.

Third, social and health services offered within the school must be coordinated with the educational program offered. Many students in urban schools require related services such as health care, dental care, and social supports. Too often, these services are not coordinated with the educational program, which leads to fractured and duplicated services that are costly and inefficient.

Fourth, large urban schools must be personalized. Far too many students attend the urban school campus without knowing even one adult well. Not only are these students at higher risk for dropping out, but also their achievement often suffers in these hostile environments (Darling-Hammond, Ancess, & Ort, 2002).

Fifth, it must be ensured that assessment and placement practices do not result in de facto segregation into special education programs. In too many school systems, African American and Hispanic/Latino students (especially males) are overidentified for special education services (Meyer & Patton, 2001; Patton, 1998; Wehmeyer & Schwartz, 2001). Predictably, these students do not have access to general education classrooms. Rather, they are segregated from their peers who have not been identified as needing such services. Along these lines, it must be remembered that overidentification can occur as a by product of increased school accountability and state assessment systems (McGill-Franzen & Allington, 1993).

Finally, no discussion of urban schools is complete without a discussion of school safety. It goes without saying that this is a priority in any school. Students should feel safe—and actually be safe—at school. Students also need to feel that they are part of a learning community. It has become apparent that too often, violent students are isolated, ostracized, and marginalized by both peers and teachers (Garbarino & DeLara, 2002).

The challenges of urban education and inclusive schooling overlap considerably. By coordinating the efforts of educators and the community on increasing achievement, access to meaningful instruction, and safe environments, success can take place on both fronts. Researching and reporting these efforts creates a spread of effect that occurs across additional schools. This book has been written with this effect in mind.

OVERVIEW OF THIS BOOK

Inclusive Urban Schools focuses on urban schools in which inclusive education has become part of the overall reform effort. The book contains examples of success and stories of ongoing challenges, as both are instructive for change agents who want to push the special education service delivery system further. In addition, commentaries from prominent scholars follow each chapter; these extend the implications from one school district to many.

In reading this book, we encourage the reader to consider several questions. These guiding questions are not easily answered, but they are important and will likely be the focus of significant discussion as IDEA enters its fourth decade of defining special education for students with disabilities.

- Is a common core of knowledge about effective instructional practices shared by inclusive educators and urban educators?
- How can supports and services for all students be provided in inclusive environments?
- How can related services be coordinated, and how can these services be integrated into the general education classroom?
- Given the diversity in urban schools, how do schools create effective environments that support the diverse learning needs of students?
- Is disability part of the human experience like race, gender, and culture? If so, how do and should schools respond?
- What should schools do when the majority of their students live in poverty?
- What are effective school and district change models and initiatives?
- How can individuals create change if outdated models drive the system?
- What changes in referral and assessment systems are needed to ensure that students receive the necessary assistance to be successful?
- What should the special education system be accountable for—process, product, or both?
- How have lawsuits helped or hindered special education reform?
- What new roles and responsibilities do special educators, general educators, family members, and administrators need to assume in inclusive urban schools?
- What role should the district office or state department of education play in promoting inclusive schooling practices?

And, finally, the essential question that frames the work of all of this book's contributors:

- What will it take for inclusive schools to become the norm?

Now, sit back and explore the range of possibilities that exist for inclusive schooling in urban schools. Enjoy the range of perspectives that this book's authors bring to the discussion.

REFERENCES

Bondy, E., & Ross, D.D. (1998). Confronting myths about teaching black children: A challenge for teacher educators. *Teacher Education and Special Education, 21,* 241–254.

Centers for Disease Control and Prevention. (2001). *Web-based Injury Statistics Query and Reporting System (WISQARS).* Atlanta, GA: Author.

Council of the Great City Schools. (2001). *Educating English language learners in the nation's urban schools.* Washington, DC: Author.

Cushing, L.S., & Kennedy, C.H. (1997). Academic effects of providing peer support in general education classrooms on students without disabilities. *Journal of Applied Behavior Analysis, 30,* 139–151.

Darling-Hammond, L., Ancess, J., & Ort, S.W. (2002). Reinventing high school: Outcomes of the Coalition Campus Schools Project. *American Educational Research Journal, 39,* 639–673.

Feldman, S. (2001). Closing the achievement gap. *American Educator, 25*(3), 7–9.

Fisher, D., & Frey, N. (2001). Access to the core curriculum: Critical ingredients for student success. *Remedial and Special Education, 22,* 148–157.

Fisher, D., & Ryndak, D.L. (2001). *The foundations of inclusive education: A compendium of articles on effective strategies to achieve inclusive education.* Baltimore: TASH.

Fisher, D., Sax, C., & Pumpian, I. (1999). *Inclusive high schools: Learning from contemporary classrooms.* Baltimore: Paul H. Brookes Publishing Co.

Garbarino, J., & DeLara, E. (2002). *And words can hurt forever: How to protect adolescents from bullying, harassment, and emotional violence.* New York: The Free Press.

Hart, D., Atkins, R., & Ford, D. (1998). Urban America as a context for the development of moral identity in adolescence. *Journal of Social Issues, 54,* 513–530.

Haycock, K. (2001). Youth at the crossroads: Facing high school and beyond. *Thinking K-16, 5*(1), 1–3.

Kennedy, C.H., & Itkonen, T. (1994). Some effects of regular class participation on the social contacts and social networks of high school students with severe disabilities. *Journal of The Association for Persons with Severe Handicaps, 19,* 1–10.

Koegel, L.K., Koegel, R.L., & Dunlap, G. (Eds.). (1996). *Positive behavioral support: Including people with difficult behavior in the community.* Baltimore: Paul H. Brookes Publishing Co.

Langer, J.A. (2001). Beating the odds: Teaching middle and high school students to read and write well. *American Educational Research Journal, 38,* 837–880.

McGill-Franzen, A., & Allington, R.L. (1993). Flunk 'em or get them classified: The contamination of primary grade accountability data. *Educational Researcher, 22*(1), 19–22.

McGregor, G., & Vogelsberg, R.T. (1998). *Inclusive schooling practices: Pedagogical and research foundations. A synthesis of the literature that informs best practices about inclusive schooling.* Pittsburgh: Allegheny University of Health Services, Consortium on Inclusive Schooling Practices. (Available from Paul H. Brookes Publishing Co., Baltimore)

McLeskey, J., & Waldron, N.L. (2000). *Inclusive schools in action: Making differences ordinary.* Alexandria, VA: Association for Supervision and Curriculum Development.

Meyer, G., & Patton, J.M. (2001). *On the nexus of race, disability, and overrepresentation: What do we know? Where do we go?* Newton, MA: National Institute for Urban School Improvement.

Meyer, L.H., Park, H.S., Grenot-Scheyer, M., Schwartz, I.S., & Harry, B. (Eds.). (1998). *Making friends: The influences of culture and development.* Baltimore: Paul H. Brookes Publishing Co.

Oswald, D.P., Coutinho, M.J., Best, A.M., & Singh, N.N. (1999). Ethnic representation in special education: The influence of school-related economic and demographic variables. *Journal of Special Education, 32,* 194–206.

Patton, J.M. (1998). The disproportionate representation of African-Americans in special education: Looking behind the curtain for understanding and solutions. *Journal of Special Education, 32,* 25–31.

Roach, V., Ashcroft, J., Stamp, A., & Kysilko, D. (1995). *Winning ways: Creating inclusive schools, classrooms, and communities.* Alexandria, VA: National Association of State Boards of Education.

Sax, C.L., & Thoma, C.A. (2002). *Transition assessment: Wise practices for quality lives.* Baltimore: Paul H. Brookes Publishing Co.

Schaffner, C.B., & Buswell, B.E. (1995). *Connecting students: A guide to thoughtful friendship facilitation for educators and families.* Colorado Springs, CO: PEAK Parent Center.

U.S. Census Bureau. *American FactFinder.* Retrieved January 28, 2003, from http://factfinder.census.gov

U.S. Department of Education. (2000). *To assure the free appropriate public education of all children with disabilities (Individuals with Disabilities Education Act, Section 618): Twenty-second annual report to Congress on the Implementation of the Individuals with Disabilities Education Act.* Washington, DC: Author.

U.S. Department of Education. (2001). *To assure the free appropriate public education of all children with disabilities (Individuals with Disabilities Education Act, Section 618): Twenty-third annual report to Congress on the Implementation of the Individuals with Disabilities Education Act.* Washington, DC: Author.

Wagner, M., Blackorby, J., Cameto, R., Hebbeler, K., & Newman, L. (1993). *The transition experiences of young people with disabilities: A summary of findings from the National Longitudinal Transition Study of special education students.* Menlo Park, CA: SRI International. (ERIC Document Reproduction Service No. ED365086)

Wehmeyer, M.L., & Schwartz, M. (2001). Disproportionate representation of males in special education services: Biology, behavior, or bias? *Education and Treatment of Children, 24*(1), 28–45.

chapter 2

LEARNING TOGETHER AND FROM EACH OTHER

Inclusive Practices at the O'Hearn in Boston

BILL HENDERSON

PARENTS OF CHILDREN with significant disabilities had demanded that it happen. Families and advocates had been arguing that under federal and state laws, their children had the right to attend general education class-rooms in their neighborhood schools. The Boston Public Schools (BPS) system wanted to wait, but the parents were tenacious. The superintendent acquiesced, and at his recommendation the Boston School Committee, the governing body for BPS, decreed that Patrick O'Hearn Elementary School would become an inclusive school beginning in September 1989.

UNDERSTANDING OUR SCHOOL COMMUNITY

BPS boasts a storied legacy in American education. It was the first school district in the United States, established in 1647. The first elementary school in the country, Mather Elementary in Dorchester, opened in 1639 and is still in operation. More than 350 years of providing public education to Boston's school children has continually challenged our ways of think-ing and working. Our constituency continues to reflect the changing face of America. BPS serves a student body that is 48% African American, 28%

Hispanic, and 15% Caucasian. As of 2002, 74% of the students enrolled in the BPS system qualify for free or reduced lunch, and 19% of all students have individualized education programs (IEPs). This last figure stands well above the national average of 11.8%.

The profile of the O'Hearn, as it is known in Boston's unique vernacular, reflects BPS. The O'Hearn serves 220 students in early childhood (3- and 4-year-olds) through grade 5. Students have diverse ethnic and linguistic backgrounds, and the majority qualify for free or reduced lunch. Approximately 25% of the students have a disability. Looking at the indicators of success used to rate schools in Boston, the O'Hearn has become one of the district's higher performing schools. Student attendance is usually at or above 95%. Discipline problems resulting in office referrals or suspensions are relatively few. Since 1993, standardized test scores have exceeded the national median and have been near the top of the district median. In addition, under Boston's Controlled Choice Assignment Plan, which allows families to enroll in any elementary or middle school in their controlled choice assignment zone, the school is very popular and perennially oversubscribed. However, the O'Hearn looked vastly different prior to 1989.

BRINGING INCLUSION TO THE O'HEARN

In the spring of 1989, after the superintendent declared that the O'Hearn would become inclusive, BPS designated a task force of O'Hearn staff, parents, and administrators. The task force decided that inclusion would start that September in two kindergarten classrooms, then be phased in through grade 5 across the following 5 years. Staff already working at the O'Hearn could elect to stay or to transfer to other schools. A new principal was appointed, and four new teachers were hired. I am happy to report that I was that new principal, and I remain in that position.

The O'Hearn's first year as a school in transition was difficult. In 1989–1990, the standardized test scores of the first through fifth grades were below the national average and near the bottom of the city's test scores. There were frequent behavior problems in the upper grades, resulting in many discipline referrals to the office. The school experienced low enrollment at every grade level because not enough parents had selected the O'Hearn, opting instead to send their children to other schools in the controlled choice assignment zone. Although the kindergarten students in the inclusive classrooms seemed to make considerable progress, there were concerns about introducing inclusive practices into the other grades. After all, academic results indicated that the school could not afford to take attention away from the goals of increasing student achievement.

How did the O'Hearn develop into a successful inclusive school? The answer is in its mission statement. At the O'Hearn, all members of the school community "learn together and from each other." We have discovered that inclusive practices do not exist apart from the goal of increasing student achievement. Indeed, inclusive practices have been a key component in meeting and exceeding those goals.

First Steps

Soon after the decision was made for the O'Hearn to become an inclusive school, the school's staff and community members moved to a site-based management model (Patterson, Purkey, & Parker, 1986). A team of elected representatives from all stakeholder groups formed a School Site Council to serve as the governing body for the school. On a monthly basis, parent leaders met with teacher representatives and the principal to make decisions about personnel, programs, and the budget.

Developing a Mission Statement

The first responsibility of the School Site Council was to craft a school mission statement. The entire school community was solicited for ideas. Teachers, support staff, and parents wrote about their hopes and dreams for the school. Students themselves drew pictures depicting whom the school should serve and what the school should do. The council then discussed all of the entries and used a consensus process to draft the mission statement. The initial statement read,

> The O'Hearn is an inclusive school. Students in regular education, students with special needs, and students considered talented and gifted learn together and from each other. Teachers and support staff team to work with all children in integrated classrooms.

Each year, the council reviews the mission statement and revises it to reflect the O'Hearn's goals and values. Yet, the school's commitment to inclusion has been steadfast, as articulated in the mission statement of 2002:

> The overall goal of our school is to help all students learn and succeed. We are committed to helping each child develop intellectually, socially, emotionally, and physically to his/her fullest potential. O'Hearn students will learn skills, increase their knowledge, and develop positive values. They will demonstrate growth in confidence, capabilities, and character.

Establishing Ways of Work

The School Site Council has set the ground rule that no conversations criticizing individual students, staff, or parents are acceptable in this public shared decision-making forum. At council meetings, teachers and parents regularly discuss topics ranging from literacy instruction to recess procedures. The members neither identify nor discuss the individuals responsible for implementing the programs but, rather, the needed goals, procedures, and resources.

Finding and Keeping the Best Personnel

Another responsibility of the School Site Council is to craft job descriptions for all new teacher and paraprofessional positions. All O'Hearn staff must demonstrate a commitment to inclusion, an ability to collaborate with many staff, an ability to make curricular adaptations, a willingness to learn new instructional techniques, and a willingness to connect with families. The council has also recruited specialists who can integrate the arts with the general curricula and therapists who can work creatively in classrooms. The School Site Council has a personnel subcommittee—consisting of two teacher representatives, a parent representative, and the principal—that interviews and selects new teachers, specialists, therapists, and paraprofessionals.

The job description for all new special or general education teachers is nearly identical. Although special and general education teachers have different certifications and areas of expertise, all assume responsibility for effectively teaching students with and without disabilities. This means that general education teachers might need to learn some things about specialized instruction, including the use of assistive technology, and special educators might need to learn more about the general curriculum and strategies for teaching reading, writing, and math. Certain tasks might not be a teacher's primary responsibilities, but each teacher's assistance in inclusive classrooms is necessary and expected. Therefore, professional development for teaching staff is ongoing and extensive. Both the insights of outside partners and the growing expertise of the school's staff contribute to the O'Hearn's knowledge base of effective practices for teaching all children.

Addressing the Budget and Funding

Although the district sets general staffing positions and salaries, the O'Hearn School Site Council has the authority to solicit and designate additional discretionary funds. For example, Title I federal funds may be used to hire an additional homeroom teacher, thus reducing all classroom sizes. Commonwealth transition funds that are earmarked to support students working below grade level are used to provide small group and tutoring support. Many of these services occur after school. Under the auspices of the O'Hearn After School Program, a parent leader works with a staff member to coordinate this extension of the school day and to offer a range of enrichment activities. Funds from the State Department of Mental Retardation have been solicited and provided to ensure that supports are available for students with more significant disabilities. These funds cover most overhead expenses of the after-school programs that now serve 70% of the total school population.

Reconfiguring Staffing Patterns

As discussed previously, the O'Hearn committed to a 5-year plan to develop inclusive practices at all grade levels. Negotiating with the school district to obtain the staffing patterns necessary to support this plan proved to be somewhat difficult. Would the school be able to justify and sustain the co-teaching model developing in the first two kindergarten classrooms and use it throughout the other grades? It was decided that beginning with the 1990–1991 school year, teachers previously assigned to the Title I room and the resource room would work in inclusive homerooms. General education teachers would be allocated based on the BPS system formula of 1 teacher for every 25 students at the upper grades and 1 teacher for every 22 students in the lower grades. Special education personnel would be allocated according to the funds already being spent for students with disabilities if these students were otherwise served in separate classrooms or private placements.

The following example demonstrates how staffing for special education personnel was determined: Students who were considered "multiple handicapped" (a state designation) had been traditionally served in classrooms of six students, with one special education teacher and two paraprofessionals. In other words, each student in that class cost one sixth of the three adults' combined salaries and benefits. Thus, for every child with the "multiple handicapped" designation who had or might have attended such a classroom in another Boston school, the O'Hearn requested and received an equivalent amount of funds from the school district.

Of course, this calculation represents a theoretical cost. Students with similar disability designations may still vary in their needs. Yet, the general staff funding principle still applies—the funds that would have been spent on personnel for students with disabilities in separate classrooms or private placements should continue to be used in general education classrooms.

Having a relatively large number of students with significant needs has allowed the O'Hearn to afford a co-teaching model throughout the other grades. A few classrooms also have a paraprofessional working with particular students on a full- or part-time basis. Therapists are allocated as they are in any other school—by the nature and frequency of the services stipulated in the students' IEPs. The major difference between traditional and inclusive schools is that in an inclusive school like the O'Hearn, most of the instruction and specialized services provided by educators and specialists occur in general classroom areas. This has created the added bonus of freeing up space on campus that once was used solely for separate special education services.

The O'Hearn attributes much of its success to its attention to these structures. The creation of a School Site Council to serve as a shared decision-making body composed of teachers, administrators, and families has been central to subsequent innovations. The development of a mission statement keeps the school on track toward achieving its goals while adhering to its values. The realities of running a school have continued to be challenging. The O'Hearn has been creative in its pursuit of funding and its staffing pattern design. In addition, the school is committed to finding and keeping personnel who reflect both the excellence and equity that has come to be associated with the O'Hearn.

Collaboration

In its first year as an inclusive school two teachers—a general educator and a special educator—were assigned to each of the two inclusive kindergarten classrooms. Initially, much attention was given to sensitizing the general education teacher regarding disability issues. Insights about specific disabilities and appropriate special education instructional strategies were shared. There were indeed wheelchairs and other pieces of adaptive equipment to accommodate, feeding and toileting techniques to learn, and IEPs and other paperwork to complete.

It soon became apparent that the special education teachers had as much to learn. Certification in special education did not mean that teachers had experience working with students with all varieties of disabilities. In addition, working in general education classrooms meant that they had to become familiar with the principles and practices of the general curriculum—literacy, math, and other subject areas. Finally, the special education teachers also needed to learn appropriate instructional strategies for students working at and above grade level.

The O'Hearn also learned together that having more than one adult in a classroom requires some changes. Historically, teaching has been a fairly isolated profession. In inclusive classrooms, teachers, therapists, and paraprofessionals not only have to figure out how to share space and responsibilities but also how to plan for individual children and specific lessons. Setting aside designated times to plan is important, but a willingness to touch base periodically throughout the day is critical as well.

As of 2003, the dynamics of working so closely with other adults varies from room to room at the O'Hearn. In some situations, one adult assumes responsibility for most of a classroom's students and another adult for just a few of the students. In other situations, the adults share their responsibilities. In both scenarios, it is critical that the professionals communicate regularly and appropriately before, during, and after lessons. Finding the time and best ways to do this are challenging. However, inclusion will not be successful unless professionals collaborate well.

At the O'Hearn, the teachers quickly learned to work collaboratively with noninstructional school staff. Lunch monitors needed to learn and reinforce certain special eating techniques. The school secretary had to become familiar with and employ particular greeting strategies for students who used alternative communication tools. The school's custodian, popular with all of the students, became one of the best motivators. The reward of having special time with him has been worked into quite a few positive behavior support plans and student schedules.

Faculty, staff, and administrators have learned to collaborate with the students as well. This has been one of the most pleasant surprises of inclusive schooling because we have witnessed what the children do for each other. Whether it is staying in line on the way to the library, painting the picture for the class mural, thinking of a good topic for the writing journal, figuring out the best way to do a multistep math problem, or encouraging someone to eat all of his or her lunch, the students themselves are sometimes the best teachers. This was initially humbling to professionals, but it soon became an important teaching strategy.

The O'Hearn has added an early childhood classroom to the campus, so the presence of young learners along with some students with significant disabilities means that many extra hands are needed at arrival and dismissal times. Each week, one of the upper-grade classes is designated to work as helpers. The students from this class wait by the door with the supervising teachers and escort those needing assistance to their classrooms or the breakfast area. It is important to note that all students—with and without disabilities—are expected to be morning helpers. Although this means that one group has a slightly delayed start each day, more teachers are freed up to be in classrooms to greet their students and get them working as quickly as possible. It also allows the helpers to start their day knowing that they are a real asset to their school.

Peer Tutoring

Encouraged by this success with the morning helpers and recognizing the many other requests for additional assistance, a peer tutoring program was established. Students have 40 minutes for lunch and recess. Students in grades 3–5 are encouraged to serve as peer tutors during one 40-minute lunch/recess period per week. After these older peer tutors finish eating, they proceed with a special pass to another location in the school to provide assistance. This might entail reading to a younger student, helping another with classwork, assisting a class during lunch and recess, or playing with children in kindergarten. This work is voluntary, and peer tutors only keep their jobs if their own classwork is satisfactory. Students with and without disabilities serve and contribute. They enjoy this opportunity immensely and gain a great sense of accomplishment.

These structural supports have become mainstays at the O'Hearn. The school's continued attention to site-based governance, budget, staffing, and collaboration are essential factors in its ability to offer coordinated, sophisticated services to students with and without disabilities. Nonetheless, these are the tent poles of the learning experience at the O'Hearn. With these structural matters well in hand, attention is now given to the curriculum.

RESPONSIVE CURRICULUM AT THE O'HEARN

The O'Hearn's standards-based curriculum is organized around Boston's Citywide Learning Standards, which seek to create stimulating and challenging learning environments that are sensitive to students' needs and learning styles. The school focuses on literacy for all. Students are expected to read at or above grade level or to achieve the goals stipulated in their IEPs. The arts and technology are utilized extensively to enhance students' learning and performances. However, the school does not subscribe to a philosophy of lockstep curriculum, materials, and instructional strategies. This "one size fits all" approach is not good pedagogy even in so-called homogeneous classes. At the O'Hearn, every classroom contains students working at, above, slightly below, and well below grade level, so using a single approach was never an option.

Many of the students with disabilities participate in activities at grade level with adaptations, an umbrella term for accommodations and modifications. Accommodations are changes in the ways students use and respond to instruction and materials (Fisher, Frey, & Sax, 1999). Other students with disabilities need modifications. Modifications are changes to the content that the student is responsible for mastering (Fisher & Frey, 2001).

Some students need modifications because the grade level material is too difficult or too easy. Others need more extensive modifications, including reduction of test items, IEP objectives that are infused into classroom activities, or access to additional peer or professional supports (Fisher et al., 1999). For these students, it is important to determine the most essential and relevant aspects of the general curriculum and then streamline the curriculum appropriately. An IEP team—consisting of at least a special education teacher, a general education teacher, a parent, an administrator, related services staff, and the student (as appropriate)—makes decisions regarding the nature, level, and frequency of the specialized materials and instruction necessary for a student with a disability. The following subsections show how these adaptations are utilized in classrooms at the O'Hearn.

Reading

Teachers regularly read aloud—an important activity in a balanced literacy program (Gambrell & Mazzoni, 1999). Children with and without disabilities enjoy listening to their teacher reading an interesting book aloud, and it is essential for all learners to hear fluent models of reading (Beck & McKeown, 2001). Adaptations are easily created for students who need them to benefit from the reading. For example, a child with visual impairments might need further descriptions of pictures, whereas a student with a hearing impairment might sit closer to the teacher or use an audio trainer microphone and headset. A student with a very limited attention span might be required to stay seated with the group for a shorter period of time.

Independent reading also occurs on a daily basis in all classrooms. During this time, students quietly read a book of their own choosing (Worthy & Broaddus, 2001–2002). Again, students with disabilities are easily included in this instructional activity. Those who have difficulties processing print might listen to their books on cassette tapes or through a talking computer. Other students might read a book using simplified print or picture versions. Of course, this means that a wide variety of books on many levels are available in each classroom. However, providing a broad range of materials is sound instructional practice, not a compromise for students with disabilities.

During guided reading, students work directly with general or special education teachers, reading specialists, vision or speech-language therapists, or instructional aides to read material that is on the child's instructional level. Children usually receive guided reading on a daily basis either in small groups or individually (Fountas & Pinnell, 1996). Decoding, word analysis, and comprehension strategies are taught according to children's levels and needs during this activity. Because guided reading is delivered at the student's instructional level, any accommodations are subsumed within the context of the lesson. Again, this is not done only for students with disabilities—it represents sound pedagogy for all students.

Shared reading is a time when all students participate in activities around a particular story. The selected text is chosen to provide instructional opportunities around a strategy and to build background knowledge related to the content (Allen, 2000). Shared reading in the primary grades is often taught using an oversized book that allows all students to see the text while they are seated in a circle around the teacher. In the intermediate grades, text is projected on an overhead while students view their own copies at their desks. For instance, a third-grade class might read a newspaper article off an overhead transparency while the teacher discusses the processes that a fluent reader uses to make meaning of the text. Again, because the instructional arrangement already lends itself to differentiation of instruction, the teacher can model a variety of strategies using the same text.

Writing

Another important component of the O'Hearn's focus on literacy is writing. Students at all grade levels engage in writing as a means to consolidate the skills, strategies, and information that they learn across the day (Fearn & Farnan, 2001). As with the elements of balanced literacy instruction discussed previously, writing presents further opportunities to create adaptations that ensure access to general education curriculum. For instance, students in a third-grade classroom were asked to compose a report in response to the central themes of farm life and friendship in *Charlotte's Web* (White, 1952). Some students wrote long reports independently with pencils or pens or on a computer. Other students needed pencils or pens with special grips; adapted keyboards; or computer programs that talk, facilitate word retrieval, and feature predictive software for spelling. A few students wrote simplified responses and included many pictures. One child showed his responses by pointing to objects and pictures on charts and computer screens.

Home Reading

Literacy instruction at the O'Hearn extends to collaboration with the family. Like every other aspect of the curriculum, students with and without IEPs participate in the family literacy program. The School Site Council decided to implement a program that promotes reading at home at least four times per week for at least 20 minutes for the younger students and at least 30 minutes for the older students. Parent volunteers have been integral in helping make the home reading program a success. They visit the homes of new students assigned to the school and provide a free book as they describe the home reading and other programs. These parents also contact the homes and offer suggestions to the families whose children do not participate regularly. (Regular participation is defined as completion of the assignments at least 75% of the time.) An invaluable contribution from the parent volunteers is helping families of children with disabilities make accommodations to increase participation. In addition, they oversee the many awards given to students who return the contracts regularly or who make progress. Finally, they coordinate fundraisers and other programs to solicit and distribute plenty of appropriate reading material. At the inception of the home reading program, only 50% of students fulfilled and returned their home reading contracts on a regular basis. As of 2003, almost 95% do so on a regular basis. Reading performance in class and on standardized tests has also increased during this time. This finding is consistent with the research on the impact of family literacy programs on student achievement, especially for diverse learners (Yaden & Paratore, 2003).

Mathematics

Like reading, math has undergone major changes in schools across the country. Increased emphasis is being placed on investigations and multiple-step problem solving. As of 2003, principles of mathematics instruction focus on algebraic thinking, data analysis, number sense and operations, geometry, and probability (National Council of Teachers of Mathematics, 2000). The use of manipulatives has given all students more concrete ways to explore mathematics. This has been particularly helpful for students with and without disabilities who have difficulties with abstract concepts and operations.

For example, computing sales tax can be a challenging task for many fourth-grade students. In Massachusetts, sales tax is 5%. Most students can be taught the operation of multiplying by .05, but many do not understand the concept or do not know that they have made a mistake if they misplace the decimal. Students gain a clearer understanding of the concept when they are shown objects that represent 5% (e.g., a stack of 5 pennies next to a stack of 100 pennies, 3.2 ounces of water in a gallon bottle next to a full gallon of water). Students who are then asked to find and compare two objects, with one representing 5% of the other (e.g., 2 sticks, 2 piles of books), are better able to demonstrate their understanding. These concrete experiences provide ample opportunities to engage all students, including those with disabilities, in percentage activities.

The school store is a large, ongoing project designed to promote use of the mathematics. This structure, built by volunteers, is located in the cafeteria and is well stocked with school items like pencils, rulers, and stickers. Students created charts that describe the merchandise, and all transactions are conducted in cash. Students with and without disabilities love working in the store, and they do so on a regular basis in both sales and stocking capacities. The school store gives all students opportunities to become literate in mathematics.

Social Studies

The teaching and learning of social studies in Boston is a particular joy for staff and students because they live in a place considered by some to be the cradle of American history. The city offers amazing opportunities for active participation and immersion in events that students from other parts of the United States can only read about or view on a computer screen (Gallagher, 1998). The opportunity for experiential learning serves students with disabilities particularly well. For example, in this environment with authentic, hands-on opportunities for learning about historical events, students studying the Boston Tea Party used the Internet to gather and then share information. Other students created murals or dioramas depicting the event. In another corner of the classroom, students wrote a description of the arguments made for and against the Boston Tea Party and the actions taken by the colonists. They later acted out these arguments for the class. By creating multiple ways of entry into the study of a historical event, students with and without disabilities can make meaningful contributions to their classmates' understanding of the major concepts and themes.

Science

Experimentation should occur regularly in science instruction to promote development of scientific reasoning skills (Zimmerman, 2000). Whether it is measuring baking soda, connecting wires and bulbs, examining rocks, or growing plants under different conditions, students with a wide range of abilities have ample opportunities to participate. As with social studies, science teachers sometimes lecture or ask the students to read from a book. Many of the strategies previously described in the Reading subsection are utilized in science instruction to promote learning through content area reading (McKenna & Robinson, 1990). Students with and without disabilities are invited to discover the practical applications of their learning.

Visual and Performing Arts

As with so many aspects of the O'Hearn experience, the school collaborates with Boston's artistic community. Visiting artists regularly work with teachers on a variety of projects, including weaving and tapestries, murals, dance, music, and drama. Student products are exhibited during classroom presentations or schoolwide productions. Parents are eager to see their children shine, and attendance at these events is very high. Students also regularly make their presentations at local senior centers and nursing homes. Community service is not only a value but also a practice at the O'Hearn, and these experiences are beneficial to all involved.

Based on initial successes with the visiting artists, the O'Hearn strove to recruit specialists who had experience with the arts and with students with disabilities. The School Site Council wrote job descriptions, recruited, and hired teachers of the arts who would best serve the inclusive school. The physical education position was also converted into a dance position, and no loss of exercise and teamwork has occurred.

It is the belief at the O'Hearn that all children benefit from the arts. The arts provide insights into the world, other people, and oneself. Children find the arts exciting, so they are easily engaged. Through the arts, children with and without disabilities have a chance to excel, to communicate, to leave their mark, and to make their statements in a manner that focuses on opportunities, not obstacles.

The arts teachers have worked with classroom teachers, supporting classroom teachers in their efforts to cover a comprehensive curriculum. As a result, choreographing a dance highlighting the skeletal structure of the body, creating masks representing Egyptian pharaohs and mummies, singing and playing a Wampanoag tribal song on simple instruments, painting a mural on colonial times, and dramatizing a scene from a favorite book are all common occurrences at the O'Hearn. Student productions have dazzled many audiences in the school auditorium. Some groups of students have also been invited to perform at the Wang Center (a major public performing center), universities, conferences, and special functions.

Recess

Although recess is not a formal subject, many students consider it the highlight of the day. Indeed, recess is an important time not only to exercise and unwind but also to interact with peers. When students with disabilities first enrolled at the O'Hearn in 1989, the outdoor play space was a 40-yard by 60-yard area covered by macadam and a small grass perimeter. There were no play structures or equipment beyond the balls and jump ropes that students took outside with them. Parents and staff wanted to install an accessible play structure in the corner. It took the school 6 years to raise the $22,000 for the excavation, equipment, and 95 cubic yards of wood chips, but when the time finally came, parent volunteers assembled the structure and scattered the wood chips using buckets and wheelbarrows.

Children who use wheelchairs are now able to roll up the long ramp onto the main platform of the play structure. From there, they can get adult assistance if they want to hang on the monkey bars, bounce on the clatter bridge, or go down the slide. Other students with milder mobility impairments can do these activities independently or with peers. This interaction serves as yet another reminder of the opportunities that have opened for all children because, initially, the needs of a few had to be met.

There is no doubt that including students with disabilities in all curricular and extracurricular activities of a school requires many adaptations. The insights of many staff, parents, and students are needed to devise and implement the most appropriate adaptations. There is also no question that many of the adaptations for students with disabilities have proven to be tremendously beneficial for students without disabilities.

This chapter began by recounting how the O'Hearn changed when parents of children with disabilities sought to right inequality. Simply put, their actions have profoundly altered who teachers, students, administrators, staff, and parents are and how we view one another. Therefore, it is fitting that the final section of this chapter ends where it began—with family leadership.

SHAPING THE O'HEARN'S FUTURE THROUGH FAMILY LEADERSHIP

School administrators often mention the importance of family involvement, although often as a euphemistic phrase for a marginalized role that is confined to bake sale contributions and gift wrap sales (Gettinger & Guetschow, 1998). The O'Hearn is seeking to change that paradigm through parent leadership. Many of the innovations brought to the O'Hearn during the 1990s were initiated by families. Family leaders sought and received funds from a number of organizations, including the Institute for Responsive Education, the Boston Foundation, ReadBoston, and the Hyams Foundation. Through their tireless efforts, family members have provided leadership on many projects that have greatly benefited the school. They edit a school newsletter, the *O'Hearn Star*, which features articles from parents, staff, and students. Parent leaders coordinate special evening events, such as interactive math family nights and literacy demonstrations. They organized a family center dedicated to offering families an opportunity to socialize while learning about selected topics. They manage a weekly book-swap program and an annual book fair and established a partnership with the Museum of Fine Arts, Boston. In addition, they coordinate volunteer activities serving in classrooms, on field trips, in the library, and at many shows. It is hoped that the sustained leadership of families of the community will continue to redefine the school and how the vision and mission are realized.

CONCLUSION

In 1989, when demanding that their children with significant disabilities attend a neighborhood school with typically developing peers, parents had no idea what inclusion would look like. Their initial concern, particularly as pioneers, was simply trying to get their children with disabilities enrolled. Existing teachers and new staff banded together to welcome these students, and their commitment to inclusive practices for all students was critical.

In determining how to work together to create meaningful education for students with disabilities, staff had to identify and test new strategies. Four dynamics of teaching and learning—collaboration, adaptation, a focus on the arts, and family leadership—have become essential. They have transformed the O'Hearn and also helped to improve teaching and learning for all students at the school.

The O'Hearn views education as an ongoing and collaborative process. Family members are very involved, as evidenced by the school's family center and family outreach program. Parent and teacher representatives work together on school-based management. In addition, staff are involved in extensive professional development activities. Students serve as peer tutors and as community helpers. Many participate in after-school enrichment programs. The O'Hearn also works closely with local universities, businesses, cultural agencies, and neighborhood organizations to benefit its students to the utmost.

Collaboration started as a necessity at the O'Hearn. Including students with disabilities throughout the building meant that supports and services had to be made available throughout as well. The spirit and practice of collaboration now permeate the school. There is a genuine sense that the O'Hearn is a community of learners and a community of helpers. At times, trying to get the highest grade on a math test and playing hard to win the kickball game are still important. Yet, the commitment to and practice of determining how to help all learn and succeed together has made the school a better learning community for all. Everyone at the O'Hearn truly is "learning together and from each other."

REFERENCES

Allen, J. (2000). *Yellow brick roads: Shared and guided paths to independent reading 4–12.* Portland, ME: Stenhouse Publishers.

Beck, I.L., & McKeown, M.G. (2001). Text talk: Capturing the benefits of read-aloud experiences for young children. *Reading Teacher, 55,* 10–20.

Fearn, L., & Farnan, N. (2001). *Interactions: Teaching writing and the language arts.* Boston: Houghton Mifflin.

Fisher, D., & Frey, N. (2001). Access to core curriculum: Critical ingredients for student success. *Remedial and Special Education, 22,* 148–157.

Fisher, D., Frey, N., & Sax, C. (1999). *Inclusive elementary schools: Recipes for success.* Colorado Springs, CO: PEAK Parent Center.

Fountas, I.C., & Pinnell, G.S. (1996). *Guided reading: Good first teaching for all children.* Portsmouth, NH: Heinemann.

Gallagher, G.W. (1998). Using historical sites to help teach the United States survey. *Teaching History: A Journal of Methods, 23*(2), 77–80.

Gambrell, L.B., & Mazzoni, S.A. (1999). Principles of best practice: Finding the common ground. In L.B. Gambrell, L.M. Morrow, S.B. Neuman, & M. Pressley (Eds.), *Best practices in literacy instruction* (pp. 11–21). New York: The Guilford Press.

Gettinger, M., & Guetschow, K.W. (1998). Parental involvement in schools: Parent and teacher perceptions of roles, efficacy, and opportunities. *Journal of Research and Development in Education, 32*(1), 38–52.

McKenna, M., & Robinson, R. (1990). Content literacy: A definition and implications. *Journal of Reading, 34,* 184–186.

National Council of Teachers of Mathematics. (2000). *Principles and standards for school mathematics.* Reston, VA : National Council of Teachers of Mathematics.

Patterson, J.L., Purkey, S.C., & Parker, J.V. (1986). *Productive school systems for a nonrational world.* Alexandria, VA: Association for Supervision and Curriculum Development.

White, E.B. (1952). *Charlotte's web.* New York: Harper.

Worthy, J., & Broaddus, K. (2001–2002). Fluency beyond the primary grades: From group performance to silent, independent reading. *Reading Teacher, 55,* 334–343.

Yaden, D.B., & Paratore, J.R. (2003). Family literacy at the turn of the millennium: The costly future of maintaining the status quo. In J. Flood, D. Lapp, J.R. Squire, & J.M. Jensen (Eds.), *Handbook of research on teaching the English language arts* (2nd ed., pp. 532–545). Mahwah, NJ: Lawrence Erlbaum Associates.

Zimmerman, C. (2000). The development of scientific reasoning skills. *Developmental Review, 20,* 99–149.

Of Diamonds and Schools

Reflections on the O'Hearn in Boston

Barbara E. Buswell

Over the course of my career, I have had the opportunity to visit countless schools as they struggle to implement inclusive practices and are rewarded with the success of their efforts. As I visit schools, I sometimes think about diamonds. This metaphor helps me consider why some schools and classrooms outperform others. Some diamonds are rough, not yet shaped or cut. Others are cut but waiting to be polished. Still others are cut, polished, and set in beautiful surroundings. To my mind, schools are like that. Every school is a diamond—some have been polished and set. Others are uncut, unpolished, and waiting for the right forces to emerge. All have potential beauty and value.

As I read the chapter by Bill Henderson, Principal of Patrick O'Hearn Elementary School, I realized how fortunate the families and children are to be educated there. Though many schools have waiting lists, most are fairly exclusive. How exciting to know that a school has a waiting list because people are interested in inclusion! This commentary focuses on why it is important to learn from the O'Hearn. I share some of the lessons that I have learned from the O'Hearn and from my work at PEAK Parent Center. I conclude with a challenge—a challenge to help every student attend a school that is priceless.

LESSONS FROM THE O'HEARN IN BOSTON

Traditional measures of quality for diamonds—clarity, cut, carat, and color—organize this section. First, it is obvious that the O'Hearn has clarity of vision for itself, the children who attend it, and their families. The vision is respectful and honest. How powerful it is that each teacher at the school is able to articulate the vision of inclusion. It is important to note that this vision is driven by the families themselves, who are essential members of decision-making bodies at the school. It is reasonable to suggest that schools looking to learn from the O'Hearn might want to first examine their mission, vision, and beliefs. They must move past the rhetoric of "all children can learn" and "no child left behind" and help every member of the school community share the vision of inclusion with the same clarity as the teachers at the O'Hearn.

The cut for every diamond is based on what the diamond has to offer. Different cuts are appropriate for different diamonds, with the goal being to reflect as much light as possible. The O'Hearn has done just this. Each child can shine as a result of authentic assessments, the tapping of individual strengths, and individualized instruction. With the school's integrated curriculum and sophisticated arts program, children do not experience a narrow curriculum but, rather, a broad one that allows each student an opportunity to sparkle. A discussion about cut cannot overlook the importance of the light. In schools, the light that illuminates every child is a meaningful, vibrant, and responsive curriculum and instruction. Without these elements, access to general education curriculum is a hollow exercise—just as a diamond in the dark is a lump of coal.

On to the tricky subject of carat. The common perception is that size matters, but this misses the point. One size does not fit all. Diamonds are cut to different sizes for different purposes. This approach maximizes their potential, as value is based not only on size but also on cut. Each cut highlights the unique beauty and features of the raw element. The O'Hearn has learned this lesson. Students are not expected to be cut in the same shape or to perform at the same developmental level at the same moment in time. Instead, students are nurtured, instructed, and valued for the unique individuals they are. Again, curriculum and instruction play an integral role. When students are given multiple ways of processing information and demonstrating mastery, the lesson becomes neither too large or too small for learners, and they demonstrate success.

Finally, when I think about the multiple colors of diamonds, I am reminded of the diversity of experience in urban schools. In too many places, this diversity is a source of frustration or fear instead of an element of beauty. At the O'Hearn, diversity is honored as a strength. The teachers and families celebrate difference rather than hide it. Most important, the faculty of the O'Hearn hold a very broad definition of diversity and do not limit their views to race or ethnicity. As the director of a parent center, I am especially pleased to see the school's attention to nontraditional families who sometimes are forgotten or ignored by schools.

WAYS FOR LOCAL COMMUNITIES TO INVOLVE FAMILIES

In this commentary, I have identified traditional measures of quality for precious stones—clarity, cut, carat, and color—to compare diamonds and schools. In earlier work, I focused on a different set of C's to describe family involvement in inclusive schools (Buswell & Sax, 2002). I argued that parent involvement should be based on the following:

- *Credibility:* View parents as valued members of the team.
- *Continuity:* Assist families and schools in keeping records of success to prevent needing to relearn the supports a child needs.
- *Conscientiousness:* Pay attention to the details that influence success.
- *Constancy:* Acknowledge endurance or tenacity and the fact that parents are with their children for the long haul.
- *Creativity:* Understand that there are unique ways to achieve the dream of a happy and successful life.

Chapter 2 suggests that the O'Hearn has addressed each of these critical factors for success. However, every family cannot move to Boston so their children can attend that school. Many parents are unsure about how to locate schools like the O'Hearn in their own communities and to identify the quality indicators for inclusive education. PEAK Parent Center has assembled a number of guiding questions (see Table 2C.1) that parents can use when they visit schools to assess the schools' practices and commitment to educating all students well. For more information on using these questions to gain access to inclusive services and on advocating through the IEP process, see *Individual Educational Plans: Involved Effective Parents* (Seyler & Buswell, 2001).

Having said that, I would like to comment on traditional family involvement efforts. I cannot say how many times I have been asked to make cookies for the class or to cut papers for a teacher with the assumption that this is the primary way in which I can contribute to my children's classes or school. I am happy to do these things for my children and our schools. However, families can and should be involved in more substantial ways. For example, family members can serve on governance teams and work on school improvement plans. Innovative schools invite parents to attend and present at their professional development events. The O'Hearn stands as a case in point. Of course, O'Hearn families participate in the typical activities associated with parent involvement; however, their work goes well beyond the roles customarily assigned to parents. As active members of their School Site Council, they oversee hiring, budget, and grant funding. Their

Table 2C.1.   Guiding questions to ask when visiting schools

High standards for all students	Does the school believe that all students can achieve high standards—both academically and socially?
	How are those beliefs demonstrated?
	How are students expected to demonstrate the standards?
	How do the administrators, teachers, and family members communicate the value of excellence and the belief that all students can continually learn?
An emphasis on thinking skills	How does what the students learn reflect the purpose and goals of the school?
	How does the design of what the school teaches (curriculum) support all students in reading, writing, speaking, listening, math, technology, creative thinking, critical thinking, and problem solving?
	How do the instructional activities help students achieve high performance standards?
	How do individualized education programs (IEPs) show a commitment to high standards for students with disabilities?
Frequent monitoring and evaluation of student performance	How often are students provided feedback on how well they are doing?
	Who provides the feedback?
	Are students encouraged to evaluate their own performance?
	How are families provided with feedback on their son's or daughter's performance?
	What kinds of tests and other evaluation processes are used and what do they measure?
	Are accommodations provided and modifications made to tests and other evaluations so that all students can participate?
	How are student accomplishments spotlighted and celebrated?
An atmosphere of order and discipline	Is there agreement among teachers, administrators, and students on basic rules of conduct?
	How many rules are students expected to follow?
	How are the rules stated?
	Are there other aspects of the school that contribute to a sense of order? If so, what are they?
	How does the schedule promote learning?
	Is the schedule flexible with space and time? How?
An atmosphere of caring	How does the school ensure a safe environment for learning?
	How are alternatives to violence taught?
	Does the staff model tolerance and respect?
	Are students being taught to respect diversity and difference?

	How are students being taught to view situations from different perspectives?
Supports for students with unique learning needs	How are teachers modifying and accommodating a wide variety of student work?
	How are students helped to develop friendships and positive relationships?
	How are support and related services given to students with IEPs?
	Do all students at the school receive a diploma after graduation? If no, how is this determined?
	How are students with IEPs graded?
Teacher skills and beliefs	Do teachers believe they can teach all students?
	Are individual learning styles and needs taken into account?
	How do teachers use content and skill learning to facilitate both academic and socialization goals?
	How well do teachers know their subject areas?
	How well do teachers know their students?
Teacher styles	How do teachers instruct?
	How do the teachers manage the classrooms?
	How do the learning activities take multiple intelligences and cultures into account?
	How are teachers involved in advising and mentoring students, in addition to teaching?
Teacher support	How is common planning time made available to teachers?
	How and when do teachers think about what, why, and how they are teaching?
	What kinds of training and development options do staff have access to and use?
	Do school or staff members participate in a national network concerned with school reform or inclusive schooling?
Shared sense of organizational purpose	Is there a clear, schoolwide vision and set of goals for behavior and achievement? If so, where do you see them?
	How are the school's priorities clearly communicated to students, parents, and community members?
	Do you see a shared understanding of the goals among students, staff, administration, and parents?
	How is the school governed?
	Who makes which kinds of decisions?
Strong administrative leadership	Is collaboration in learning among faculty, staff, and students noticeable?
	How do the administrators foster vision building, ongoing improvement, and problem solving?

(continued)

Table 2C.1. *(continued)*

	How do the teaching staff and administrators get along?
	Do administrators encourage teachers to try new ways to teach more effectively to a diverse group of students?
A learning organization	Does administration support ongoing professional growth of the staff?
	How does administration encourage productive inter- actions with district-level programs? With families? With community partners?
	How is success with all students measured?
	How are families involved as full partners in decisions that affect them?
Family and community involvement	How does the school invite and expect family and com- munity involvement?
	How does the school create regular two-way, meaning- ful communication with families?
	How are families invited to help their sons and daugh- ters in the learning process?
	How does the school show appreciation of the tradi- tions of families from diverse cultures?
	What kind of parent involvement in academics occurs beyond the parent-teacher organization, parent's night, and extracurricular activities?
	Are other community organizations engaged in part- nerships with the school? How?
	How does the school involve community members, local businesses, and human services agencies to help students succeed?
	Does the school have a relationship with colleges or universities?
	Does the school have any agreements with local employers to place students in internships?

From Seyler, A.B., & Buswell, B.E. (2001). *Individual educational plans: Involved effective parents* (pp. 9–15). Colorado Springs, CO: PEAK Parent Center; adapted by permission.

outreach and community programs have become part of the fabric of their com- munity. Thousands of schools across the nation are faced with incredible chal- lenges that can strain their thin resources. The O'Hearn has figured out how to tap one of its most important reserves—the community itself.

CHALLENGE

Returning to the diamond metaphor, remember that these precious and valu- able stones began as lumps of coal. They become precious gems because of the pressures placed on them. They become valuable when someone attends to them, notes unique characteristics, polishes them, places them in settings that highlight their unique beauty, and provides them room to shine. My challenge for us all is to achieve no less for every child in the U.S. school system. The O'Hearn demonstrates that inclusive practices can be implemented and result in strong student achievement. We must attend to the children in our schools, to polish them, to carefully tailor their setting to ensure they have access to a setting in which they can shine! I know that parents often place pressure on educators. However, just as children are diamonds in the rough, educators—with pressure, polish, and light—shine as at the O'Hearn. In turn, they serve as diamonds for others to view and emulate. It is never too late to become a precious gem.

REFERENCES

Buswell, B., & Sax, C.L. (2002). The three C's of family involvement: Things I wish I had known. In C.L. Sax & C.A. Thoma, *Transition assessment: Wise practices for quality lives* (pp. 39–49). Baltimore: Paul H. Brookes Publishing Co.

Seyler, A.B., & Buswell, B.E. (2001). *Individual educational plans: Involved effective parents.* Colorado Springs, CO: PEAK Parent Center.

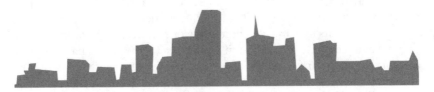

A Triangle of Supports in South Florida

Denyse Patel Henry and Nancy Frey

SUN AND SURF. Hot sand, hotter salsa. High fashion models and music from all over the Caribbean. These are the images readily associated with Miami by many Americans, especially those who live in colder climates. Although these carefully crafted marketing images are enviable, they obscure the real South Florida. Given the heavy emphasis on tourism, the region of Miami and Fort Lauderdale may not always be recognized as a major urban center with the challenges of rapid growth, a diverse population, stratified economic distribution, and an educational system straining to meet the needs of its students. A brief review of the history of the region illuminates these issues.

Early in the 20th century, heavy development began in the southeastern portion of Florida when entrepreneurs like Henry Flagler started building railroads and hotels. In 1925, development reached a peak, only to be devastated by several major hurricanes and the Depression of the 1930s. Economic development was once again revitalized by the armed forces training held in South Florida during World War II, and returning war veterans settled in the Miami area, spurring a new round of major population growth. The region again experienced an important change when Fidel Castro came to power in 1959, forcing thousands of refugees to flee Cuba. Many settled in Florida, especially in the Miami area. In 1980, South Florida experienced another population shift when Castro briefly opened Cuban ports and thousands of refugees fled the island. During the 1990s, the military coup in Haiti had an impact when thousands of refugees fled and settled in South Florida. In 1992, Hurricane Andrew spurred further growth shocks when tens of thousands of Miami-Dade residents permanently relocated to Fort Lauderdale to escape the devastation, placing tremendous strain on schools and other infrastructure.

At each turn, South Florida has endeavored to absorb the influx of large groups resetting in the area. Whether refugees fleeing oppressive governments, immigrants in search of a better life, or "snowbirds" relocating from the cold climates of the northeastern United States, the region has grown to accommodate new arrivals. At the beginning of the 21st century, the region celebrates its great diversity. Influenced by Cuban and Caribbean cultures, Miami is considered a trade center for Latin America. This growth has been both a blessing and a challenge. In the 1990s, Miami-Dade County grew by 9.8% overall (Bureau of Economic and Business Research, 1999); Broward County, where Fort Lauderdale is located, grew 29.3% (U.S. Census Bureau, 1999). South Florida now boasts a population of 3,681,000 people.

Miami is a city where "minorities" are the majority: 57.4% of Miami-Dade County residents are Hispanic/Latino, meaning that Miami is the second-largest Hispanic/Latino population center in the United States after Los Angeles (U.S. Census Bureau, 1999). Nowhere is this more evident than in Miami's public schools. In 2000, more than 54% of the students were Hispanic/Latino, and 11% were Caucasian (Miami-Dade County Public Schools, 2001). Broward County has a diverse student body as well: 57 languages are spoken by students from 155 countries (Broward County Public Schools, 2002). The region's 569 public schools educate more than 618,000 students, 87,000 of whom qualify for special education services under the Individuals with Disabilities Education Act (IDEA) Amendments of 1997 (PL 105-17). Although these urban schools continue to struggle with the challenges of population growth, as well as cultural and linguistic diversity, success stories are emerging regarding successful and meaningful inclusion of students with significant disabilities. These successes share several elements, including a framework for articulating student support and the availability of technical assistance.

SUCCESSES OF INCLUSIVE EDUCATION

Inclusive education in South Florida shares features with successful practices around the United States. Several essential elements emerged from a study researching useful practices for inclusion of students with significant disabilities (Ryndak, Jackson, & Billingsley, 1999–2000):

1. Promotion of inclusive values in the school
2. Collaboration between general and special educators
3. Collaboration between teachers and related service providers
4. Family involvement
5. Planned curriculum
6. Scheduled delivery of services
7. Assessment of and reports on student progress
8. Instructional and behavioral supports

However, cataloging important features of inclusive education is not enough. Successful practice necessitates the deliberate construction of these elements to increase the likelihood of sustained change. In South Florida, designing and implementing inclusive practices sometimes emerges through the collaboration of technical assistance networks, districts, and schools.

One source of technical assistance is the Florida Inclusion Network (FIN), funded by the state department of education. FIN was established in 1992 to develop a statewide network of people who would provide technical assistance to schools and school districts that wanted to establish, increase, or refine inclusive educational practices. Financial support is allocated from Florida's IDEA Part B dollars, and the total amount of funds set aside for the network is unmatched by any other state of similar size or demographics.

This chapter shares the stories of three students with significant disabilities from Miami and Fort Lauderdale. In each case, technical assistance from the network enhanced the work of administrators, educators, and families in creating a successful inclusive educational experience. Although each student has unique strengths and needs that demand an individualized approach, each plan began with a common framework to create an educationally responsive learning environment—a triangle of supports (Castagnera, Fisher, Rodifer, & Sax, 1998).

A TRIANGLE OF SUPPORTS

Including students with significant disabilities can be challenging when a one-size-fits-all approach is utilized in an attempt to conform students' experiences to existing practice. As each student is unique, so are the systems that support their learning in general education classrooms. Therefore, no single formula exists for supporting a student—it is more than just

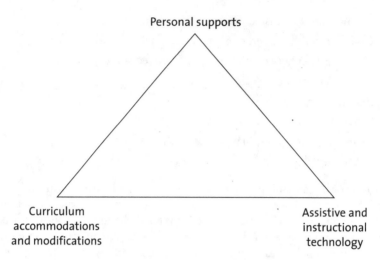

Personal supports

Curriculum accommodations and modifications

Assistive and instructional technology

Figure 3.1. Triangle of supports. (From Castagnera, E., Fisher, D., Rodifer, K., & Sax., C. [1998]. *Deciding what to teach and how to teach it: Connecting students through curriculum and instruction* [p. 18]. Colorado Springs, CO: PEAK Parent Center; reprinted by permission).

relying on the presence of a paraprofessional to "smooth over" the bumps that might occur. For instance, although experience has shown that students do need a system of personal supports to be successful, those supports may or may not include a paraprofessional. In addition to personal supports, all students require curriculum accommodations and modifications to ensure that learning is meaningful. Finally, assistive and instructional technology creates opportunities for access to enriching learning experiences (see Figure 3.1). These components comprise a triangle of supports (Castagnera et al., 1998). The following subsections examine these elements.

Personal Supports

All students, with or without identified disabilities, require a system of personal supports. For example, young students may need help with fasteners on clothing, and older students may need help locating reference materials in the media center. Educators have long known that anticipating student support needs and then strategically locating those supports ensures a smooth learning environment. This is no different for students with disabilities. However, a common error is failing to consider the full range of supports. Personal supports available to students generally fall in one of two categories—natural supports or specialized supports (Frey, 2001). Natural supports are those available to all students enrolled in a class, and they include the teacher and peers. They also include the supports available schoolwide, such as counseling services, social workers, and reading specialists. Specialized supports are associated with specific compensatory education programs like special education and Title I. Supports in this category include the special education teacher, paraprofessionals, and related service personnel (e.g., speech-language therapists, translators). These personal supports are more fully explained in Table 3.1.

When designing personal supports for a student with a disability, it is important to remember that uniform supports are rarely necessary across the entire day. One should consider the demands of the academic task or activity and tailor supports accordingly. The detrimental effects of excessive support on the academic and social development of students with individualized education programs (IEPs) are well documented (Brown, Farrington, Knight, Ross, & Ziegler, 1999; Giangreco, Broer, & Edelman, 1999; Jones & Bender, 1993). By utilizing a sophisticated system for describing and deploying a range of personal supports, social and academic isolation can be avoided.

Curriculum Accommodations and Modifications

Curriculum accommodations and modifications form the second element in the triangle of supports. Accommodations and modifications allow the student to gain access to the general education curriculum and successfully participate in general education classes.

Accommodations

Accommodations are changes in how the student obtains information and in how he or she demonstrates learning. When a student receives accommodations, the content and performance criteria does not change (Castagnera et al., 1998). Examples of accommodations include calculators, braille textbooks, and oral versions of tests. The accommodations are designed to support the student and provide the opportunity to demonstrate mastery.

There are four major forms of accommodations: format, response mode, assessment procedures, and setting (Beech, 1999). Some students have difficulty with the format or the manner in which information is presented. If students have difficulty with lists of vocabulary terms, small-print text, or printed directions, then the manner in which the information is presented should be adjusted. For example, rather than present a list of vocabulary terms for students to define at the beginning of an instructional unit, break the terms into small sets of related terms, then introduce each set as the information is discussed throughout the unit. Students with visual

Table 3.1.   Levels of personal support

Level of support	Description
Full-time	The staff person remains seated in close proximity to the student. This person may need to assist the student with materials and supplies needed to complete class assignments and group work. He or she acts as a role model for cooperation, collaboration, acceptance, and respect for all.
Part-time	The support staff provides assistance to the student at a predetermined time or on a rotating basis. The staff person maintains an awareness of curriculum and assignments to encourage the student's productivity, completion of assignments, tutorial, or organizational support.
Intermittent	Peer tutor and natural support, as well as support from paid staff, provide assistance in the classroom on a daily basis or every other day to troubleshoot immediate challenges and assist with surprise assignments or projects.
Peer tutor	A peer tutor provides support to the student in a variety of ways. He or she may assist in mobility to and from class, carrying or remembering materials, taking notes, completing assignments, and facilitating communication. The peer tutor may act as a role model for social and friendship interactions as well. The peer tutor may also participate in the development of support strategies. The tutor receives elective credits for providing this support.
Natural	Natural support is provided by students who are enrolled in the class. These students usually volunteer to provide support by taking notes, recording homework assignments, and so forth.
Supplemental	Supplemental support is provided by speech-language pathologists, orientation and mobility specialists, and physical and occupational therapists. These individuals provide their services within general education classrooms.

From Frey, N. (2001). Tying it together: Personal supports that lead to membership and belonging (p. 121). In C.H. Kennedy & D. Fisher, *Inclusive middle schools*. Baltimore: Paul H. Brookes Publishing Co.; adapted by permission.

impairments may require large-print versions of text, books on audiotape, or braille materials. If a series of directions is overwhelming for some students, use a flow chart to illustrate the sequence of the directions. In these cases, the students with disabilities receive information in alternative formats but are responsible for the same curriculum as their peers.

For some students, the manner for responding to an assignment or prompt may need to be adjusted. Students who struggle with fine motor skills often find writing assignments to be laborious and frustrating. Providing a computer allows such students to complete the response while providing a more meaningful experience. Other alternative methods of responding include writing on the test rather than on an answer sheet, providing an oral rather than a written response, or demonstrating understanding through role-play or the use of objects.

Many accommodations can be provided while maintaining the integrity of assessments. Examples include assessing content first and then mechanics, providing partial credit for responses, allowing extra time to complete the test, allowing the use of a calculator, allowing a change of environment (e.g., from a desk to a study carrel), or allowing small breaks during testing periods. Accommodations like these are available in the test manuals for standardized tests such as the Florida Comprehensive Achievement Test. Teachers should refer to test manuals prior to administering assessments.

Modifications

Some students may require modifications to the curriculum. These are changes to the course content, although the subject area matches that of the rest of the class. Modifications fall into four categories (Fisher, Frey, & Sax, 1999):

1. Same only less: The assignment is the same, but the number of items to complete is reduced. For example, a science multiple choice test may feature four possible answers, while the modified version has only two.

2. Streamlined curriculum: The assignment is reduced to focus on key elements. For example, while others write a persuasive essay on the use of recycling, a student may create a list of disposable classroom items that the school can recycle.

3. Same activity with infused objective: The activity remains the same, and IEP objectives are infused into an assignment. For example, a student with measurement objectives participates in a chemistry lab experiment and is responsible for measuring the ingredients needed by the group.

4. Curriculum overlap: The assignment for one class may be completed in another class, or the student may receive credit in more than one curricular area. For example, a poster presentation in mathematics may also receive a language arts grade.

As with all supports, curriculum accommodations and modifications should be used strategically. Rarely are these adaptations necessary across the day, for every curricular area and assignment. Rather than apply accommodations and modifications in a blanket fashion, one should consider the demands of each task and then only make changes that are necessary to ensure success. The purpose of instruction is to scaffold a student's ability to perform increasingly complex tasks independently. Although some support may be needed, the goal of increased independence should always remain a central focus.

Assistive and Instructional Technology

Instructional and assistive technology constitute a third consideration for creating a triangle of supports. *Instructional technology* refers to resources such as computers, CD-ROMs, the Internet, and multimedia tools that provide access to information (Sax, 2001a). Students increasingly rely on hardware and software applications for communication purposes. The use of instructional technology is considered to be a standard of effective instruction for all students, and most states have created technology standards for educational practice. The emphasis on infusion of technology in sound instruction is a boon for all students, especially for students with IEPs in general education classrooms.

In addition, some students require assistive technology to obtain higher educational goals and strengthen independence. According to federal guidelines, *assistive technology* is "any item, piece of equipment or product system, whether acquired commercially off the shelf, modified, or customized, that is used to increase, maintain, or improve functional capabilities of individuals with disabilities" (Sax, 2001b, pp. 89–90). Some available devices can be placed on a continuum from low-tech to mid-tech to high-tech items.

Low-tech devices are readily available and do not require an external power source. Many of these items are helpful for students who need assistance with writing, grammar, note taking, or organization. These students may benefit from specialized pens or pencils with comfortable grips, paper with raised lines, erasable highlighters, magnifiers for reading, or tilt laptrays. Other low-tech devices are customized for the individual student rather than purchased as commercial products. Examples include picture schedules attached by Velcro for transitions throughout the day or customized school bags for carrying materials to class.

Mid-tech devices are commonly available and may require an available power supply. Electronic devices such as tape recorders, talking calculators, and electronic spell checkers are considered mid-tech assistive technology. These devices are commercially available and range in price.

High-tech devices require specialized knowledge and may rely on an available power source. They are often purchased for use by a specific student and are therefore usually not readily available at schools. Examples include alternative computer keyboards; augmentative and alternative communication devices that allow students to communicate using a communication board or a computer with specialized software for speech; and devices for mobility, such as wheelchair lifts or walkers. Because the approval and ordering process for most schools is time consuming, becoming familiar with the district procedures for obtaining such items is recommended.

Most school districts require an evaluation prior to providing a student with assistive technology support. Such evaluations are often requested through the IEP process, although there may be other, less formal procedures in place as well. Once an evaluation is complete and the use of the assistive technology is approved, the information is documented in the student's IEP to provide continuity of services and supports across districts and states. Additional information on this topic is available through national and state organizations, including the Rehabilitation Engineering and Assistive Technology Society of North America (http://www.resna.org). The Florida Alliance for Assistive Services and Technology (http://faast.org) provides additional information about assistive technology in Florida.

TRIANGLE OF SUPPORTS FOR THREE STUDENTS

The triangle of supports consists of personal supports, curriculum accommodations and modifications, and assistive and instructional technology. This framework for creating responsible and effective supports for students with significant disabilities was utilized for each of the three South Florida students profiled in this chapter, and their educational experiences serve as a portrait of inclusive education. These students with moderate to severe disabilities were able to participate successfully in a general education setting. In each case, the district, school, and family collaborated with the technical assistance network to move the student from a segregated classroom. We believe that these efforts have been sustained across the students' school careers because the personal, curricular, and technology supports that each requires to be successful have been clearly articulated. Although initial resistance to inclusion was voiced by some teachers and school administrators, the available parent and district-level support ensured that appropriate supports and services were in place and that questions regarding these students were answered.

Maria: Making the Most of Personal Supports

Maria is a sociable and energetic student with Down syndrome and a full-time participant in a general education classroom. When Maria was in kindergarten, she was sent to an elementary school with a "cluster" program, where students with cognitive disabilities were transported to receive special education services. At that time, Maria spent her entire day in a special day program. As the year progressed, Maria's mother became increasingly concerned about the lack of opportunity for interaction with students without disabilities. At the end of kindergarten, Maria's mother enrolled

Maria in her neighborhood school. After several meetings with the administrators from the new school, school district personnel, the school's general and special education teachers, and the FIN facilitator, Maria was placed in a general education classroom for first grade. Maria was the first student with a moderate disability to receive special education services in a general education environment at this particular school. After this team reviewed Maria's IEP, it became evident that Maria would benefit from the structure of Mrs. Jimenez's first-grade classroom. Mrs. Jimenez, a general education teacher, emphasized cooperative learning, as students worked in small heterogeneous groups to complete activities. Mrs. Jimenez and the special education teacher, Mrs. Terrance, collaborated in developing strategies that would work best for Maria, and they quickly created a system for planning. Mrs. Jimenez would deliver weekly plans with attached worksheets and assignments, and Mrs. Terrance would prepare curriculum accommodations and modifications to ensure that Maria's academic, social, and behavioral goals were met in the general education classroom.

The IEP team later met to review the types of personal supports that would best meet Maria's needs. Mrs. Jimenez believed that she could meet many of Maria's academic needs within the classroom; however, from time to time, Maria would benefit from additional support for special projects. It was decided that Maria would benefit most from intermittent support from a paraprofessional on an as-needed basis. As the special education teacher for the school, Mrs. Terrance supervised the two instructional aides assigned to the department. Therefore, during their weekly meetings, Mrs. Jimenez and Mrs. Terrance would determine whether additional support was needed for any upcoming activities. Mrs. Terrance would then create the weekly schedule for the instructional aides to cover these activities. Many of Maria's other needs could be met with natural support—that is, her classmates. These students could help Maria read books and make transitions from one subject to another, help her with lunch in the cafeteria, and provide other assistance as Maria became familiar with the school campus.

Now in fifth grade, Maria continues to receive services in the general education classroom, and her peers continue to provide support as needed. As Maria attends the neighborhood school with her friends and participates in extracurricular activities, she and her family, teachers, and friends have also begun to look to Maria's future.

Julie: Making the Most of Curriculum Supports

Julie is presently in middle school, but her journey to inclusive education began in elementary school. She has a rare migratory brain disorder that affects her speech and language, fine motor skills, and cognition. She communicates with gestures and expressions, as well as two- or three-word verbal responses, and her impairments meet the federal definition of severe disability. Julie's early school experiences consisted of attending special day classes with other students with significant cognitive disabilities. Although she participated in some general education activities, she remained a "visitor" to her peers, like Peter in Schnorr's (1990) article. Julie was likeable and friendly, but true membership in the community of the classroom eluded her.

When Julie was in third grade, her mother realized that she wanted her daughter to receive services in the general education classroom. Having a highly inclusive life outside of school, Julie's mother felt that her school day should be inclusive as well. Julie's parents, teachers, and school district personnel met to discuss these changes in placement and to reflect these changes in Julie's IEP. That day, Julie became the first student with a significant cognitive disability to be included in the general education classroom at her school. With the support of the school district, Julie's teachers received support on how to meet Julie's needs in the general education environment. The following year, Julie entered a newly constructed school and attended general education classes every year thereafter.

When Julie entered middle school, the changes in curriculum and scheduling posed a challenge for educators. The FIN facilitator provided assistance in designing ways for Julie's teachers to develop curriculum accommodations and modifications that increased her participation in the class. Because the school is organized in "houses" (clusters of approximately 160 students, four general education teachers, and a special educator), the potential for collaborative practices already existed. In additions, the houses also included students with less severe disabilities, English language learners, and students with Section 504 plans (which, under the Rehabilitation Act of 1973 [PL 93-112], protect individuals from discrimination on the basis of disability in programs that receive federal financial assistance). To provide support that meets the needs of this diverse student population, Julie's special education teacher and subject area teachers met regularly to plan instruction and curricular supports for all students. With the support of the school's administration, teachers were given a common planning period as well as a meeting day once every 6 weeks to develop long-term plans. Julie's general education teachers used an interdisciplinary approach to curriculum design (Jacobs, 1989), which made modification and accommodation significantly more meaningful. The team organized the curriculum around a central question or problem, and the students developed solutions that directed their instruction and research (Wiggins & McTighe, 1998). By providing learning experiences that linked to the central questions, students were able to understand how the curriculum related to the real world.

In Julie's sixth-grade year, the central question was derived from news of rapid amusement park expansions in Florida. "Can you educate and entertain at the same time?" became the organizer for all of the curriculum areas, and the entire grade level was challenged to create an educational and entertaining American History amusement park. All of the students first participated in creating a concept map for an amusement park. This graphic organizer enabled the students to visualize the steps involved in developing the project, and it became an important tool in designing meaningful instruction for Julie.

The success of students in need of specialized support, including Julie, depended heavily on the collaboration between the subject area teachers and the special educator, Mrs. Parker. Using the concept map as a guide, the general education teachers identified the standards to be taught through the project. Mr. Lee, the social studies teacher, focused on the standards related to American history for sixth grade. Mrs. Martinez, the science teacher, outlined the physics and energy standards involved in the development of this project.

Although the general educators were very knowledgeable about their subjects, they were not certain how to successfully include students with disabilities in these activities. Mrs. Parker, the special education teacher, was able to support Mrs. Martinez and Mr. Lee with these concerns. Mrs. Parker suggested that the social studies and science teachers place students in cooperative groups for activities. By using cooperative grouping and assigning students tasks based on students' strengths, all students were able to participate. As a member of the group, Julie had responsibilities that related to the class project. She worked in a ride development group, assisted in the construction of a model of the park, and co-produced a multimedia presentation with her peers. Mrs. Parker was able to provide Mrs. Martinez and Mr. Lee assistance in assessment by reviewing Julie's goals, then developing a rubric that reflected her IEP objectives. Julie was assessed on her final project, a carousel of wagons to symbolize the westward movement across the prairies in the mid-19th century. Julie presented her project to the class with the assistance of a peer; she then presented her westward movement multimedia presentation using her IntelliKeys keyboard. Mrs. Parker later remarked, "The best part of the project was Julie's presentation to her peers. Not only was Julie proud of her work, but so was her group."

Julie continues to participate in general education, where she prospers educationally and socially. She enjoys typical teenage activities such as going shopping with friends or to the movies. Her peers have become her strongest advocates in both social and academic activities. At her last IEP meeting, Julie's mother summed up her daughter's experiences in middle school:

Julie's always going to have a disability. The goal is not to "cure it." But unless kids know Julie, and Julie knows kids, then she goes from having a disability to having a handicap. Being unknown and a stranger in your own school—that's the only real handicap.

Leon: Putting it All Together

Leon enjoys music, spending time with friends, and visiting the local skateboard park. Like many other teenagers, he likes having sophisticated gadgets. The type of gadgets in his everyday life, however, distinguish Leon from his peers. Leon relies on a sophisticated array of technology to participate in general education classes at his neighborhood high school. Leon uses an electric wheelchair to negotiate the sprawling campus, uses BIGmack switches to activate a variety of items in his classes, and is exploring his new Delta Talker communication device.

Leon's early academic years consisted of attending special day classes with other students with severe disabilities. As Leon approached the end of his elementary school years, his father attended a conference on inclusive education and determined that it was the best approach for his son. This experience is consistent with the reports of many other parents of children with disabilities, who cite attending a conference as an important catalyst in their journey toward inclusive education (Grove & Fisher, 1999). During fifth grade, Leon began spending his lunchtime and art class with the general education students. Although this was an important first step, it left everyone involved feeling that more could be accomplished.

Upon entering middle school, Leon became the first student with a significant disability to be included in a general education classroom at his school. With the support from the school district offices, school administration, faculty, and a facilitator from the FIN, Leon spent 90% of his school day with peers without disabilities. At this time, Leon strengthened his communication skills and level of independence. To prepare for Leon's transition from middle school to high school, high school staff became very involved in Leon's eighth-grade year. High school teachers visited Leon's middle school to observe and participate with Leon in inclusive environments and to discuss successes and challenges with their colleagues. Collaborating across schools led to proactive measures that eliminated or minimized many of the barriers anticipated in Leon's move to a new school.

By the end of eighth grade, teachers from both schools were prepared for Leon's transition. When Leon entered high school, the FIN facilitator provided additional support by facilitating meetings among the various departments as well as designing and delivering staff development for the paraprofessionals at the school. This support was essential to Leon's success in his first year of high school, and a schedule that rotated instructional aides for each class ensured that Leon would not become dependent on a single paraprofessional. Curricular supports were also essential, and the general education teachers quickly rose to the challenge, especially when it came to applying Leon's technology supports. For instance, Leon was enrolled in a ceramics class. After meeting with the district's assistive technology coordinator, the teachers devised a way for a switch to be attached to the potter's wheel. Leon became responsible for activating the water spray and rotating the wheel. Leon quickly learned a cause-and-effect relationship (that of turning the wheel on and off while watching his peers throw pots)—an important objective that had been on his IEP for 4 years. Inspired by this success, the 2-D art teacher used switches on the Spin Art machine. In his English class, his peers assumed the responsibility of programming his communication device and added a number of colloquialisms unique to teenagers.

As Leon's social and academic worlds expanded, it seemed logical to capitalize on the energy generated by his enthusiastic supporters. During the second semester of his freshman year, Leon's teachers, friends, relatives, and other community members gathered to discuss Leon's future and to create a PATH (Planning Alternative Tomorrows with Hope) person-centered plan (Pearpoint, O'Brien, & Forest, 2000). The technical assistance network facilitated the meeting, and everyone left with a common understanding of Leon's dreams of becoming an advocate for individuals with disabilities and creating his own art business. His PATH became a reference for designing his remaining school years. Leon enrolled in many art courses throughout high school in preparation for his future business. He also expanded his skills in advocacy by participating in classes that required presentations. Leon also has spoken at conferences and meetings throughout Florida on his experiences as an individual with a disability. He is looking forward to graduating and entering the next phase of his life. Leon's family cites his high school experiences as a major influence in shaping his future. We further suggest that Leon has fundamentally shaped educational practices at his high school, which now offers similar supports to nearly 30 students with disabilities.

CONCLUSION

Good inclusive practices emerge from responsive personal supports, thoughtfully designed curriculum, and creative use of technology—a triangle of supports. The students in this chapter represent the potential of all students with significant disabilities. Sadly, many students with IEPs in

South Florida, as well as in the other urban areas discussed throughout this book, cannot tell similar tales. Yet, as educators committed to inclusive education, we believe that exploring success stories allows the replication of sound practice for other students. When students have specialized and natural supports, access is increased. When units of instruction based on a diverse student population and an understanding of various learning styles are developed, meaningful learning takes place. Finally, technology provides access to places and activities previously thought to be inaccessible for those with significant disabilities. The real challenge is in "going to scale"— that is, creating systems of support for districts, schools, and classrooms that will streamline their ability to design responsive supports for diverse learners. Like students, these organizational systems also need a triangle of supports, or ways to readily obtain the technical assistance required to make inclusive education a reality for every student with an IEP. The existence of such a network in Florida is an important step in creating access to the general education curriculum. We hope that these complex organizational structures "ramp up" their capacity to provide inclusive education so that the marketing slogans for the region will be a reality for all students with IEPs—"Welcome to Miami/Bienvenidos a Miami."

REFERENCES

Beech, M. (1999). *Accommodations: Assisting students with disabilities: A guide for educators.* Tallahassee, FL: Bureau of Instructional Support and Community Services.

Broward County Public Schools. (2002). *Interesting factoids.* Retrieved January 31, 2002, from http://www.browardschools.com/about/factoids.htm

Brown, L., Farrington, K., Knight, T., Ross, C., & Ziegler, M. (1999). Fewer paraprofessionals and more teachers and therapists in educational programs for students with significant disabilities. *Journal of The Association for Persons with Severe Handicaps, 24,* 250–253.

Bureau of Economic and Business Research. (1999). *Florida estimates of population.* Gainesville: University of Florida.

Castagnera, E., Fisher, D., Rodifer, K., & Sax, C. (1998). *Deciding what to teach and how to teach it: Connecting students through curriculum and instruction.* Colorado Springs, CO: PEAK Parent Center.

Fisher, D., Frey, N., & Sax, C. (1999). *Inclusive elementary schools: Recipes for success.* Colorado Springs, CO: PEAK Parent Center.

Frey, N. (2001). Tying it together: Personal supports that lead to membership and belonging. In C.H. Kennedy & D. Fisher, *Inclusive middle schools* (pp. 119–138). Baltimore: Paul H. Brookes Publishing Co.

Giangreco, M.F., Broer, S.M., & Edelman, S.W. (1999). The tip of the iceberg: Determining whether paraprofessional support is needed for students with disabilities in general education settings. *Journal of The Association for Persons with Severe Handicaps, 24,* 281–291.

Grove, K.A., & Fisher, D. (1999). Entrepreneurs of meaning: Parents and the process of inclusive education. *Remedial and Special Education, 20,* 208–215, 256.

Individuals with Disabilities Education Act (IDEA) Amendments of 1997, PL 105-17, 20 U.S.C. §§ 1400 *et seq.*

Jacobs, H.H. (1989). *Interdisciplinary curriculum: Design and implementation.* Alexandria, VA: Association for Supervision and Curriculum Development.

Jones, K.H., & Bender, W.N. (1993). Utilization of paraprofessionals in special education: A review of the literature. *Remedial and Special Education, 14*(1), 7–14.

Miami-Dade County Public Schools. (2001). Retrieved November 2001 from http://www.dadeschools.net

Pearpoint, J., O'Brien, J., & Forest, M. (2000). *PATH: A workbook for planning possible positive futures: Planning alternative tomorrows with hope for schools organizations, businesses and families* (2nd ed.). Toronto, Ontario, Canada: Inclusion Press.

Rehabilitation Act of 1973, PL 93-112, 29 U.S.C. §§ 701 *et seq.*

Ryndak, D.L., Jackson, L., & Billingsley, F. (1999–2000). Defining school inclusion for students with moderate to severe disabilities: What do experts say? *Exceptionality, 8,* 101–116.

Sax, C. (2001a). Using technology to enhance learning. *California Reader, 34*(2), 14–19.

Sax, C. (2001b). Using technology to support belonging and achievement. In C.H. Kennedy & D. Fisher, *Inclusive middle schools* (pp. 89–103). Baltimore: Paul H. Brookes Publishing Co.

Schnorr, R. (1990). "Peter? He comes and goes . . . ": First graders' perspectives on a part-time mainstream student. *Journal of The Association for Persons with Severe Handicaps, 15,* 231–240.

U.S. Census Bureau. (1999). *Counties ranked by Hispanic population, July 1, 1999* (CO-99-18). Washington, DC: Author.

Wiggins, G.P., & McTighe, J. (1998). *Understanding by design.* Alexandria, VA: Association for Supervision and Curriculum Development.

SCALING UP

Expanding the Triangle of Supports

VIRGINIA ROACH

For decades, parents and advocates have fought for the inclusion of students with disabilities (particularly significant disabilities) in public education. Although the initial focus was on access to public schooling, since the mid-1980s the focus has shifted to advocacy for inclusion in the general education school program (Case, 1992; Mills & Hull, 1992; Moscovitch, 1993). There is evidence that the number of students with disabilities served in separate schools and classrooms is diminishing. According to the *Twenty-Third Annual Report to Congress on the Implementation of the Individuals with Disabilities Education Act,* 47% of the school-age students receiving special education during the 1998–1999 school year were removed from the general education classroom less than 21% of the time (U.S. Department of Education, 2001).

There are at least three influences on the inclusion of students with disabilities in the typical classroom. First, the Individuals with Disabilities Education Act (IDEA) of 1990 (PL 101-476) specifically requires it, and the Individual with Disabilities Education Act (IDEA) Amendments of 1997 (PL 105-17) strengthen the degree to which local providers must ensure that the general education program is the placement of first consideration (Final Regulations, 1999). Second, families have continued to request, and in some instances demand, that their children receive services in the general education classroom. Third, increasing diversity in the overall student population is placing pressure on schools to serve a broader range of learning styles, student cultures, and linguistic backgrounds. In short, school officials, teachers, and the faculty that train them are being forced to more broadly define "normal" and to move away from Anglo, typically male, cognitive constructs (Aronson & Gonzalez, 1988; Fordham, 1991).

Although the increased inclusion of students with disabilities in the typical classroom is a positive trend, educators must guard against repeating the mistakes of the past. When the federal special education law was initially enacted, it spawned the development and growth of a vast, separate special education bureaucracy. Like all bureaucracies, as special education grew, it differentiated and specialized, creating standard, automatic responses to the education of students with disabilities (National Association of State Boards of Education, 1992). The result was the delivery of individualized supports and special services to students with disabilities on an almost universal basis that wasn't very "individualized" or "special" (Smith, 1990; Smith & Simpson, 1989). Similarly, as inclusion is promoted on a wide-scale basis, the fear is that students will be "dumped" wholesale back into general education classrooms without appropriate supports and services. In fact, there is evidence that this has happened in many schools across the country (Viadero, 1993). As the nation moves toward wide-scale acceptance of inclusion, families, educators, and policymakers must avoid a bureaucratic, lockstep response from the system that leads to maximum general education classroom placement but perhaps minimal real inclusion.

In Chapter 3, Henry and Frey provide an informative road map for including students with disabilities in general education programs based on a three-point framework for support. This triangle of supports includes personal supports, curriculum accommodations and modifications, and assistive and instructional technology. Their chapter is helpful for teachers and families because it is well grounded in the experiences of actual students, as illustrated by the three student examples used in the chapter. It also gives educators and families specific guidance about what to do in the classroom. Many inclusion texts speak more generally and do not specifically connect student learning characteristics with teaching strategies. Henry and Frey emphasize that the programmatic approach to inclusion must be fundamentally student specific. It is important to note that the authors caution against excessive support for students with disabilities: "Uniform supports are rarely necessary across the entire day.... The detrimental effects of excessive support on the academic and social development of students with individualized education programs (IEPs) are well documented" (p. 37). In addition, Henry and Frey specifically note that starting at the system level without a grounding in the actual student–teacher interchange is doomed to fail. Regarding important elements of inclusive programs, they write, "Successful practice necessitates the deliberate construction of these elements to increase the likelihood of sustained change" (p. 35).

Henry and Frey provide a rich description of their work with three different students; however, they note, "The real challenge is in 'going to scale'" (p. 47). The key is to move from this student-specific understanding to systemwide inclusion approaches that do not lose sight of the individual student. Scaling up is not just a matter of adding more. There is both a quantitative and qualitative element to moving from an individual student focus to a whole school focus on inclusion. Scaling up has implications for student placement, the provision of technical assistance, and the focus of teacher professional development. These differences compose the next step to expanding the triangle of supports.

STUDENT PLACEMENT

Scaling up inclusion involves changing the actual placements of students with disabilities. Roach, Ascroft, Stamp, and Kysilko (1995) discussed a continuum of implementation that appears to be a common pattern for schools and districts in determining student reassignment and inclusion. At its slowest pace, inclusion is implemented on a case-by-case basis, as families request inclusion for their children. This leads to a gradual process, with little systemic change to support inclusion from one building to the next. Hence, districts often duplicate start-up costs as each new student is included in the general education classroom. Following on the continuum are districts that initiate inclusion through the introduction of a special or pilot project. These pilot projects serve as models to "sell" inclusion to a broader audience of educators in the community. Next on the implementation continuum is the "comprehensive phase-in" approach. In this approach, the district phases in inclusion in a purposeful way: grade by grade, building by building, or teacher by teacher within buildings. In addition, new schools in the district open as inclusive schools. The most rapid, wide-scale implementation seems to be districts that convert entirely to inclusive classrooms within a period of a few years.

Although districts report using these various approaches to implementation, it is important to note that there is not a linear relationship between one end of the continuum (one-by-one student placement) and the other end (whole school transformation). That is, a whole school transformation is not achieved by simply adding all individual placements of students with disabilities into general education classrooms. In general, the first two implementation strategies are programmatically based, whereas the last two rely on a policy foundation (Roach et al., 1995).

TECHNICAL ASSISTANCE

Scaling up inclusion also means changing the way that technical assistance is provided. In reviewing examples provided by Henry and Frey and other rich descriptions of inclusive schools, one can deduce a shift in focus from providing direct guidance and support to individual students to focusing on schoolwide schedules and staffing plans, teacher (rather than student) schedules, and schoolwide curriculum change. When technical assistance providers focus on supporting the success of one student in an inclusive placement, their assistance typically emphasizes the development of the specific program for that student. Technical assistance providers may be involved in making modifications or accommodations to the curriculum to support the student in the general education classroom, demonstrating co-teaching with the general education teacher, or meeting with district personnel to coordinate the transfer of a student from a segregated placement to a neighborhood school. This direct contact equates to additional personnel resources, as the technical assistance provider is, in effect, acting as a part-time special education teacher or inclusion specialist.

When students are included as part of a pilot or demonstration project, technical assistance typically still focuses on the student rather than on the school. In these programs, individualized technical assistance is multiplied in an effort to show multiple "inclusion success stories." Technical assistance focuses on designing student programs and schedules that are feasible schoolwide. Technical assistance providers still engage in designing specific accommodations and modifications for students, demonstrating best practices and attending meetings such as the student's IEP meetings. These efforts are designed to demonstrate successful inclusion as well as to mitigate any additional burden that an individual classroom teacher may experience as a result of inclusion. In this way, the program creates staff advocates that will, it is hoped, lead to the greater success and expansion of inclusion in the school and district. As with student-by-student inclusion, technical assistance translates into real additional staffing at the building level. Depending on the size of the pilot program, this can mean adding one half-time or full-time position.

A fundamental shift occurs in providing technical assistance when a school or district moves toward inclusion as a matter of policy. These districts and schools seek to create sustainable, systemic support for the effort by changing administrative structures, staffing patterns, and teacher relations across classrooms and departments. Technical assistance providers typically shift their unit of analysis. Instead of individual students, the focus shifts to the school as an organization. Technical assistance providers determine the schedules of special education teachers and classroom aides to provide maximum support to general education teachers who are implementing curriculum modifications and accommodations, which may or may not have been developed by the technical assistance provider. As an outside catalyst, the technical assistance provider convenes meetings among elementary school teachers or across departments at the high school level to facilitate the planning for individual students. Various modifications and accommodations may be developed as exemplars for teachers to use when planning for individual students. In the absence of a whole school transformation, the technical assistance provider may spend a considerable amount of time spanning the interface between those working in inclusive classrooms and those maintaining traditional, segregated programs. Activity accelerates at the beginning and end of each year, as issues associated with transitioning from one grade to the next must be negotiated.

Technical assistance in a whole school reform model is different still. In this model, the technical assistance provider works with building administrators as much as with teachers to plan building schedules that coordinate the support needs of teachers and develop new staffing patterns to fully integrate the special and general education staff. Rather than focus on individual curriculum, modifications, and accommodations, technical assistance providers may engage staff in discussions about new curriculum constructs, such as thematic instruction, cross-disciplinary curriculum, and student-centered curriculum (Jorgensen, 1998). Moving from inclusion on a student-by-student basis to a whole school reform model that supports all students requires a shift in focus for the technical assistance provider. In the former case, the provider delivers direct instructional services to students with disabilities. In the latter case, the technical assistance provider operates in a quasi-administrative role to ensure that the school develops systems to support all children.

TEACHER PROFESSIONAL DEVELOPMENT

Teacher development also changes when scaling up from placing individual students in typical classrooms to supporting an inclusive student body. When students are included in an isolated fashion, administrators typically ask teachers to volunteer to work with the student with a disability. Support emphasizes ensuring that the student with disabilities "fits into" the general classroom with a minimal amount of disruption. Teacher development in this instance does not typically expand beyond the specific classroom teacher(s) with whom the student is placed and the special education teacher assigned to the student. Depending on the situation, the general classroom teacher may be given some information on the child's specific disability. Otherwise, support is targeted to curriculum modifications and accommodations and to addressing any behavioral issues that a student might present in the general education classroom.

In contrast, professional development may be a key component of special or pilot inclusion projects. Often, these projects have a special focus on providing professional development to teachers as an incentive for schools to participate. Professional development typically encompasses both generic accommodation and modification strategies and specific planning strategies for individual students. Teachers may receive additional release time to engage in professional development and planning activities like personal futures planning (e.g., PATH: Planning Alternative Tomorrows with Hope, as mentioned in Henry and Frey's chapter). Although intensive, the professional development provided through special inclusion projects is not typically integrated with a school or district's other professional development activities. Such development may be part of an individual teacher's professional development plan, although this is more typical for special education teachers than for general education teachers.

As with technical assistance, the professional development provided to teachers who are involved in school- or districtwide inclusion differs somewhat from that which is provided to teachers involved in isolated inclusion programs. Rather than provide student-based professional instruction, teacher development tends to focus on more generic support strategies that teachers may apply to individual students as the need arises. In addition, inclusion as district or school policy, by definition, relies on the work of teachers, who have a variety of attitudes toward supporting students with disabilities in the general education classroom. Therefore, professional development also tends to address teachers' attitudes. Technical assistance providers may structure several professional development sessions that provide opportunities for teachers with concerns and reservations to voice those concerns. More intensive professional development may be provided to teachers who will soon implement inclusion. For example, if all of the rising third graders will be included in fourth grade next year, a focus of professional development may be on helping the fourth-grade teachers prepare for the coming year. Peer tutoring among teachers, co-teaching, and mutual planning times are typically utilized in a school that is transforming to an inclusive school as a matter of policy.

Professional development in a building undergoing a whole school transformation often differs from professional development involving only some staff. Because of the transformative nature of such inclusion, more time may be spent in faculty-wide discussions about the nature of education in the school and the ways in which teachers want the school to change. These discussions may be led by teachers, working in teams or as a whole faculty, rather than by a building administrator or technical assistance provider. Such professional development stresses changing the instructional orientation of teachers toward all students, not just toward those with disabilities. Ideally, faculty discussion and development is as focused on curriculum as instruction but in a general education, not special education, context. Because of the sweeping nature of the change, professional development activities may begin 1–2 years before the school is actually restructured. Table 3C.1 summarizes the general focus of placement,

Table 3C.1. Focus of training and technical assistance at each point on the placement continuum

	Inclusion as discrete, isolated incidents		Inclusion as district or school policy	
	Individual basis	Pilot program	Policy movement	Whole school transformation
Student Placement	Students included in typical classrooms one-by-one, based on a specific teacher or family request	Students included in general education and neighborhood school as a result of a special pilot program	Heretofore segregated students are included grade by grade as a whole school initiative (e.g., all kindergarten students included the first year, kindergarten and first graders the second year)	Whole school transformation; all students who would normally attend the school attend with typical age-grade peers
Technical Assistance	Technical assistance focuses on program development and instruction for individual students; specific advocacy for individual students; extra resources provided	Technical assistance focuses on individual students or class and designing student programs and students' schedules; individual curriculum modifications and accommodations; extra resources provided; focus on ensuring success with minimal extra work for the regular classroom teacher	Technical assistance focuses on schoolwide orientation and supports; designing grade-level programs and supports; typically focus on individual and group curriculum modifications and accommodations	Technical assistance focuses on schools; schoolwide schedules and staffing; focus is on teacher schedules, rather than students' schedules; schoolwide curriculum may change (Jorgensen, 1998)
Teacher Development	Individualized, as needed	For teachers across the program; some discussion of generic support strategies, but specific assistance offered in designing programs for individual students; typically intensive support	Schoolwide, typically by grade; focus more on generic support strategies that teachers then may apply as needed to individual students; also must attend to teacher attitudes	Schoolwide; attention in early planning stages to teacher attitudes, concerns; focus on changing instructional orientation of teachers toward all students

From Roach, V., Ascroft, J., Stamp, A., & Kysilko, D. (1995). *Winning ways: Creating inclusive schools, classrooms and communities.* Alexandria, VA: National Association of State Boards of Education; adapted by permission.

technical assistance, and teacher professional development at each point of the inclusion continuum.

CONCLUSION

In Chapter 3, Henry and Frey offer an excellent template for supporting students with disabilities in the general education classroom. Although they work as technical assistance providers in a network that is more oriented toward the left side of Table 3C.1, they ask readers to contemplate how systems can scale up their work in inclusion. This is no easy task. As previously discussed, technical assistance providers must change the nature of their assistance when "going to scale" as well as mitigate the natural tendency of large bureaucracies to standardize inclusion, just as segregated special education services were standardized. Fortunately, Henry and Frey suggest some ways in which to approach this task. First, adopt an orientation that is student focused, not service focused. Ultimately, this can lead to less expensive, less intrusive services. Second, keep inclusion efforts focused on student achievement and placement. This is a better fit with general education reform and accountability in schools today. Finally, operate from a simple, flexible framework to avoid "one-size-fits-all" inclusion. A triangle of supports—personal supports, curriculum accommodations and modifications, and assistive and instruction technology—is the recommended framework. As schools and districts go to scale with inclusion, these elements should be considered when designing technical assistance structures and teacher professional development. It is hoped that in this way, districts can be grounded in the needs of teachers yet attend to the triangle of supports of the larger system.

REFERENCES

Aronson, E., & Gonzalez, A. (1988). Desegregation, jigsaw, and the Mexican-American experience. In P.A. Katz & D.A. Taylor (Eds.), *Eliminating racism: Profiles in controversy* (pp. 301–314). New York: Kluwer Academic/Plenum Publishers.

Case, A.D. (1992). The special education rescue: A case for systems thinking. *Education Leadership, 50*(2), 32–34.

Final Regulations for the Individuals with Disabilities Education Act (IDEA) Amendments of 1997, PL 105-17. (1999). Retrieved January 20, 2003, from http://www.ideapractices.org/law/downloads/Fullregs.html

Fordham, S. (1991). Racelessness in private schools: Should we deconstruct the racial and cultural identity of African-American adolescents? *Teachers College Record, 92,* 470–484.

Individuals with Disabilities Education Act (IDEA) Amendments of 1997, PL 105-17, 20 U.S.C. §§ 1400 *et seq.*

Individuals with Disabilities Education Act (IDEA) of 1990, PL 101-476, 20 U.S.C. §§ 1400 *et seq.*

Jorgensen, C.M. (1998). *Restructuring high schools for all students: Taking inclusion to the next level.* Baltimore: Paul H. Brookes Publishing Co.

Mills, R.P., & Hull, M.E. (1992). State departments of education: Instruments of policy, instruments of change. In R. Villa, J. Thousand, W. Stainback, & S. Stainback (Eds.), *Restructuring for caring and effective education: An administrative guide to creating heterogeneous schools* (pp. 245–266). Baltimore: Paul H. Brookes Publishing Co.

Moscovitch, E. (1993). *Special education: Good intentions gone awry.* Boston: Pioneer Institute for Public Policy Research.

National Association of State Boards of Education. (1992). *Winners all: A call for inclusive schools.* Alexandria, VA: Author.

Roach, V., Ascroft, J., Stamp, A., & Kysilko, D. (1995). *Winning ways: Creating inclusive schools, classrooms and communities.* Alexandria, VA: National Association of State Boards of Education.

Smith, S.W. (1990). Individualized education programs (IEPs) in special education: From intent to acquiescence. *Exceptional Children, 57,* 6–14.

Smith, S.W., & R.L. Simpson. (1989). An analysis of individualized education programs (IEPs) for students with behavioral disorders. *Behavior Disorders, 14,* 107–116.

U.S. Department of Education. (2001). *To assure the free appropriate public education of all children with disabilities (Individuals with Disabilities Education Act, Section 618): Twenty-third annual report to Congress on the implementation of the Individuals with Disabilities Education Act.* Washington, DC: Author.

Viadero, D. (1993, April 14). Special educators' group weighs in on 'full inclusion' [Electronic version]. *Education Week.* Retrieved January 20, 2003, from http://edweek.com/ew/ewstory.cfm?slug=29cec.h12&keywords=Viadero

PREVENTING READING DIFFICULTIES AND ENSURING ACCESS TO THE GENERAL EDUCATION CURRICULUM

Early Grade Literacy Instruction in Houston and Fort Worth

KERRI L. BRIGGS AND MEAGHAN S. EDMONDS

EDUCATIONAL REFORMS have driven much of the conversation about school improvement since the 1980s. Nowhere is this more true than in the state of Texas, where the average demographics for its largest urban districts are challenging: 63% of all students are identified as coming from low socioeconomic backgrounds, 20% are English language learners, and 11% are students with disabilities. In addition, these districts face increased expectations for achievement while providing equitable educational opportunities for students at risk, including those with disabilities.

Reform efforts, however well intended, can derail learning if they are focused on too many narrow objectives. For instance, emphasis on reform in inclusive practices can fail if they are designed and implemented outside the general educational reform efforts. When forced to choose, teachers and administrators may forego reform efforts that appear to only address the needs of a small segment of the school population in favor of efforts with more widespread impact. For this reason, inclusive school reform efforts are increasingly becoming embedded into general education restructuring. A linchpin of this infused approach to school reform lies in understanding the complexities of policy politics that drive school change efforts.

In his book about agenda setting in governments, Kingdon (1995) described a "policy window," wherein for a period of time, there is an opportunity for government action around a particular public issue. As this policy window opens, three key elements—knowledge about problems, politics, and policies—converge to address an issue. Such was the situation in Texas around the issue of reading, particularly reading in the primary grades. The issue of early reading achievement has bearing on inclusive schooling efforts as well because 11% of all Texas schoolchildren are served under the Individuals with Disabilities Education Act (IDEA) of 1990 (PL 101-476) (Texas Education Agency, 2000). This chapter examines these three key policy elements at the state and national levels, then in more detail at the local level through case studies of two large urban districts, Houston and Fort Worth. This analysis describes how educators in these two districts seized the opportunity created by the policy window to reform reading instruction while improving educational opportunities for students with disabilities.

The three key elements are briefly considered at the state level and used as a model to establish an outline for the case studies. The greater part of the chapter is devoted to 1) the problems urban districts face in ensuring that students, particularly students with disabilities, become successful readers; 2) the political actors involved in initiating and implementing these districtwide reading reforms; and 3) the policies crafted and implemented by two urban districts to address reading for students with and without disabilities.

KNOWLEDGE OF THE PROBLEMS

As described by Kingdon (1995), one reason that a policy window opens is because an old problem becomes more severe. In the 1994–1995 school year, more than 20% of Texas students had not passed the state's reading assessment, and this figure only represented scores from about two thirds of students in the tested grade levels. Many of the students excluded from testing were those with disabilities. Then governor George W. Bush, upon considering these numbers, concluded that the number of students struggling with reading was significant and the situation warranted action (Walt, 1996). With that determination, the Texas Reading Initiative (TRI) was launched in January 1996 and the policy window opened.

Following on the heels of the TRI were two seminal consensus documents in reading research that brought the reading issue to the forefront of the national policy agenda: *Preventing Reading Difficulties in Young Children* (Snow, Burns, & Griffin, 1998) and *Teaching Children to Read: An Evidence-*

Based Assessment of the Scientific Research Literature on Reading and its Implications for Reading Instruction (National Reading Panel, 2000). These research syntheses yielded a truce in the "reading wars," as they had been known (Manzo, 1998). Prior to the publication of these two research syntheses on reading, Texas had issued its own document, *Beginning Reading Instruction: Components and Features of a Research-Based Reading Program* (Texas Education Agency, 1997). This collective knowledge base allowed Texas educators and politicians to approach the problem of low reading achievement with confidence.

KNOWLEDGE OF POLITICS

Since the TRI's inception in 1996, the state political environment has been supportive of reading instruction reforms. Taking great efforts to put reading high on the agenda of local educators, the governor and first lady of Texas, the state commissioner of education, and countless others traveled the state to ensure that the TRI message was heard and the state reading programs were visible. The message conveyed the initiative's goal: to ensure that every student could read on or above grade level by the end of third grade and remain on grade level throughout his or her school career. It is important to note that students with individualized education programs (IEPs) were included in these statements about "all students." The message was palatable among citizens and business representatives, as the economy continued to move toward the service sector and the need for educated workers increased (Bass, 1996). In 1996, the Governor's Business Council began hosting regional meetings about reading to determine the best course of action. By bringing the issue to the legislature, the governor made the provision of resources and increased accountability at the state level a high priority.

KNOWLEDGE OF POLICY

The TRI is an assortment of capacity-building initiatives, funding opportunities, and state policies established to assist local districts in their efforts to teach students to read. Since 1996, the reading initiative provided educators with goals, standards, accountability measures, resources, and capacity-building opportunities to improve reading achievement for students in Texas schools. Furthermore, expectations about the participation of students with disabilities in statewide assessments was also identified. In other words, the policy made clear that improvements in reading achievement must also include students with IEPs.

One foundation of the TRI has been the Texas Essential Knowledge and Skills (TEKS) curriculum, a set of instructional objectives that took effect in all core content areas in 1998. These standards clearly established expectations for student learning and serve as benchmarks for state assessments. Other policy components (e.g., competitive grant opportunities) encouraged innovative reading programs at the local level and facilitated the development of intervention programs for struggling readers. One comprehensive capacity-building component of the reading initiative was the Student Success Initiative. As a measure of prevention and intervention, this initiative aimed to provide teachers with the knowledge and skills necessary to address the reading instructional needs of all students and to support schools with additional funding for accelerating reading instruction. Again, a core assumption is that the TEKS curriculum is designed for all students, thereby ensuring that students with disabilities can benefit from general education curriculum.

Local Policy Window

One could consider the TRI as the final output from the open policy window. Yet, the state's substantial efforts to influence local education policy and practice were only the first steps. In a state where local control is the guiding principle, change occurs only when the local districts act (Fullan & Miles, 1992). With respect to the TRI, change was not evident until each district considered the state's direction, determined its own needs, and designed a response.

From the beginning of the reading initiative, two districts in particular— Houston and Fort Worth—responded enthusiastically and have been highly engaged in the difficult work of reforming reading in the early grades. Located in large urban areas, both districts recognized a need for an increased focus on reading instruction for students with and without disabilities and led the way in reform, earning reputations as active districts in the TRI. Unique among urban districts, Houston and Fort Worth have sustained fairly ambitious reading reforms for several years.

LEARNING FROM THE DISTRICTS:
CASE STUDIES OF HOUSTON AND FORT WORTH

The following sections focus on how knowledge of local problems, district-level politics, and comprehensive reading policies converged in the Houston and Fort Worth school districts to address the issue of reading for all students, as well as how these reforms have influenced the education experiences of students with disabilities. The sections also explore how these initiatives unfolded in several elementary schools, paying particular attention to the effect on students with IEPs. The exploration of these initiatives was guided by several questions:

1. What are the central components of these urban reading initiatives?

2. What role did the policy window and its three key elements (knowledge of the problem, knowledge of politics, and knowledge of policies) play in the districts' reading initiatives?

3. What can be learned about serving struggling readers with and without disabilities from these local reading initiatives?

Key Demographics of the Districts and Schools

Located in urban centers, Houston and Fort Worth schools are heavily populated by students from minority groups, students who have limited English proficiency, and students from low socioeconomic backgrounds. Nationally, these groups of students have experienced higher rates of reading failure than other students (Simmons & Kameenui, 1998). Houston's student enrollment was more than 209,000 in 2000–2001, with 75% qualifying for free or reduced lunch under federal guidelines, an accepted measure of socioeconomic status (SES) of schoolchildren. In addition, 24% of the district's students were identified as English language learners, and 10% of all students possessed an IEP (Texas Education Agency, 2000; Young, 2000). Fort Worth has a similar demographic profile, with 58% of its 78,000 students qualifying for free or reduced lunch. Like Houston, Fort Worth identified 24% of its students as English language learners, and 11% of its students have disabilities.

This chapter analysis is organized according to the Kingdon (1995) framework—that is, knowledge of the problem, the political environment, and policy solutions. Within those three primary elements, meaningful sources of information were identified (see Table 4.1). This gave the chapter's inquiry structure regarding where to find relevant information, as well as a means for summarizing it according to agreed-on themes. Reading leaders in both districts were given the opportunity to comment on and clarify findings as needed.

What Was Learned: Local Knowledge About the Problem

Each district began with an in-depth assessment of the current state of reading instruction for students with and without disabilities. Factors inside and outside of the classroom were identified to create a plan for linking the in-

Table 4.1.   Urban reading initiatives and the policy window

Knowledge of the problem	Political environment	Policy solutions
Students with special needs	Superintendents	Content
	District reading leaders	Instruction
Risk factors for reading difficulties	Principals	Finances
	Teachers	Assessment
Language issues	Parents	Professional development
Instructional materials		Monitoring progress
Teachers		

tent of the TRI and the TEKS curriculum to widespread instructional practice in these urban schools. The results of their findings are summarized in the following subsections.

Specializing Education within the General Environment

As stated previously, in the 2000–2001 school year, 10% or more of Houston and Fort Worth's students qualified for special education services. However, changes in state assessment policies, the Individuals with Disabilities Education Act (IDEA) Amendments of 1997 (PL 105-17), and Title I programs meant that districts like Houston and Fort Worth needed to approach instructional reform such as districtwide reading initiatives under a new paradigm of service delivery. This meant that students with disabilities must be decreasingly relegated to specialized classes or teachers and increasingly included in the general curriculum through the addition of preventative and early intervention programs. To accomplish this change, neither district designed a separate initiative, ensuring that students with disabilities would be full participants in innovative reading reform from the beginning. Instead, they designed a comprehensive reading initiative to address the needs of *all* students.

Risk Factors for Reading Difficulties and Their Prevalence in Urban Areas

Developmental and physical disabilities often accompany reading problems (Snow et al., 1998); however, these did not seem to be the salient concerns of urban educators. Rather, Fort Worth and Houston educators tended to describe the risk factors for reading difficulties among their students in social and economic terms. For instance, a detailed list of problems facing Fort Worth "high-need campuses" included social conditions such as 1) an increased incidence of single-parent families; 2) students being raised by grandparents; 3) increased rates of students transferring from one school to another; 4) neighborhoods with significant substance abuse, crime, and gang activity; 5) homes with little access to print material or technology; 6) parents being isolated from schools; and 7) adult illiteracy (Fort Worth Independent School District [ISD], 1999).

Adverse economic circumstances can also influence the occurrence of reading difficulties, and urban areas, including the schools, contain concentrated instances of poverty (Wilson, 1991). In grant applications for state funds to improve reading, Fort Worth noted that 53 of their 69 campuses had students with low SES at or in excess of the state average of 48% low SES (Fort Worth ISD, 1998). Houston noted that in 17 of its elementary schools selected for a state reading grant program, more than 90% of students received free or reduced price lunches (Houston ISD, 1998).

Student Language Issues

Numbers from Houston and Fort Worth reveal that almost one in four students is not proficient in English. For the most part, the students' native language in these districts is Spanish, although both districts document a number of other languages spoken by students, such as Vietnamese and Korean (Texas Education Agency, 1998). Although attending a school of low quality is more problematic than having limited English skills, children who lack English proficiency are more likely to experience difficulties in learning to read in English (Snow et al., 1998). These districts were acutely aware that their reading initiatives needed to address the increasing numbers of non–English-speaking students.

The Basal Is Good, but Not Enough

Texas schools receive adequate basic instructional materials because of the statewide textbook adoption process. This process equalizes *basic* instructional materials throughout the state. However, differences are likely in other supplementary materials—materials that are needed to provide students with balanced literacy instruction. For this reason, reading leaders in Houston and Fort Worth actively sought supplemental instructional materials as part of the reading initiatives. This approach was particularly aligned with effective instructional practices for students with disabilities (Fisher & Frey, 2001).

Teachers as the Key to the Initiatives

Research results concerning teachers and reading instruction indicate that most teachers are not equipped to adequately address the extensive range of reading needs among today's children (Moats, 1994; Nolen, McCutchen, & Beringer, 1990; Snow et al., 1998). At the earliest stages, Houston and

Fort Worth identified teacher professional development in effective instructional strategies as an area that needed attention. For instance, an internal survey of Houston teachers recognized that several areas were lacking: follow-up training for new teachers, instructional consistency, skill in using effective instructional techniques for English language learners and students with disabilities, and knowledge about developing a child's oral language use and vocabulary (Houston ISD, 1999).

Local Politics: Participants in the Initiatives

Support by the local school boards, district leaders, teachers, principals, and others was instrumental to the design and implementation of these large-scale reading initiatives. Without the combined efforts of each stakeholder group, the initiative may have failed. Fortunately, the groups worked toward common goals using their areas of expertise to ensure that the reading initiative was valuable for all students.

Superintendents Leading with Vision

In addition to the very public focus on reading from state leaders, these districts had local spokespeople who were equally vocal and persuasive. Then superintendents Rod Paige (Houston) and Thomas Tocco (Fort Worth) made reading reform a high priority in their districts. Both had an ambitious vision of what reading could be and were willing to allocate the resources to achieve their goals. Once sold on the merits of the new reading plan, Tocco pushed the pace of reform by quickly expanding the number of schools implementing direct instruction programs. Paige and Tocco also made it clear that local educators had a choice: They could implement these programs or they could leave the district. It appeared that both leaders' tenure with their districts may have been a critical factor in allowing them to see their visions through to fruition. The average tenure for urban superintendents ranges from 2½–3 years (Council of Great City Schools, 2000). Before his appointment as U.S. Secretary of Education in 2001, however, Dr. Paige had been superintendent of Houston schools for 7 years. Dr. Tocco also beats the average for urban superintendents, remaining head of the Fort Worth school system since 1994. By characterizing the state of reading as a "crisis situation," each was able to allocate resources, gain the support of school boards, and keep these complex organizations focused on the goal at hand.

District Leaders Implementing the Plans

Behind the scenes, both districts had passionate leaders who were shaping policy and ensuring that the initiatives were implemented as intended. In particular, Phyllis Hunter (Houston) and Marsha Sonnenberg (Fort Worth) were key individuals throughout the process. As local reading leaders, they took the message to the field, held fast in the face of resistance to change, ensured that decisions were made with the end goal in mind, and worked to bring in additional resources. Ms. Hunter, along with a team of others, identified research-based programs, applied for grants, and organized training. Furthermore, as Director of Reading for the Houston school district, Ms. Hunter and her successors had cabinet-level status, reporting directly to the superintendent (Bowler, 2001). Ms. Sonnenberg organized training, met with principals and teachers to discuss the Forth Worth reading initiative, and monitored its implementation. Both were committed to keeping the reading initiatives at the top of their districts' agendas.

General and Special Education Teachers Accepting Change

Resistance from general and special education teachers in implementing the direct instruction programs adopted as part of the initiatives would not have been unexpected. However, teachers in both districts have not opposed the reading initiatives as an organized group. There was some limited resistance within individual schools in Houston, but leaders expected that in a big implementation of this kind. To overcome resistance, the district relied on the specialized teaching staff to guide teachers and principals and actively cultivated administrative support. Furthermore, the infusion of additional resources to implement the initiative eased the pressure and inspired commitment.

Principals Monitoring Progress and Supporting Efforts to Change

The role of principals in reading reform primarily began after the initiatives were designed. In these large districts, principals have been charged with ensuring that teachers have the necessary materials and are implementing the programs as intended. Explained one Houston district leader, "Principals have the most crucial role. In general, the district is in the support role and the principals have the main responsibility for implementation" (W. Sexton, personal communication, May 24, 2001). Although Fort Worth has numerous individuals collecting field data to monitor implementation, the principals understand their roles as facilitators, implementors, and evaluators of the reading initiative on their campuses. One Fort Worth principal explained that he and his fellow administrators also were instrumental in smoothing teachers' transition from a whole language reading program to the new direct instruction reading program.

Parents Supporting Literacy in the Home

In both districts, parents participated in initiative activities and were given information about how to enhance literacy outcomes. In neither district were parents included as designers of the reading initiative itself. Both districts devised plans for involving parents by providing free children's reading materials, literacy classes, and information about the reading assessment results. The information about reading progress is of particular interest to parents as their children approach the third grade. Beginning in 2003, students in grade 3 and above will be required to pass the state reading assessment to be promoted. By making parents aware of this promotion policy and of efforts to improve reading, the two districts hope to reduce problems that may occur when that policy is enacted.

Local Policy Solutions

Once Houston and Fort Worth education leaders understood the issues in their districts, they quickly moved into the design and implementation phase. Eager to take advantage of state and national resources, both districts focused on improving reading programs and reading achievement for all students.

Content of the Reading Initiatives

An important similarity between the reading initiatives in both Houston and Fort Worth was a strong sense of vision and purpose. Eager to correct problems, prevent chronic reading difficulties, and reduce referrals for special education, Fort Worth reading leaders created "Imperative 1" to ensure that "all students will be able to read by the end of grade two" (Tocco, Sonnenberg, Brinson, Ware, & O'Brien, 2000, p. 4). Houston, similarly ambitious in its reading initiative, set the bar even higher by claiming that its students would "read on grade level by the end of first grade" (Markley, 2000, p. A17). These goals were clearly reflected in reading initiative details that focused on prevention and intervention.

With clear goals in mind, district leaders reached a consensus on the primary grade reading principles that would shape decisions. In each district, a framework was developed as district leaders reviewed reading research, state policy, state curriculum standards, and nationally accepted conclusions about reading. These frameworks established standards and expectations for the instruction that students would receive in early grade reading and served as the foundation on which subsequent policies were built. Although the frameworks differed in the amount of detail offered, they shared the following expectations that students will (Fort Worth ISD, 1998; Houston ISD, 1996):

1. Expand their use and appreciation of oral and printed language
2. Understand and manipulate phonemes through direct, systematic instruction

3. Learn the relationship between the sounds of spoken language and the letters of written language
4. Use and expand decoding strategies
5. Write and relate their writing to spelling and reading
6. Practice accurate and fluent reading in multiple texts, including decodable stories
7. Learn and apply comprehension strategies
8. Hear well-written stories and informational books read aloud daily
9. Read and comprehend a wide assortment of books and other texts

These frameworks also had much in common with the findings of the National Reading Panel (2000) and the work of Snow and colleagues (1998). In addition, these principles of balanced literacy instruction are viewed as sound components of reading instruction for students with disabilities (Pressley, Roehrig, Bogner, Raphael, & Dolezal, 2002).

A districtwide advisory committee in Houston incorporated into their consensus document specific components for core reading instruction and reading interventions that would reflect the goal of developing balanced reading programs, as outlined by the framework. The *Balanced Approach to Reading (BAR)* components are summarized in Table 4.2. By detailing the programmatic aspects of the reading initiatives, the Houston and Fort Worth districts made their expectations accessible to general and special educators, forming a directive for future instructional practices in classrooms and schools.

Core Curriculum

Once the vision and principles were defined, the districts used them as guides for operationalizing the initiatives. Both districts selected core curricula for schools to implement that were supported by research and would bring a new level of consistency to the districts' reading programs. Over the course of 3 years, all but three Fort Worth elementary schools adopted one of two direct instruction programs for their core reading curriculum: Open Court (SRA/McGraw-Hill, 1995) or Reading Mastery (Engelmann et al., 1995). These particular curricular programs were selected because they were determined to be particularly effective in addressing the reading needs of children with low SES and who are at risk (Tocco, Sonnenberg, Brinson, Ware, & Wright, 1999). In Houston, kindergarten and first-grade classrooms used Open Court; the Harcourt Brace series (Harcourt School Publishers, 1995), which is a state adopted basal series; or the Scott Foresman (1995) series for Spanish-speaking students. Both districts made exceptions to the mandated adoptions for schools that had already demonstrated high

Table 4.2.   Components of Houston's *Balanced Approach to Reading (BAR)*

Provide ongoing professional development
Showcase children's literature
Present reading programs to parents
Organize reading days with all faculty, staff, and students
Monitor implementation of reading programs
Intervene with struggling readers
Use classroom assessments regularly
Create family literacy programs
Allocate money for classroom and school libraries

performance levels; a small number of Houston schools that participated in a separate locally funded direct instruction intervention were also excluded from curriculum mandates.

Interventions

Both districts closely examined reading interventions, although, comparatively speaking, Fort Worth focused more on the core reading curriculum, whereas Houston devoted more resources to reading interventions. These distinctions were driven in part by the use of state grants and district size. Fort Worth used several state funding opportunities to bring the core reading program to more schools. Alternatively, Houston used these opportunities to support specialized interventions in more schools. In both cases, inclusive practices through access to general education curriculum by students with disabilities remained a core issue. Details about Houston's intervention efforts follow.

Houston's intervention programs were funded through different sources and crafted to achieve specific goals. For example, one summer program was specifically designed to address the reading needs of primary grade students with and without disabilities *and* to provide additional professional development for teachers. The 2000 summer program served approximately 9,400 primary grade students, reflecting a higher turnout than usual at this grade level. Seeking to create a professional development opportunity, the district's reading office developed three summer school curricula around the core reading programs. The summer program was seen as "an opportunity for teachers to deepen their understanding and training with the three basal programs" (W. Sexton, personal communication, May 24, 2001).

In addition to the summer program, Houston had several other intervention efforts underway, including the following:

- Federal class-size reduction funds of $8.3 million supported 169 teachers in delivering reading instruction during the regular school year, as funds reduced the number of students per class.
- The Houston Livestock and Rodeo Show sponsored implementation of Reading Mastery in 20 elementary schools by providing additional funding for program materials and coaches to train teachers and monitor implementation.
- Several state grants funded research-based reading interventions such as Language for Learning, Read 180, Soar to Success, Reading One-to-One, and Si Puedo in elementary and middle schools. These interventions were designed for students with and without disabilities.

Alignment

Since the 1990s, Texas has designed a system whereby state standards for student learning are tied to state assessments. In a similar manner, both Fort Worth and Houston aligned their reading curriculum to assessments and benchmarks. Fort Worth developed comprehensive scope and sequence documents for kindergarten through second grade that aligned their direct instruction reading programs with state curriculum standards. These guides offered modifications for students who exceeded the standards, reluctant readers, students with limited English proficiency, and students with IEPs (Fort Worth ISD, 2000). An important intention of this policy was to increase participation of students with disabilities in district and state assessments. Houston leaders designed a comprehensive set of curriculum guidelines that incorporated objectives with the state curriculum standards in several subject areas, including reading and language arts.

Direct Instruction in the Classroom

As stated previously, both districts relied on curriculum programs typical of direct instruction: Open Court and Reading Mastery. In practice, direct instruction entails grouping students by ability so they can participate in reading instruction through general education classrooms. The Fort Worth programs included the following elements (Tocco et al., 2000):

- Consistent daily practice of reading skills
- High rates of teacher–child interaction
- Continuous assessment
- Immediate correction of errors
- Enhancement of comprehension with vocabulary building and literature

Again, these instructional approaches are noteworthy for their alignment with generally accepted principles of sound practice for the education of students with disabilities (Simmons & Kameenui, 1998).

Professional Development for General and Special Education Teachers

A critical component of these district reading initiatives was comprehensive professional development for teachers. With the introduction of new curriculum in Fort Worth and the balanced approach to a reading program in Houston, both districts provided opportunities for all primary grade general and special education teachers to learn about the programs. Instead of relying on the less expensive approach of training a small cadre of campus representatives who would then convey the information to others, the two districts allocated significant resources to provide training for *every* primary grade teacher involved with reading. By 2001, Houston had trained almost 11,000 teachers in the balanced approach to reading; by 1999, 1,100 Fort Worth teachers had participated in professional development for Reading Mastery or Open Court. In addition to these formal professional development opportunities, Fort Worth provided individualized training upon request, as well as problem-solving sessions about these reading programs. The "make-and-take-it" sessions gave teachers an opportunity to develop classroom materials that could immediately be used in conjunction with reading instruction. These local professional development initiatives were added to the state-supported reading academies for primary grade teachers.

Specialized Teacher Roles

Implementation in both districts was a top priority, as evidenced by the allocation of scarce human resources to the initiative. In Fort Worth, coaches, mentors, and researchers were employed to ensure that general and special education teachers implemented programs as intended as well as to document areas of progress and continued need. Similarly, Houston identified Reading Teacher Trainers to provide mentoring and coaching to teachers. The role of these specialized trainers was to offer support, model lessons, arrange for additional training, or assist with materials. The intent within both districts was to improve implementation and develop the capacity to effectively meet the needs of struggling readers with and without disabilities.

Principals

Principals in Fort Worth participated in professional development throughout the initiative. District staff expected principals to monitor implementation of the direct instruction reading programs. To realize that expectation, principals went to training sessions about program monitoring. Furthermore, Fort Worth organized ongoing training and ensured that each principal had a teacher's manual so he or she knew what to look for during classroom observations. The sense from principals was that the training was very helpful and enabled them to be intelligent observers of reading instruction for diverse learners.

Finances

The National Research Council stated that "schools with greater numbers of students at risk for reading difficulties must have extra resources" (Snow et al., 1998, p. 328). With support from private foundations and the state and federal governments, the Houston and Fort Worth districts were able to follow this recommendation. The funds were significant for several reasons. In particular, with each new funding source, both districts targeted high-need campuses to make certain that these schools received instructional materials, training, and other resources. As new resources became available, the next set of campuses was targeted for special assistance. The funding tapped for these initiatives was used to support increased reading achievement for students with and without disabilities.

Fort Worth adopted a reading curriculum that initially was not on the list of state-approved reading materials, so the curriculum had to be purchased with local funds. Fort Worth leaders recognized that their newly selected curriculum would be successful only if teachers were trained to use the curriculum with all the appropriate materials. Therefore, an identified priority of district leaders was securing funds to support these programs. The increased financial backing brought credibility and authority to these local initiatives. As noted by a Fort Worth principal, the infusion of funds "is great compared to the past. Of course, we could always use more. We had scraps for years; now we have meat and potatoes."

Both districts sought and received financial assistance from community organizations and corporations. Another source of support came from university faculty, who offered advice on research, evaluations, curriculum design, and planning. Garnering community support contributed to the stability and credibility of these initiatives.

Assessment

Texas has a significant statewide assessment system that measures student progress beginning in the third grade and extending through high school. In conjunction with the TRI, the state also mandates that reading inventories are administered in kindergarten through second grade. These assessment policies were integrated into the local reading initiatives. The culture in both districts respects testing information and expects teachers and principals to respond to learning trends. In addition, students with disabilities were included in the assessment systems to provide a more accurate portrait of district achievement and to ensure access to the general education curriculum.

Information from ongoing progress monitoring guided decision making about core and supplemental reading programs in the two districts. Assessment data were used to 1) identify students who would benefit from additional instruction, 2) inform reading curriculum and instruction decisions at the district level, 3) address problem areas in reading at the campus level, 4) determine the benefits of one reading program over another, 5) measure the quality of teacher implementation, and 6) monitor student reading achievement. Fort Worth in particular conducted several analyses on reading assessment data to determine the initiative's effectiveness and subsequently targeted its ongoing efforts to strengthen the programs.

Monitoring Implementation

Expectations were high for use of these new programs. As one district leader reported, superintendent Rod Paige wanted teachers "to know the strategies so well they could do them with their eyes closed" (W. Sexton, personal communication, May 24, 2001). However, processes to ensure implementation varied between the two districts. Although Houston initiated a process for monitoring the implementation of the reading initiative programs, Fort Worth clearly invested more heavily in monitoring implementation and providing assistance to teachers. During one school year, Fort Worth teachers received formal feedback on their use of the reading program an average of three times. Spending significant time in the classroom, district coaches and school-based mentors provided training and formative evaluation information to teachers while a team of researchers engaged in a summative evaluation. With each coaching session, teachers received information confidentially; the evaluation information was reported to school and district administrators only when problems were left uncorrected or ignored.

In addition to the Fort Worth coaching and mentoring process, a research team including both district personnel and external consultants conducted its own implementation study. These individuals assessed program implementation, the quality of classroom implementation, and the use of coaching sessions. Ultimately, the data that they collected through classroom observations was combined with student achievement results to determine program effectiveness and the extent to which differences in implementation affected student progress (Tocco et al., 1999). Both districts wanted to ensure that all students in need had access to these reform efforts, particularly English language learners and students with disabilities. Although Houston reading leaders spent less time in the classroom, they too looked at trends in student reading data to monitor progress and program effectiveness.

Results: Achieving the Ends

The Fort Worth and Houston districts analyzed assessment data to determine the effectiveness of their reading initiatives. Based on reports issued by the two districts, results have been promising. As evidence of program success, Houston ISD's *State of the Schools 2000* report highlighted improvements on nationally standardized tests. According to this analysis, first-grade students "topped the 50th-percentile mark in reading" for the English SAT-9 and Spanish Aprenda 2. Fort Worth framed success differently, comparing assessment scores of students involved in the initiative with scores of those on campuses not participating. One early statistic showed that kindergarten and first-grade students attending campuses involved with the reading initiative were making greater gains than Fort Worth students in traditional programs (Ware & Brinson, 1999). Kindergarten, first-, and second-grade students in reading initiative schools also had higher average SAT-9 scores than the national sample (Tocco et al., 2000). For instance, first-grade students in schools using Open Court demonstrated greater gains in scores and a higher end-of-year score than the national norm. Compared with schools not participating in the initiative, program schools had lower end-of-year SAT-9 averages, but the percent gain was larger. Regardless of how outcomes were calculated, both districts had data to support their claims of improved student reading performance. Neither district had yet to reach its goal, but initial reports suggested that these reading initiatives were leading to improvements in students' reading abilities.

Complications Along the Way

Despite the successes that the Fort Worth and Houston districts have experienced, there have been a few complications. As is typical with many urban districts, both were confronted with turnover among teachers and administrative staff. Systems were in place to recruit faculty and administrators into the district, but there were implications for professional development—namely, that the districts were constantly training new teachers and principals. Although challenging to maintain, this training was a necessary part of sustaining the reading initiatives and the work from previous years.

Data from both districts indicated that most teachers were implementing the curriculum and integrating new practices into their reading instruction. However, leaders in both districts desired increased expert levels of implementation for the curriculum and instructional methods (e.g., using small groups, managing time). In an effort to create this expertise, Houston used summer school to extend training and provide more opportunities for teachers to practice using newly adopted curriculum and key instructional methods. Fort Worth continued searching for qualified personnel to serve as mentors and coaches to teachers.

A final complication involved the logistical aspects of unfolding these comprehensive reading initiatives in large, complex environments. The logistics of training teachers, acquiring materials in a timely fashion, and distributing materials was a challenge. Both districts created systems for dealing with these operational issues, but addressing them still was not easy. For instance, grants that operated on 1-year cycles meant that districts had to be prepared to move quickly once notification of funding had arrived. Yet, even the best preparations could not account for slow delivery from publishers or training that was difficult to arrange. In addition, although both districts had infused a significant amount of instructional materials into the schools, more such materials were needed. With any reform, it is inevitable that there will be problems to solve; these two districts have met the challenges and seem prepared to achieve their goals.

Implications of Reading Reform Efforts on Inclusive Practices

Whenever general education reform results in improved outcomes for students, especially in a core area such as reading, students with disabilities benefit. There are several ways that these students have benefited from Fort Worth's and Houston's approaches to their reading initiatives.

Leaving No Child Behind

Both districts revealed that one goal of the initiatives and related interventions was to reduce referrals to special education. In practice, this meant that students who might typically receive little or no attention for their reading problems were the target of supplemental reading instruction. Thus, students who may have been left to fall further behind and then be referred for special education participated in interventions and benefited from improved overall reading instruction.

Providing Leveled Instruction and Materials

Many students with disabilities struggle with reading difficulties and are often provided inappropriate instruction and reading materials that are too challenging. The infusion of materials supported by these districts' initiatives provided teachers with a wide variety of reading materials that could then be matched to a child's ability. For example, Fort Worth used state funds to purchase several sets of leveled books for primary grade students, with and without disabilities, who struggled with reading. At the end of the school year, these books were sent home with students to prevent the regression in reading ability that tends to occur during summer vacation. Although it was an expensive endeavor, buying books on multiple levels created a situation in which all students could experience reading success.

In addition, a common thread of targeting instruction to student needs ran through the training sessions offered to teachers as part of the initiatives. In both districts, teachers are expected to individualize reading instruction. This has remained a primary goal of reform efforts, and it has been made more explicit through professional development for general and special educators and modeling of collaborative practices between the two. Therefore, it was no accident that direct instruction—built on the idea that students participate in reading instruction at their own level—lay at the heart of each initiative. Professional collaboration also has become a critical element of successful instruction in inclusive classrooms.

Providing Instruction within the General Education Classroom

By and large, the needs of students with disabilities were accommodated through the adoption of instructional strategies shown to be effective with struggling readers. To reflect inclusive practices, both districts were committed to providing general education teachers with the skills to meet the needs of all students through targeted, individualized instruction. Wherever resource room programs were still being utilized, the same materials and training were provided by the district. That is, materials and instructional methods in Fort Worth and Houston schools were consistent across programs.

Setting High Expectations

Reduced expectations for students with disabilities often result in low levels of instruction and low performance. The expectations in both Houston and Fort Worth, however, were that all students would be proficient readers. Leaders in Houston were adamant that the success of their reading initiative would not be born on the shoulders of students who had already reached high levels of achievement. The system for disaggregating assessment data for minorities and special education students allowed Houston coordinators to monitor the progress of students in these groups relative to other students and to make programmatic improvements to better serve children who were at risk. At the same time, it was imperative that these students participate in the assessment system so the district could obtain results for future decisions.

Having General and Special Educators Work as a Team

A continuing challenge is to obtain a unified education system, whereby all educators have shared goals for ensuring access to the general education curriculum for students with disabilities. The primary advantage to the reading initiatives in these two districts was that educators shared assessments and a reading curriculum regardless of the students they taught. One gained a sense that teachers were united by a shared responsibility for developing the reading skills of all students. In Houston, a committee composed of representatives from the reading, special education, bilingual, and early childhood departments collaborated to create all reading initiative policies. This collaboration occurred at the school level as well, where teachers from all specialties regularly met to discuss their practices.

CONCLUSION

Houston and Fort Worth are typical urban school districts in the problems that they face. Both, however, are atypical in their commitment to remedy these problems. Through comprehensive reading initiatives, the two districts work to prevent reading failure by introducing instructional strategies proven to be effective with students at risk for reading difficulties. Both were uncompromising in their efforts to raise reading achievement, as illustrated by the establishment of multiple interventions for students in need of additional reading instruction. Students with special needs benefit from these initiatives, as the overall capacity of both districts to teach reading has improved.

The challenges facing these two districts are not unique to Houston or Fort Worth and have been detailed extensively in other publications (Adams, 1990; August & Hakuta, 1997; Gersten, Schiller, & Vaughn, 2000; Simmons & Kameenui, 1998; Snow et al., 1998). However, efforts to consolidate multiple school reform efforts into a cohesive and well-articulated plan of action has contributed to reading success for children with and without disabilities.

These concentrated reading reform efforts by dynamic leaders in Fort Worth and Houston resulted in reading instruction that was increasingly targeted to individual student needs. The changes that these districts have undergone and the successes that they have experienced would not have been possible without the opportunities created by the open policy window experienced in Texas. Although each district has shown improvement in their students' reading achievement, the task at hand is yet to be completed. Accomplishing their goal of having successful readers in the primary grades means investing time and resources for the long term. Such a commitment may outlast the open policy window, but dedication to improving the skills of all students, regardless of ability, will likely sustain the reading initiatives and inherently inclusive practices in Fort Worth and Houston for the foreseeable future.

REFERENCES

Adams, M.J. (1990). *Beginning to read: Thinking and learning about print.* Cambridge, MA: The MIT Press.

August, D., & Hakuta, K. (1997). *Improving schooling for language-minority children: A research agenda.* Washington, DC: National Academy Press.

Bass, F. (1996, July 24). Debate over reading guidelines becomes battle in the culture wars. *The Wall Street Journal,* pp. T1, T4.

Bowler, M. (2001, January 7). A pioneer in reading set to extend reach. *The Baltimore Sun,* p. B2.

Council of Great City Schools. (2000, March). *Urban school superintendents: Characteristics, tenure, and salary. Second biennial survey.* Washington, DC: Author.

Engelmann, S., Bruner, C.E., Hanner, S., Osborn, J., Osborn, S., & Zoref, L. (1995). *Reading Mastery.* Columbus, OH: SRA/McGraw-Hill.

Fisher, D., & Frey, N. (2001). *Responsive curriculum design in secondary schools: Meeting the diverse needs of students.* Lanham, MD: Scarecrow Press.

Fort Worth ISD. (1998). *Texas Reading Academies, 1998–2000: Application to the Texas Education Agency* (Request for application [RFA] #701-98-017). Fort Worth, TX: Author.

Fort Worth ISD. (1999). *Texas Reading Academies, 1999–2000: Application to the Texas Education Agency* (RFA #701-99-005). Fort Worth, TX: Author.

Fort Worth ISD. (2000). *Pathways to excellence.* Fort Worth, TX: Author.

Fullan, M.G., & Miles, M.B. (1992). Getting reform right: What works and what doesn't. *Phi Delta Kappan, 73,* 744–752.

Gersten, R., Schiller, E.P., & Vaughn, S. (Eds.). (2000). *Contemporary special education research: Syntheses of the knowledge base on critical instructional issues.* Mahwah, NJ: Lawrence Erlbaum Associates.

Harcourt School Publishers. (1995). *Collections.* Chicago: Author.

Houston ISD. (1996). *A balanced approach to reading: A PEER review of HISD's reading program.* (Report No. 33.2600). Houston, TX: Author.

Houston ISD. (1998). *Texas Reading Academies, 1998-2000: Application to the Texas Education Agency* (RFA #701-98-017). Houston, TX: Author.

Houston ISD. (1999). *Academics 2000: First things first: Application to the Texas Education Agency* (RFA #701-98-025). Houston, TX: Author.

Houston ISD. (2000). *State of the schools 2000.* Retrieved February 2003 from http://www.houstonisd.org/HISD/portal/article/front/0,2731,20856_17267,00.html

Individuals with Disabilities Education Act (IDEA) Amendments of 1997, PL 105-17, 20 U.S.C. §§ 1400 *et seq.*

Individuals with Disabilities Education Act (IDEA) of 1990, PL 101-476, 20 U.S.C. §§ 1400 *et seq.*

Kingdon, J.W. (1995). *Agendas, alternatives, and public policies* (2nd ed.). New York: Longman Publishing.

Manzo, K.K. (1998, March 25). NRC Panel urges end to reading wars. *Education Week, 17*, 1, 18.

Markley, M. (2000, February 14). HISD to expand district's early reading classes; Studies show kindergarten, pre-k program to be effective. *Houston Chronicle,* p. A17.

Moats, L.C. (1994). The missing foundation in teacher education: Knowledge of the structure of spoken and written language. *Annals of Dyslexia, 44,* 81–102.

National Reading Panel. (2000). *Teaching children to read: An evidence-based assessment of the scientific research literature on reading and its implications for reading instruction.* (NIH Pub. No. 00-4754). Washington, DC: U.S. Department of Health and Human Services.

Nolen, P.A., McCutchen, D., & Beringer, V. (1990). Ensuring tomorrow's literacy: A shared responsibility. *Journal of Teacher Education, 41*(3), 63–82.

Pressley, M., Roehrig, A., Bogner, K., Raphael, L.M., & Dolezal, S. (2002). Balanced literacy instruction. *Focus on Exceptional Children, 34*(5), 1–14.

Scott Foresman. (1995). *Lectura Scott Foresman.* Glenview, IL: Author.

Simmons, D.C., & Kameenui, E.J. (Eds.). (1998). *What reading research tells us about children with diverse learning needs: Bases and basics.* Mahwah, NJ: Lawrence Erlbaum Associates.

Snow, C.E., Burns, M.S., & Griffin, P. (Eds.). (1998). *Preventing reading difficulties in young children.* Washington, DC: National Academy Press.

SRA/McGraw-Hill. (1995). *Open Court: Collections for Young Scholars.* Columbus, OH: Author.

Texas Education Agency. (1997). *Beginning reading instruction: Components and features of a research-based reading program* (Report No. CU7 105 01). Austin, TX: Author.

Texas Education Agency. (1998, January). *Policy Research Report #10: Academic achievement of elementary students with limited English proficiency in Texas public schools* (Pub. No. GE8-600-03). Austin, TX: Author.

Texas Education Agency. (2000). *Snapshot 2000.* Retrieved August 2001 from http://www.tea.state.tx.us/perfreport/snapshot/2000/

Tocco, T.S., Sonnenberg, M., Brinson, P., Ware, A., & O'Brien, D. (2000, August). *Implementation and evaluation of direct instruction reading programs.* Fort Worth, TX: Fort Worth ISD.

Tocco, T.S., Sonnenberg, M., Brinson, P., Ware, A., & Wright, M. (1999, June). *Implementation and evaluation of a reading program that works.* Fort Worth, TX: Fort Worth ISD.

Walt, K. (1996, February 1). The crisis at hand: Governor wants $65 million to ensure that Texas schoolchildren learn to read. *Houston Chronicle,* pp. 1A, 8A.

Ware, A., & Brinson, P. (1999). *Fort Worth ISD reading program: First year evaluation report.* Fort Worth, TX: Fort Worth ISD, Department of Research and Evaluation.

Wilson, W.J. (1991). Another look at the truly disadvantaged. *Political Science Quarterly, 106,* 639–656.

Young, B.A. (2000). *Characteristics of the 100 largest elementary and secondary school districts in the United States: 1998–1999* (Report No. NCES 2000-345). Washington, DC: National Center for Education Statistics.

Urban Literacy

Ensuring Access to the Curriculum
for All Students in Houston and Fort Worth

Jacqueline Thousand and Alice Leilani Quiocho

Chapter 4's rich description of the Houston and Fort Worth school districts' sustained early literacy efforts not only offers readers a template for promoting school reform and systems change, but stresses the importance of watching for, encouraging, and taking advantage of "policy windows" of opportunity, where politics and public policy can be harnessed to address critical problems (Kingdon, 1995). Chapter 4 also recognizes that change in and of itself is not necessarily progress. That is, change does not necessarily lead to better results—in this case, the literacy skills of young people. Progress can only be determined through multidimensional data collection, which is a central component of the Houston and Fort Worth initiatives.

Furthermore, although Briggs and Edmonds do not expressly discuss other models for thinking about and planning systems change, their description of these two Texas school districts' literacy initiatives illustrates dimensions of other frameworks that have been very useful in helping people succeed at change endeavors. For example, building on Michael Fullan's work in the 1980s and 1990s (Fullan, 1982; Fullan & Stiegelbauer, 1991), Villa and Thousand (1992) described four stages of change—visionizing, introducing, expanding, and selectively maintaining. The Houston and Forth Worth districts have demonstrated a clear understanding of having and spreading a strong *vision* and providing rich resources in *introducing* their literacy initiatives.

Sometimes the districts took advantage of the political and policy situation (e.g., high-stakes state assessment of student literacy performance in the third grade), and sometimes the two districts chose to attend to an element in different ways. Nevertheless, each dimension is seriously considered and acted upon. Kingdon's (1995) policy window approach to viewing and addressing change is very useful in helping urban school districts promote change.

MOVING TOWARD UNIVERSAL DESIGN OF CURRICULUM

Universal design refers to creating environments or products so there is little to no need for modifications or specialized designs for special circumstances (Udvari-Solner, Villa, & Thousand, 2002). Curb cuts are an example of universal design. If designed in up front, they cost virtually nothing, and they allow wheelchairs, strollers, walkers, and joggers easy and safe access. So, then, what would universal design look like when applied to a curriculum—a literacy curriculum or any other curriculum? Up front, curriculum would be selected/designed with the broad range of all students' learning and language differences (not deficits) in mind. Alternative materials at multiple levels of difficulty and interest and research-based instruction would be available for all teachers to use. Teachers would be trained and coached to use the curriculum and instructional methods being introduced. This would lead to early identification, intervention, and individualized instruction for students who need it. Special educators would have and use the same curriculum materials as general educators when they provide supplementary supports to help move students to grade level and out of the need for special education.

The Briggs and Edmonds chapter shows that both Texas districts are attempting to do this, at least in content (i.e., curriculum) and process (i.e., instruction). They are attempting to move toward a universal design rather than a retrofit, "fix it when it finally is broken" approach in early literacy curriculum and instruction. They are also paying attention to the movement of students with disabilities out of segregated settings and into the general education classroom. Finally, these districts view prevention of special education referrals to be an important goal. We applaud urban school districts that work proactively to reverse the disproportionate representation of English language learners, Hispanic/Latino, and African American students in special education.

LESSONS THAT OTHER COMMUNITIES CAN USE

Several lessons learned in Houston and Fort Worth resonate with us, given our own experiences in developing inclusive practices in our communities. They include the emphasis on ongoing and meaningful professional development and the commitment to seeking resources, both fiscal and human, from inside and outside their systems. A third lesson that Briggs and Edmonds identified as a gap can be included as well: the importance of working through, with, and by parents to establish and implement school reform efforts.

Lesson #1: Engage in real professional development beyond initiation and surface coaching.

Those in the field of education are quite familiar with the usual "dog and pony" or "spray and pray" approach to professional development. Commonly, a prestigious "expert" comes in for a day to introduce a teaching innovation. The expert then leaves, and little follow-up is done to ensure that the innovation is carried out with integrity or is personalized for the unique characteristics of the district and the students it serves. In Houston and Fort Worth, attention and resources were directed to professional development by providing every primary grade teacher with direction instruction in the use of the newly adopted reading programs. The districts also structured ongoing implementation support and monitoring via coaches, mentors, and researchers in Fort Worth and Reading Teacher Trainers in Houston. Briggs and Edmonds do not specify the exact nature, intensity, and frequency of the mentoring and coaching. However, our experiences may serve to illuminate the pitfalls of professional development.

One of this commentary's authors was for many years the director of professional development for a consortium of 14 school districts in southern California. In this position, she became painfully aware of the importance of going beyond "surface coaching," the practice of having a coach visit, observe, and provide feedback on two to three occasions and then never return. Such surface coaching often occurs because schools districts allocate too few resources for the endeavor (e.g., one coach for seven or eight schools). The sad outcome is that teachers often feel let down and do not develop the level of confidence or competence to integrate the innovation into their routine teaching practice. Just as some students need more scaffolding than others, teachers need different types and amounts of modeling, coaching, and support to achieve mastery of a complex instructional innovation. The lesson we learned is that for initiatives to have any hope of systemic effectiveness, educators need varying degrees (i.e., intensity and duration) of support (i.e., coaching) to integrate the practice into their repertoire. We hope that in the case of the Houston and Fort Worth reading reforms, thoughtful plans have been designed to avoid these pitfalls in developing teacher learning.

Lesson #2: Seek resources from within and without.

Clearly, within most school systems, there are not enough human or material resources to "go it alone" when attempting to make a dramatic change in practice or policy. Briggs and Edmonds' chapter describes how the two Texas districts took advantage of federal programs and state competitive reading intervention grants to launch their reading initiatives. Houston's tapping of a *local* resource, the Livestock and Rodeo Show, demonstrates how additional funding for education can be tapped in the private sector. Going after private resources does take time. It is necessary to meet face to face with potential investors, to clearly explain the program and its benefits, to negotiate what is doable and affordable for them, and to guarantee that their contribution not only will assist children but also will be advertised to the community. It takes human resources to tap resources, so districts must be willing to dedicate a proportion of someone's responsibility to capture the attention of these people who have a desire to contribute to the future of their community. The positive side benefits of such efforts are tremendous community goodwill and active involvement. Community members come to feel a part of the school rather than spectators on the sidelines.

Lesson #3: Include parents as a linchpin of the improvement process.

Briggs and Edmonds make a strong case for the importance of involving stakeholders in the creation and implementation of a school reform effort. However, although the two Texas school districts did an admirable job of involving its professional constituency, parents were not involved in the design process. Instead, they were included only at the implementation portion of the process, even while many of the risk factors for reading difficulty identified in the Texas study were family-related environmental factors. Specifically, many parents were emerging in their own literacy development and had not been active in promoting their children's literacy. To their credit, the Houston and Fort Worth school districts provided parents with literacy classes and free reading materials for their children. Based on our experiences, we would encourage these districts to reconsider the role of families, making them a linchpin of this improvement process. This requires adopting family involvement efforts as part of their districtwide reforms and can be addressed through four principles of family involvement.

Go to the Families

One important principle of family involvement that we have learned over the years is to be more proactive—that is, to go to the families rather than expect the families to come to us. In urban and low-income areas, go to the apartment complexes, churches, and other places where people gather. Talk about the projected change, get the input of community members about their dreams and concerns for their children, engage them there to see how the change initiative can positively affect their children, and help them discover how they can get involved in some way.

One of the authors of this commentary is familiar with such actions as the new principal of a very impoverished school district. In the summer before school opened, she visited the homes of every family in the school to introduce herself and her vision for the school. She told families that she would be holding weekly community luncheons to which all were invited to learn about the school's needs and how families could help. By the end of her first year as principal, parents had held several successful fundraisers. Those who were local business people had donated equipment and materials and offered their unique expertise to make school improvements (e.g., setting up and training teachers to use a homework hotline, writing and securing grant funds). Many parents now come to the school on a regular basis, volunteering in a variety of capacities.

Make Literacy Development a Family Affair

Parents who are developing their own literacy must be considered and treated as knowledgeable people who are concerned about their children and who can be active partners in their children's literacy development. These parents can listen to their children read to them and, through the process, learn to read along with their children.

Rethink What Is Considered Reading Material

It is important to encourage creativity when considering potential reading material available in the home. Teachers often think only of storybooks and textbooks when considering what constitutes suitable reading or print material for the home. All types of nonbook print material exist in every home. Print is found on cereal boxes and "to do" lists, in letters to friends and family, in comic books and teen magazines, and in newspapers in the languages of the home and community. Educators can help parents value these materials and give them ways to help their children use the materials. For example, parents can have their children make their own lists (e.g., "list all the items in the kitchen drawers," "list everything that you see in the back yard"). Or parents can ask their children to recreate, in comic book format, a story told by a member of the family, to write letters to other family members, and so forth.

Ask "What Can We Do?"

A fourth family involvement principle is to ask parents, "What can we as educators do to help you help your children with reading?" Parents often reply, "Teach us ways to help; we don't know how to do it!" One of the commentary's authors did this and offered families a weekly 1-hour workshop to teach literacy strategies. Collectively, families agreed on a convenient day and time for them to come to school. Each family then identified which member would attend each week (e.g., grandmother would come the first week, older brother the next, mother the next, aunt the next, a neighbor the next). Once per week, they gathered and learned a new literacy strategy, often creating "make and take" materials. They were charged with trying out the strategy with their children and reporting on their success and challenges at the next week's meeting. In the subsequent session, they would refine their techniques and learn yet another new strategy.

Summary

The progress made by these two Texas districts in designing and implementing a complex school reform effort that involves reading curriculum design, academic achievement targets, and access to general education curriculum for students with disabilities is an enormous undertaking. By strengthening family involvement in the process, we believe that their goals are even more likely to be met.

THREE THINGS TO PROMOTE
INCLUSIVE PRACTICES IN COMMUNITIES

The lessons shared in the experiences of the Houston and Fort Worth school districts to establish a complex school reform effort in an urban school provide valuable insight for all districts, large and small. Attentiveness to the policy and politics of a community is essential for change to occur. Leadership at all levels can accelerate change through coordinated effort as well. Ongoing professional development, active pursuit of fiscal and human resources, and family involvement are also key to the accomplishment of long-range goals. All of these elements appear to be present at varying levels of sophistication in Houston and Fort Worth. We offer three additional action items to strengthen the links between academic reform efforts and school restructuring for inclusive practices.

Action #1: Differentiate curriculum and
instruction for every teacher and student.

Chapter 4 is particularly important for the promotion of inclusive education because it models that "all does mean all." In Houston and Forth Worth, students with disabilities and their special education support personnel are not given or expected to use different literacy materials or do not have different literacy goals. The outcomes are the same for all students; that is, the highest level of literacy achievement that quality materials and instruction can afford each individual learner. Teachers received common training in the new curriculum approaches, and special educators are not exempt or separated from their general education colleagues. In this way, these two Texas districts serve as a model of how to actualize the requirement in the Individuals with Disabilities Education Act (IDEA) Amendments of 1997 (PL 105-17) that students with disabilities have access to the general education curriculum. This is a very positive outcome for students, and it unites educators, students, and families against two common enemies: reading difficulty and failure.

Briggs and Edmonds did not discuss whether or how teachers are held accountable for differentiating instruction with the newly adopted literacy materials and interventions. Simply providing quality materials does not ensure differentiated use of the materials with students with and without disabilities, who have varying learning styles and who benefit from varying instructional interventions. Figure 4C.1. offers a series of questions that teachers can ask themselves and their colleagues to guide themselves through the process of differentiating curriculum, instruction, and assessment. The questions and process are based on the principles of universal design previously discussed and help teachers avoid retrofit remediation or specialized instructional referral (e.g., special education referral).

Action #2: Listen to teachers and address their needs.

Also not discussed in the Briggs and Edmonds chapter was just how the concerns and perceived needs of the teachers in the school systems were given forum and if and how they were addressed. The two districts did recognize that there would be resistance, which naturally arises when it is not yet evident that the incentives and resources that are needed will be forthcoming. The districts' strategies for providing incentives and resources to rally support was to provide teachers with adequate instructional material resources and to deploy specialized teaching and coaching staff to help. Yet, how were the voices of teachers systematically elicited to determine which other skills, resources, incentives, and actions were perceived as needed?

One of the authors of this commentary was a principal when inclusive education had come to the forefront as a best educational practice (McGregor & Vogelsberg,1998; Villa & Thousand, 1992, 1995, 2000). She deeply wanted to restructure the school into cooperative teaching teams in which all students—with and without disabilities, with and without English language proficiency—could be included in all classes. Knowing the importance of giving voice to participants of change initiatives, she took advantage of staff meeting time to structure cooperative learning triads, in which faculty could have their individual

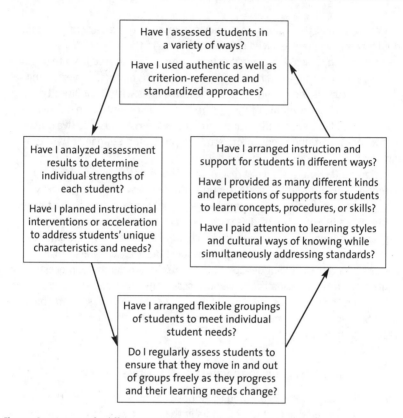

Figure 4C.1. A process for differentiating curriculum, instruction, and assessment.

voices heard and then reported to the whole group following their discussions. To promote the vision and incentive for change, she prompted faculty to discuss the question, "Would such a change truly represent progress; that is, would it be better for students?" Once this rationale for change was established through faculty conversation and once the principal listened and provided faculty with information that they wanted and needed, staff agreed to restructure their departmentalized, factory model of schooling into heterogeneous teaching teams that included special educators and other specialized support personnel.

The other commentary author worked with a southern California district, using a series of small focus forums to enable every teacher, paraprofessional, and principal, as well as a number of parents in the district, to articulate 1) what schools currently did to support students in literacy and mathematics, 2) which procedures and processes successfully avoided special education referrals, 3) what teachers needed to successfully support the academic success of all students, and 4) what else the district could do to promote student access to and success in the core curriculum (Thousand, 2000).

An analysis of their responses revealed that teachers in the primary grades overwhelmingly wanted additional human and instructional support for students who were not eligible for any of the existing reading or math intervention programs but who were at risk for failure and future referral to special education. They also wanted to incorporate these interventions into the school day rather than keep children after school or bus them in early. This information was reported back to all stakeholders, again in focus forums. As a consequence, resources were shifted to include kindergarten and first-grade students in intervention programs. In one school, this happened within days.

Ownership and "buy-in" occur when teachers see their ideas integrated into the change process rather than having the change imposed on them. Both of these examples illustrate how educators (and others), when given the opportunity to voice their concerns and articulate their perceived needs, can become active agents in a change effort. One obvious lesson here for the inclusive education movement is to elicit and listen to the voices of those who will be on the front line in carrying out inclusive practices. Yet, educational leaders should only engage in this process of eliciting voices if they will truly listen to and act on what teachers say. Otherwise, leaders are engaging in a false community and participatory process that only angers people, diminishing their trust in and respect for leaders and the system that they represent. A related lesson is to respect the limited amount of time that teachers have by capturing already structured forums (e.g., regular faculty meetings, retreats, scheduled in-service times) for vision and incentive building, problem solving, and creative thinking. Discussions regarding inclusive education should never become "just one more thing" that teachers have to do.

Action #3: Practice bold and courageous leadership.

Villa and Thousand, in their discussion of the most frequently cited reasons for lack of school change, identified "naïve and cowardly" leadership as a primary contributing factor (1995, p. 56). Leaders—superintendents, school boards, and district middle managers—are naïve when they fail to recognize just how much emotional energy, planning, and time it takes to change a complicated system, such as a school system, and to install a complex practice such as inclusive education. They are naïve when they fail to link what already is going on in the district with new movements such as inclusive education or early literacy intervention. The result is chaos, with neither teachers nor community members able to see the relationships among the many initiatives. Consequently, often none of the initiatives fully develop, and students do not fully benefit.

Leaders are cowardly when they are so focused on what they want to happen that they are unaware of or dismiss the emotional turmoil and conflict that naturally arises from change. They also are cowardly when they do not see the change through, moving on to something else prematurely or actually leaving their leadership position before the change has taken hold. The average tenure of a superintendent is fewer than 5 years. No wonder people say, "This is only a fad," and hope to wait it out until the change endeavor dies from lack of attention.

Central to any successful change effort is bold and courageous leadership such as that demonstrated by the superintendents and the passionate district reading leaders in the Houston and Fort Worth districts. Leaders are bold and courageous when they are aware of and deal with the usual resistance and barriers to change. Bold and courageous leaders know to motivate others, who in turn commit to the work of accomplishing the vision by communicating on an ongoing basis to every person who comes on the scene (e.g., teachers, parents, school board members, community leaders) a compelling picture of the desired future state. These leaders also are willing to engage in hard, time-consuming, and often very personal and emotional work (e.g., research best practices; apply for grants; organize training; meet face to face with teachers, principals, parents, and community and business leaders). In addition, leaders need another dose of courage—the courage to step out of the "leader" mode and be co-learners and co-teachers with their staff.

CONCLUSION

The promise of the work begun by the Houston and Fort Worth districts lies in its embedded commitment to consolidating general and special education reforms to improve teaching and learning for all students. The focus on reading, therefore, becomes a staging platform for fostering collaboration between educators that is not dependent on matching the credentials on their teaching certificates. Both of these districts seek to use a philosophy of universal design in curriculum, thus ensuring that students with disabilities have access to general education curriculum.

We believe that access can be enhanced by creating a larger role for the parents and families of the community. Access to curriculum by students is vital; access by their families is imperative. Furthermore, our experiences have taught us that when we develop pathways to curricular access for families, students benefit the most. When families can move to the forefront of leadership roles in a district, the complex job of educating students with diverse needs is shared.

Perhaps the most encouraging work coming out of Texas is the commitment to ongoing professional development. The skills associated with effective teaching continually evolve for each teacher; therefore, it is logical that coaching and support for these teachers grows and changes as well. As educators who have worked both within and alongside school districts, we are heartened by Houston's and Fort Worth's investment in developing collaborative partnerships among K–12 staff and knowledgeable others in the community. Again, students are the beneficiaries of these partnerships.

Finally, we offer that leadership plays a critical role in the success or failure of any school reform. These initiatives are not for the faint-hearted; indeed, bold and courageous leadership is necessary to weather the challenges of steering a large district on a new course that affects every classroom in the organization. Briggs and Edmonds suggest that Houston and Fort Worth are blessed with such leadership.

Access to the general education curriculum does not come easily, nor does it occur in isolation of the larger context of education. Briggs and Edmonds remind readers that an understanding of the problems, policies, and politics of the community provide both a path and a plan for creating these possibilities. We concur and add that the human resources available to the school—including parents, teachers, administrators, and the community at large—are essential in marrying general and special education reform.

REFERENCES

Fullan, M.G. (1982). *The meaning of educational change*. New York: Teachers College Press.

Fullan, M.G., & Stiegelbauer, S.M. (1991). *The new meaning of educational change* (2nd ed.). New York: Teachers College Press.

Individuals with Disabilities Education Act (IDEA) Amendments of 1997, PL 105-17, 20 U.S.C. §§ 1400 *et seq.*

Kingdon, J.W. (1995). *Agendas, alternatives, and public policies* (2nd ed.). New York: Longman Publishing.

Knoster, T.P., Villa, R.A., & Thousand, J.S. (2000). A framework for thinking about systems change. In R.A. Villa & J.S. Thousand (Eds.), *Restructuring for caring and effective education: Piecing the puzzle together* (2nd ed., pp. 93–128). Baltimore: Paul H. Brookes Publishing Co.

McGregor, G., & Vogelsberg, R.T. (1998). *Inclusive schooling practices: Pedagogical and research foundations. A synthesis of the literature that informs best practices about inclusive schooling*. Pittsburgh: Allegheny University of the Health Sciences, Consortium on Inclusive Schooling Practices. (Available from Paul H. Brookes Publishing Co., Baltimore)

Thousand, J.S. (2000). *Solana Beach School District strategic plan strategy #7 self-study of student supports summary report*. Unpublished report, available from author at California State University–San Marcos, College of Education.

Thousand, J.S., & Villa, R.A. (1995). Managing complex change toward inclusive schooling. In R.A. Villa & J.S. Thousand (Eds.), *Creating an inclusive school* (pp. 51–79) Alexandria, VA: Association for Supervision and Curriculum Development.

Udvari-Solner, A., Villa, R.A., & Thousand, J.S. (2002). Access to the general education curriculum for all: The universal design process. In J.S. Thousand, R.A. Villa, & A.I. Nevin (Eds.), *Creativity and collaborative learning: A practical guide to empowering students, teachers, and families* (2nd ed., pp. 85–103). Baltimore: Paul H. Brookes Publishing Co.

Villa, R.A., & Thousand, J.S. (1992). Restructuring public school systems: Strategies for organizational change and progress. In R.A. Villa, J.S. Thousand, W. Stainback, & S. Stainback
(Eds.), *Restructuring for caring and effective education: An administrative guide to creating
heterogeneous schools* (pp. 109–137). Baltimore: Paul H. Brookes Publishing Co.

Villa, R.A., & Thousand, J.S. (1995). *Creating an inclusive school.* Alexandria, VA: Association
for Supervision and Curriculum and Development.

Villa, R.A., & Thousand, J.S. (Eds.). (2000). *Restructuring for caring and effective education:
Piecing the puzzle together* (2nd ed.). Baltimore: Paul H. Brookes Publishing Co.

chapter **5**

THE FORMATION OF A SPIRITUALLY
CENTERED LEARNING COMMUNITY

Congress School in Milwaukee

MAUREEN W. KEYES, ALICE UDVARI-SOLNER,
JAN BLOEDORN, RON TAYLOR, NANCY ANNAROMAO,
TAYOTIS CALDWELL, KEONA JONES, AND MARY BETH MINKLEY

MANY CONSIDER the development of inclusive school communities as the most significant school reform on the collective journey toward a more just society. At the center of this reform are teachers, administrators, students, and members of the wider school community engaged in a sociopolitical process that not only calls into question existing assumptions about teaching and learning but also requires an examination and subsequent rearticulation of the institution's attendant values and daily practice (Udvari-Solner, 1996; Wisniewski & Alper, 1994). In many U.S. schools, the journey toward inclusive education has mirrored other social movements that have at their roots just and democratic intentions for individuals who have been marginalized in some way by the dominant culture. A common characteristic in these social movements is that a core of individuals begins to interrogate the existing values, standards, and logic of the institution in which they function. In the case of inclusive education, people begin social change by seeking equal educational opportunity for all students; challenging traditional methods of categorizing learners by deficit labels; striving for equitable roles, power, and authority between general and special educators; or truly questioning the sources of students' academic failures.

This chapter features the development and the ongoing nurturing of successful inclusive educational experiences at Congress Extended Year-Round School (or Congress School, as it is commonly known) in Milwaukee, Wisconsin, where this move toward social justice has occurred. Previous research by the first author (Keyes, Hanley-Maxwell, & Capper, 1999) linked the importance of administrative leadership to successful inclusive schooling efforts. Although numerous studies connect administrative leadership to the development of successful inclusive schools (Burrello, Lashley, & Beatty, 2001; Katsiyannis, Conderman, & Franks, 1996; Rude & Anderson, 1992; Schoeller, 1989; Stainback & Stainback, 1990; Stainback, Stainback, & Forest, 1989), it is unlikely that administrators could move an entire school or organization toward more just outcomes without a committed staff.

The staff at Congress School describe their motivation and commitment to inclusive schooling as reflections of their spiritual beliefs, values, attitudes, and responsibilities. Furthermore, they attribute their resolve for social justice in the lives of children attending urban public schools—particularly those with disabilities—as being fueled by their spiritually centered beliefs and practices.

The various definitions of spirituality advanced by the staff at Congress contained three key themes. Spirituality was the unseen force that 1) unified staff, students, and families during times of stress and celebration; 2) held their roots of respect and dignity for others, particularly for children; and 3) helped in processes of discernment that teaching was a calling. Many referred to beliefs including concepts of God or Jesus and formal religion as ways they sustained their commitment to the Congress School mission of inclusion. A generally accepted phenomenon of social movements is that the principal leaders articulate beliefs, which manifest into actions because of a critical mass of like-minded individuals.

The work of Palmer (1998) was particularly helpful to the chapter authors as they worked to sustain and explain their commitment to this social movement toward equity at Congress School. After providing a description of the featured site with brief explanations of the authors' roles, this chapter contains an overview of the stages of a social movement articulated by Palmer, an account of selected events in the development of inclusive practice at Congress School that parallel the social movement stages, and a conclusion with recommendations for utilizing a social movement framework to facilitate inclusive schooling.

CONGRESS SCHOOL

Milwaukee is the 19th-largest U.S. city and reports demographic data not unlike those from other urban districts. The overall population within Milwaukee is approximately 50% European American, but only 17.5% of school-age European Americans attend a Milwaukee Public School (MPS) (Sykes, 2001). Additional demographics show that disproportionate numbers of students of differing ethnicities attend public rather than private schools, are in special education programs, and qualify for free or reduced-price lunches (Sykes, 2001).

Approximately 750 students from ages 6 weeks to 12 years attend Congress School, a MPS. Children attend one of two campuses: South Campus focuses on early childhood education with children from 6 weeks of age through kindergarten, whereas North Campus contains the first through fifth graders. Of the learners at Congress, 89.5% are African American, 3.2% are Native Hawaiian or Pacific Islander, 2.5% are Southeast Asian, 0.6% are Hispanic/Latino, and 3.7% are European American (2000–2001 Blue Ribbon Schools Program Application). Within the total population, 83% qualify for reduced or free lunch, 18% have identified disabilities, and the mobility rate is 20%. Children with various disabilities attend Congress School and receive their educational programs alongside same-age peers in general education environments. As of 2003, no students who are deaf or blind live in the school community.

Distinguishing Features

Mary Beth Minkley became the principal of Congress School in 1993. When she shared visions of an inclusive neighborhood school that would one day be well known for its excellent educational program, she brought to the school what many veteran staff described as life and hope (Capper, Keyes, & Theoharis, 2000; M. Weems, personal communication, June 4, 1997). The staff at Congress School welcomed her and many of her new ideas. One of the first changes that she suggested was an overall redesign of Congress School, taking it back to a neighborhood school concept. MPS had eliminated neighborhood schools as part of an earlier racial integration mandate.

Another idea that Mary Beth Minkley introduced resulted in a year-round educational calendar with the addition of 16 instructional days. Results of the school's restructuring efforts demonstrated improved outcomes for students. For example, in 1993, state and district assessments showed that Congress was within the lowest 20th percentile of the city's elementary schools in performance and achievement. Results from the 1999–2000 state

Table 5.1. Results for Grade 3 students on the Wisconsin Knowledge and Content Exam (WKCE)

School year	Percent at or above state standard
1996–1997	31
1997–1998	26
1998–1999	30
1999–2000	63

and district assessments revealed scores that placed Congress School in the highest quintile. Academic improvements on formal reading assessments for students in Grade 3 from the years 1996–2000 are reported in Table 5.1.

Successful recruiting efforts have diversified the 74-person faculty: 45% of teachers and 25% of administrators are people of differing ethnicities. The student to teacher ratio is 15 to 1, with an average of nearly two teachers in every classroom, which is significantly higher than the more typical 30 to 1 ratio found in other MPS classrooms. The per-pupil expenditure is approximately $50 more than in other Milwaukee public schools. Much of the school's capacity to provide additional resources to its students is credited to the entrepreneurship of its staff. Many faculty members of Congress and of the University of Wisconsin–Milwaukee (UW-M) have written successful grant proposals that bring additional funds to the school for projects such as class-size reduction. In addition, through a partnership with UW-M, the number of adults might increase by 6–10 each semester with the additional interns, student teachers, and field students.

All of the restructuring and reforms that have taken place at Congress School since 1993 have led to the final distinguishing feature—being recognized as a Blue Ribbon School of Excellence from the U.S. Department of Education. In Fall 2001, Congress School received this award for the 2000–2001 school year, becoming the first urban, nonspecialty neighborhood school in Wisconsin to achieve this distinction. Unfortunately, the enrollment of students with disabilities in general education classrooms is not a criterion for this honor. Congress distinguished itself by earning this honor while maintaining an inclusive urban school community—a vision that was shaped by many.

Role of the Chapter Authors

Several people were involved in the move toward inclusion through a partnership formed between UW-M and Congress during the 1996–1997 school year, with funds from various grants. Originally, partnerships were developed with six Milwaukee public schools to promote student achievement and to strengthen the field-based components in the UW-M undergraduate and postbaccalaureate teacher preparation programs in general and special education. The first author, Maureen W. Keyes was on the faculty of UW-M. When given the opportunity to participate in this partnership and recruit an elementary school that included students with disabilities, she became the Congress School liaison with UW-M.

Keyes enlisted Alice Udvari-Solner, a teacher-educator at the University of Wisconsin–Madison and the second chapter author, to plan and deliver longitudinal staff development in the areas of collaborative teamwork and differentiated instruction. While providing in-service and technical assistance, Udvari-Solner interacted with the entire Congress staff and established ongoing relationships with specific teaching teams that requested follow-along assistance over the course of 2 years. The other authors are part of the faculty at Congress, except for Ron Taylor, who is a community volunteer and documentary filmmaker.

STAGES OF A SOCIAL MOVEMENT

For teachers, an important message in *The Courage to Teach: Exploring the Inner Landscape of a Teacher's Life* (Palmer, 1998) is an understanding of the processes by which social movements surface. Palmer analyzed reform efforts and described a four-part process to explain social movements. His process resembles the *Movement Action Plan* used to guide grassroots and nonprofit social change organizations (e.g., Lakey, Lakey, Napier, & Robinson, 1995).

Understanding a Movement Mentality

Educators often are confronted with new ideas, methodologies, or orientations to innovate their teaching practices. In many cases, however, they halt their enthusiasm and actions, falling victim to the rather negative mindset of "it won't happen here." They can usually identify the conditions in which they work that obstruct consideration for any new ways to address pertinent issues. When they adopt a negative mindset, in essence they promote the notion that either the status quo is too powerful and resistant to change or that they have become apathetic or incapable of imagining the expense of new energy or interest necessary to develop innovative responses to meet both new and ongoing school challenges. Lakey et al. warned activists of this phenomenon with descriptions of the Perception of Failure, the second stage in *The Movement Action Plan* (1995, p. 15). To reach the Winning over the Majority stage, Lakey and colleagues predicted increased negative reactions to social reform as natural and reminded activists that the most successful social movements occurred because members struggled to enlist reluctant naysayers rather than ignore their protests.

Palmer (1998) cautioned that it is important to resist this mindset and to recognize that there is a critical if not symbiotic relationship between institutions and social movements. Often, institutions or organizations represent principles of order and regulation, safety, predictability, and permanence. Capper (1993) suggested running the particulars of school reform through a multiparadigm framework to determine an orientation toward justice. She offered a series of questions to determine whether school policies and practices lend consideration of power, voice, equity and consensus, or whether suggested changes are designed merely to perpetuate the status quo. Many restructuring efforts simply rearrange existing structures while avoiding the bold strides that are required to incite fundamental reforms. At the beginning of previous social justice movements, those asking fundamental questions about democracy not only identified their opinions but also indicated their willingness to work toward the transformation and, in so doing, found kindred spirits.

Palmer articulated that educators who want to make a difference must identify their "bottom lines" (1998, p. 167). Rather than succumb to the demands of the institution, educators for social change are led by a collective need to find another way, an alternative that upholds every child's right to dignity and access. Consequently, the first step in social upheaval occurs when the institution's reach extends beyond the tension and growing discontent felt by individual members and taps the shoulders of like-minded educators, calling them toward collective engagement. When educators face resistance, refuse to internalize the "logic of the institution," and propose alternatives that they believe are in the best interest of the children they teach, they begin the social reform. Examples of institutional logic that can erode the adoption of collaborative and inclusive efforts in schools include the following:

- Special education was designed to teach students with disabilities, and I am a general education teacher.
- We were hired to *teach* kids content, not to *care* for kids with disabilities.
- Children with significant disabilities should attend separate, special schools.

Individuals who become involved in social movements experience resistance to their social activism, and when they later return to leverage

Table 5.2. Palmer's framework for social movements

Stage 1	Isolated individuals make an inward decision to live "divided no more," finding a center for their lives outside of institutions.
Stage 2	These individuals begin to discover one another and form communities of congruence that offer mutual support and opportunities to develop a shared vision.
Stage 3	These communities start "going public," learning to convert their private concerns into the public issues they are and receiving vital critiques in the process.
Stage 4	A system of alternative rewards emerges to sustain the movement's vision and to put pressure for change on the standard institutional reward system.

Source: Palmer (1998).

reforms in their respective institutions, they are able to do so in a more systematic fashion because they have learned from their experiences. For example, Palmer (1998) studied major social movements such as the civil rights, women's rights, and gay/lesbian/transgender efforts and concluded that the processes of change began when people no longer envisaged promise within the status quo of their organization. He described this evolution in his four-part process of social change (see Table 5.2), which is further detailed in the following subsections.

Stage 1: Making an Inward Decision to Live "Divided No More"

Social movements toward just ends happen when isolated individuals who are affected by conditions that need changing decide to live "divided no more" (Palmer, 1998, p. 167). The conditions that incite concern or discouragement are often brought to life within social institutions (e.g., schools). Palmer described this as the process whereby individuals experience inwardly one imperative for their lives, yet their actions seem quite the opposite.

When the differences in personal and institutional imperatives become untenable, some individuals make a conscious decision to honor their core values. Living divided no more is about bringing personal actions into accord with one's inner life. The process of doing so forces such an individual to acknowledge self, claim identity, and sustain integrity. For many, the decision to live divided no more may require finding a center and belief system that resides outside the institution. This does not necessarily mean literally leaving an organization, although it may. It does, however, mean finding a strong spiritual center with which to be grounded. A movement may begin when multiple individuals—often unrelated or unaware of each other's stance—make these personal decisions around a social issue. Because this decision is deeply personal, a sense of vulnerability is a natural response to the process of change.

Stage 2: Forming Communities of Congruence

In this stage, like-minded people gather in communities to support their deeply cherished beliefs. People who have decided to take a stand come together and find their ideas affirmed and individual beliefs reinforced. "Communities of congruence" form to develop and translate the vision for change into a language that can be used to communicate with others. Amid a coalition of like-minded individuals, members practice the skills that are necessary to take their ideas to a wider audience—that is, members of the majority. Without this critical phase to create greater interest in the issues and to develop coalitions and channels to make change, the necessary support to effect reform does not take place.

An example is the development of TASH (formerly The Association for Persons with Severe Handicaps) in the early 1970s. A number of people with commonly held beliefs that did not fit or adhere to the organizational frameworks of existing advocacy agencies coalesced to reinvent a human services organization. This think tank of families, teachers, administrators, and scholars conceived and built a network for educating students with severe disabilities. The philosophy, language, and technology developed effectively established an enduring community of like-minded activists that continues to affect the rights of individuals with significant disabilities worldwide.

Stage 3: "Going Public" with Values and Commitments

After individuals have built strength within their coalitions of change, it is essential that they bring their ideals into the public or to the institutional majority or else they may run the risk of becoming nothing more than a "permanent counterculture sect" (Bannan, 2000). Unless the movement's vision is expressed and tested in a larger arena, others will not be given the opportunity to learn from and potentially join forces.

In the case of creating an inclusive school culture, going public may mean that the small groups of teachers or parents come forward in building-wide forums to witness their beliefs in the face of critics within a school or an institution. Those supporting the movement must be able to respond to and articulate answers to the multitude of "What ifs?" and "Yes, but . . . " counter positions. It is only in these interactions within and outside of the school or institution that understanding, persuasion, and new membership can be gained. Quite often, this is the step that requires members of a reform movement to draw on their spiritual beliefs, and in the case of rights for individuals with disabilities, to draw on their commitment to shape a society that values dignity and respect for all. Palmer summarizes the importance of this phase in these words:

As a movement goes public, the identity and integrity of its participants are tested against great diversity of values and visions at work and the public arena. We must stay close to our own integrity in this complex field of forces, where we can easily lose our way. But we must also risk opening ourselves to conflicting influences, for in that way both the movement and our integrity can grow. (1998, p. 179)

Stage 4: Creating Alternative Rewards

In the final stage, the individual and collective energies used to create the movement return to the institution to alter its logic. Termed "alternative rewards" by Palmer (1998), others suggest additional steps with different language. *The Movement Action Plan* (Lakey et al., 1995), for example, refers to "winning over the majority," "achieving alternatives," and, finally, "consolidating and moving on" to mark aspects of a social reform movement. One inherent reason that movements begin is that the institution has the power both to define the reward system and exert its control over its membership. Patricia Hill Collins refers to this in her writings on "White racism" as the logic of segregation (1998).

To level power inequities, it is essential that the institution's hold on values and practices, which denies the voice of others, becomes obsolete. Consequently, the movement must develop space to adopt new ways of collaboration, inclusion, and respect for others. For the reform or movement to thrive, the old system of rewards, opportunities, voice, and control must be reapportioned; otherwise, the institution's values remain unchanged. For many, these rewards are natural outgrowths of participating in the movement itself. For spiritually centered individuals working for justice, having the space to exercise their beliefs and practices is often reward enough. Therefore, within schools and institutions, it is critical that adherents to new collaborative inclusive ideals receive rewards—both tangible and intangible.

The Social Movement Toward Inclusive Education at Congress School

Social changes in any school organization are affected by a multitude of factors. Often, when a reform such as developing an inclusive school community succeeds, participants involved with the reform are then asked how success was achieved. In the example of Congress School, the following questions were asked: "Were students with significant disabilities always included in your school?" and "How did you extend inclusive practices to all children with disabilities in the neighborhood considering the tendency for large urban districts to cluster students by categorical label?"

In the case of Congress School, staff and this chapter's authors had the benefit of several years of hindsight and countless data on which to draw, such as taped and transcribed qualitative interviews, videotapes, surveys, and longitudinal participant observations. As transcripts were analyzed, it became clear that events had unintentionally transpired across a number of years at Congress that paralleled elements of a social movement. This section features numerous stories, events, or actions related to Congress School that fulfill Palmer's (1998) stages of a movement. Following this overview, the chapter illustrates the three components that formed the definition for spirituality listed previously in the chapter—that is, the unseen forces that 1) unified staff, students, and families during times of stress and celebration; 2) held their roots of respect and dignity for others, particularly for children; and 3) helped in processes of discernment that teaching was a calling.

Stage 1: Making an Inward Decision to Live "Divided No More"

> Words mean nothing without action. For me, to teach is to love and to love is to prize my vulnerability, and vulnerability is my essential link to reality. So, when [a student] acts in a way that says, "But you can't love me," I tell her, "I just won't *not* love you, I just can't *not* love you."

These words, spoken by chapter co-author Nancy Annaromao while a novice teacher/intern, demonstrate an epistemology that implies a regard for the dignity of all students. She reflected on a particular student who had been labeled "unreachable and unteachable" and generally forsaken as a "lost cause" by others. Nancy was but one of many teachers at Congress School who described teaching practices and beliefs about the dignity of each child as the inseparable qualities holding her epistemological framework together. She also explained that being forced to teach in a school that did not uphold these values would be unthinkable for her. Similarly, another teacher spoke explicitly of how her political beliefs and her teaching practices blended:

> I see the beauty in children, for they are gifts. My teaching is related to my political advocacy work, for righteousness, and justice. I crave peace and balance but I am always rocking the boat. (personal communication, April 2001)

The dramatic turnabout for students enrolled in Congress School occurred for many reasons, including the spiritually centered beliefs that teachers held about children. Staff members described spirituality through moments of discernment and within little events in their work lives, ascribing its nature as sustaining and challenging. They considered the challenges of their core beliefs to care and connect with children "defining moments" and "glimpses of the future." Spiritually centered beliefs guided the behaviors of many staff. These beliefs were expressed by those in various leadership positions on a regular basis as well, and staff described the importance of consistent support from the principal.

A review of the literature about principals of inclusive schools suggested that effective leaders lead by example, create plans for implementation, demonstrate collaborative leadership, involve interested teachers on a volunteer basis, solve problems proactively, and articulate their personal commitment to the inclusion of students with disabilities publicly at the outset of their administrative careers (Capper, Keyes, & Theoharis, 2000; Deering, 1996; Ewald, 1996; Janney, Snell, Beers, & Raynes, 1995; Katsiyannis et al., 1996; Keyes, 1996; Van Horn, Burrello, & DeClue, 1992; Villa & Thousand, 1990). Principal Mary Beth Minkley was just this type of leader. When she began working at Congress, she defined and maintained her views on the goals of inclusive schooling: "[C]hildren are a miracle and we are here to create loving and nurturing environments for them to learn, and that is simply my bottom line." This philosophy was seen throughout all of her activities. Assistant principal Keona Jones also ascribed her leadership and strength to make unpopular decisions to a spiritual center:

> I make decisions, not based on what's just best for today . . . but based from my spiritual connection. You don't just mak[e] a bad decision just to have a situation rectified, just to pacify a parent. It's not fair.

Another person involved in the formation of a spiritually centered community was the chapter's first author, Maureen W. Keyes, whose description of involvement in Congress School and living a life undivided follows:

> When I completed my doctoral studies and was given the position as assistant professor at UW-M, I knew that I would not be able to live with myself if I was not deeply connected to a school community and able to experience the challenges and the joys of teaching in an urban community. I had long been rather resistant to university professors who came into the schools where I taught if they were not able to reflect a lived experience or knowledge of the pertinent issues. Therefore, when I heard

of possible funding for me as a faculty liaison within an MPS school, I quickly sought permission to participate and to secure an inclusive school for the network. Another belief that I held was the need to connect with a school community that had a like-minded, inclusive principal.

All of the featured individuals began their journeys somewhat independently and autonomously. Yet, they discovered one another as they revealed their beliefs about the value of children.

Stage 2: Forming Communities of Congruence

A community of congruence was initiated by Mary Beth Minkley and Maureen Keyes, with their agreement to form a university–public school partnership. Although the relationship was designed for a multitude of reasons, it essentially cemented the role for UW-M faculty to perform their roles of "critical friends" to the Congress School staff. Doing so permitted Maureen Keyes to dialogue with staff, parents, and involved community members about the educational practices and beliefs related to teaching children with significant disabilities in inclusive classrooms.

The partnership enabled UW-M to pour additional resources and supports into the school and to offer staff opportunities to assume roles within the university. For example, Mary Beth Minkley and Maureen Keyes co-taught a seminar for all preservice general education teachers. Congress School staff had opportunities to engage in professional development alongside preservice teachers. One of the first formal staff requests asked Maureen Keyes for a 3-credit course/staff development opportunity. Approximately a third of the teaching staff enrolled, and they read *The Courage to Teach*, Palmer's (1998) popular book connecting spirituality and teaching.

A major activity within the course asked participants to reflect on their day-to-day actions and interactions with children to unearth their core values and beliefs (see Figure 5.1). After participating staff completed this and related activities, they expressed an interest in involving other staff and approached the principal for permission to lead similar activities during the opening in-service programs of the following school year.

On other occasions, Mary Beth Minkley had outwardly supported the collective efforts of staff to improve and enhance the school's inclusive practices. She suggested that members of the staff express their needs directly to Maureen Keyes in her role as a university faculty member. Staff insisted that on-site in-service programs be tailored to their needs or that they be given access to off-site programs that addressed individual concerns. A spe-

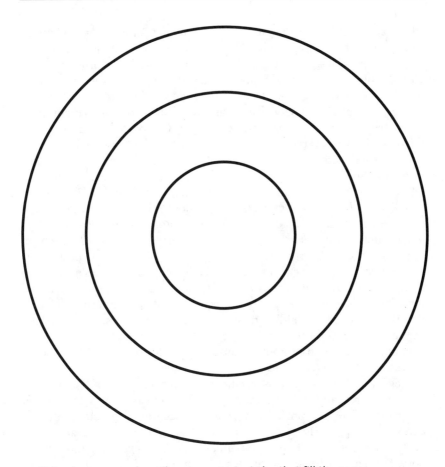

1. Using large paper, draw three concentric circles that fill the page.

2. In the inner circle, write in one phrase or sentence that describes your inner-most core values or beliefs—those you could not compromise, especially in your life as an educator.

3. In the outer circle, list five or six activities or events that immediately come to mind when you recall your most recent teaching experience.

4. In the middle circle, list descriptions of how your day-to-day activities connect with your core beliefs. In other words, how does your life reflect the concept of a life that is not divided?

Figure 5.1. Exercise for defining one's inner beliefs. (*Source:* Yoder, 1998.)

cific area of staff concern was the need for more effective collaboration among staff in accommodating the wide diversity in student needs. As described previously, Mary Beth Minkley responded by bringing Alice Udvari-Solner to Congress School for multiple and varied staff development programs. Using funds from grants and the school staff development budget, two full-day in-service programs were planned. Both days brought together the entire 75-person staff from both Congress School campuses, thus ensuring that everyone heard and engaged in the information together.

Staff were asked to come to these sessions configured in teams that were based on this guiding question: "With whom do I need to work or interact daily to instruct and support all students in this school?" This put people face-to-face to discuss teaching philosophies, negotiate roles, and produce authentic ideas for differentiated lessons that could be applied immediately in their practices. The first day focused on collaborative team processes to enhance student-centered problem solving and constructive team functioning. Participants examined the components and skills needed for effective relationships and communication. The session was organized for individuals to develop specific strategies for enhancing team collaboration that included 1) building trust among team members; 2) articulating common beliefs and attitudes; 3) structuring curriculum and instruction co-planning meetings to promote equity in the roles of general and special educators; 4) using a variety of decision-making and problem-solving strategies to address student-specific, classroom-based, or schoolwide issues; and 5) refining and expanding communication and conflict resolution approaches. The second full day session concentrated on differentiating curriculum and instruction across the areas of content, process, and product (Udvari-Solner, Villa, & Thousand, 2002). At this point, staff were supported in analyzing their own teaching and applying alternative approaches that would reach a more diverse group of students. Sessions were structured to establish a sense of parity and joint responsibility between general and special educators for the design and delivery of instruction.

Subsequent to the full days, Alice Udvari-Solner offered follow-along support to work on team-specific or curriculum-based issues. Requests came from four teams of special and general educators and the entire kindergarten and first-grade teaching staff, resulting in 4 additional days of technical assistance. The follow-up sessions were tailored to the requests that teachers made. Figure 5.2 provides one example of an activity, typical to these staff development sessions, that was designed to promote the development and articulation of shared belief systems for those who would function as instructional teams.

These professional development opportunities were designed to exemplify and reinforce trust, respect, collaboration, courage, and connect-

---

> **Articulating Our Philosophies and Practices**
>
> Listen-Share-Formulate-Create
>
> 1. Partner with a person with whom you work.
> 2. Select a topic or issue associated with inclusive practices in either early childhood or kindergarten education. For example, how are goals relative to developmentally appropriate practice, differentiation in goals and objectives, social competence, emotional behaviors, structured and unstructured play, literacy, assessment, family involvement, communication, and culturally relevant pedagogy?
> 3. Write a brief statement that represents your understanding or philosophy on the topic. (All participants complete this step independently, writing their responses on one of the three index cards given to each pair of partners.)
> 4. Compare cards with your partner.
> 5. Using the third card, create a joint statement to represent your viewpoints. You may need to compromise with each other to design this statement.
>
> **Reflection:** Were you and your partner in agreement? If not, where did you conflict and how did you compromise? In what ways did shared dialogue change your opinions or understanding? How might the activity of developing a joint statement affect your working relationship? What other applications might this procedure have?

Figure 5.2. Sample dialogue activity.

edness among all participants. As a result, these venues that brought staff together in both large group and team configurations became environments for a community of congruence to be established and nurtured.

Stage 3: "Going Public" with Values and Commitments

As explained previously, the stage that Palmer (1998) labeled "going public" involves many aspects of bringing the beliefs and demands for social reform from the local membership to the larger population, which is usually considered as the status quo or the "powers that be." Mary Beth Minkley became involved on multiple fronts. She showed her staff how to bring their needs to those who were capable of making the sort of changes needed to enact the next level of reform.

For example, Mary Beth Minkley determined that year-round schooling was a way for staff and children to remain immersed in an inclusive learning community. Staff became interested in this reform as they began to research published reports on the gains for children attending year-round schools. Of note were the gains shown by children with disabilities. Making an extended year part of the typical Congress School program meant that parents of children with disabilities would no longer have to prove the need for extended school year agreements.

On another level, including children with significant disabilities at the beginning of the 1997–1998 school year was made possible through a series of events, all of which exemplified Palmer's (1998) stage of "going public." Essentially, another example of living a life undivided took place. Neither the principal nor her staff had taught children with autism at Congress School. When the school district told Mary Beth Minkley to prepare for a "unit of severe autistics" who would be "coming for 1 year," she immediately sought the support of Maureen Keyes, requesting whatever needed to be done to maintain the school's inclusive philosophy and learning community.

Stage 4: Creating Alternative Rewards

Congress School exemplifies an institution that has developed a totally unique set of rewards per Stage 4 of Palmer's (1998) framework. This subsection shares examples of the alternative rewards that came from new "ways of doing business" at Congress School.

One special education teacher intern described her inner struggle as she learned to work within an inclusive collaborative environment. Nancy Annaromao knew that the rewards of some much-needed planning time would no longer be available to her. Instead of being able to steal time to complete required tasks whenever her teaching partner took on lead responsibilities, she remained in the general education classroom to support or team teach alongside the general education teacher. She reflected repeatedly and looked within for ways to negotiate her shifting role from autonomous special education teacher to collaborative team member:

> How can we move beyond the fear that destroys connectedness? . . . By reclaiming the connectedness that takes away fear. I realize the circularity of my case—but that is precisely how the spiritual life moves, in circles that have no beginning or end, where, as [T.S.] Eliot writes, we "arrive where we started and know the place for the first time."

Nancy and other staff openly discussed how difficult it is to see beyond the conditions that divide. The following vignette by Jan Bloedorn and

Tayotis Caldwell, two of this chapter's authors and teachers at Congress School, exemplifies their ongoing negotiation for role definition and ends with their descriptions of the ultimate rewards of a true collaborative relationship. Neither teacher planned on teaching children with autism or was keen on collaboration. When asked to recall their early months in an inclusive collaborative classroom, these teachers recalled how workdays were punctuated with disagreements over things like use of the classroom bulletin boards. They described the progression of their collaboration as being motivated by their spiritually centered beliefs regarding the sanctity of childhood and their moral responsibilities to teach all children:

> It was more than skill and talent, knowledge and aplomb. Teaching in settings with high rates of poverty and disability can be demanding and draining and provided what seemed to be little recourse. The first months of our relationship were what we now call "the survival months," or "how many adults can you fit into one classroom?" During this phase the students' greatest challenges were the challenged teachers. And this led us into the next stage, the commitment, or "we will teach all of our children," phase. Emerging collaboration that soon became facilitated collaboration marked this period. We began working on our lesson plans together and considered our next phase as "putting commitment into action." We realized this was the heart of our teaching partnership and we were motivated by the results. Finally, we reached the level where our philosophy was our classroom community and we saw the blending of our beliefs, our common goals, trust, and how the blending of best practices of general and special education were building a foundation of learning.

Recommendations for Other Schools

For us, the study of Palmer's (1998) work in relation to Congress School was empowering because dramatic differences in the lives of children with and without disabilities and their families began with a personal decision—something that every individual has within his or her control. To initiate and sustain inclusive schools, we recommend the creation of a forum for educators to explore the elements of social reform, in which there is space and time to articulate beliefs, truly consider the perspectives of others, and be encouraged to make personal change. It is important to create opportunities for dialogue and action around the phases of a social movement within

Table 5.3.   Questions to promote social change

Discouragement and resignation often come when we "internalize the logic of the organization" and find our vision of hope blocked by the same organization. Give examples of the institutional logic that you believe operates in this school. How have you or others internalized this? What are the personal trade-offs involved when doing so?

Movements and their founders "abandon the logic of organizations so that they can gather the momentum necessary to alter the logic of organizations." Could you free yourself from organizational logic and continue membership in the organization? How might this happen, and what repercussions might occur?

Stage 1: Making an Inward Decision to Live "Divided No More"

1. Consider your personal choices or those of someone whom you know (either personally or through study) that indicate reprioritized thoughts, feelings, and actions toward the development of a more just society. What led to these decisions? What risks were encountered? What changes did you/the person experience?

2. In apparent displays of courage, which resources supported the actions and commitment?

3. What conditions represent congruence among thoughts, feelings, and actions in your school?

Stage 2: Forming Communities of Congruence

1. Which structures, either within or outside your school or institution, could nurture and shelter "communities of congruence" for teachers who decide to work toward social justice? What opportunities exist within your school or institution that could support your efforts toward community?

Stage 3: "Going Public" with Values and Commitments

1. What happened when you or someone you know "went public" with his or her commitment to social justice? What was the effect of this public display on a personal level? On a family level? Within the closest circle of friends?

2. With which institutions outside of the education field could you develop alliances as your movement toward more just ends/inclusive schools grows? Who or what could provide critical support of your efforts?

3. What would facilitate opportunities to join with other organizations of like-minded individuals or similar social justice organizations?

Stage 4: Creating Alternative Rewards

1. What does the idea of *rewards* mean for you as a teacher?

2. For what are people rewarded in this school? How are they rewarded?

3. If involved with a movement toward educational reform for social justice, what keeps you engaged? What do you and members of your group do to nurture commitment?

Source: Palmer (1998).

people's workplaces and personal lives. Learning the logic of a movement, then situating themselves in the midst of a movement mentality helps individuals understand their relationship to and impact on social change. If educators want to reform education in the face of obstacles, a "movement mentality" may facilitate wresting their energy to impact positive change. Table 5.3 provides an outline for dialogue that is based on Palmer's four stages.

CONCLUSION

Congress School became a successful inclusive school because its unique learning environment was built on the strong collaborative, spiritual partnerships formed among members of the staff, students, families, and community. Everyone worked so hard to keep the dream of an inclusive environment alive, especially for the children with more significant disabilities. Evidence from formal and informal assessment results indicated consistent student growth and achievement. These results proved to others that an urban, public, inclusive school with an overarching mission of justice and equity for all students could not only teach all children effectively, but also that its members could model to others what the word *all* really means (Bolman & Deal, 1995; Capper et al., 2000; Gilley, 1997; Gutierrez, 1988; Hawley, 1993, Herman, 1994).

REFERENCES

Bannan, R. (2000). *Impact of Catholic feminist dissent.* Retrieved April 2002 from http://www.womensordination.org/pages/art_impact.html

Bolman, L.G., & Deal, T.E. (1995). *Leading with soul: An uncommon journey of spirit.* San Francisco: Jossey-Bass.

Burrello, L.C., Lashley, C., & Beatty, E.E. (2001). *Educating all students together: How school leaders create unified systems.* Thousand Oaks, CA: Corwin Press.

Capper, C.A. (1993). Educational administration in a pluralistic society: A multiple paradigm approach. In C.A. Capper (Ed.), *Educational administration in a pluralistic society* (pp. 7–35). Albany: State University of New York Press.

Capper, C.A., Keyes, M.W., & Theoharis, G.T. (2000). Spirituality in leadership: Implications for inclusive schooling. In R.A. Villa & J.S. Thousand (Eds.), *Restructuring for caring and effective education: Piecing the puzzle together* (2nd ed., pp. 513–530). Baltimore: Paul H. Brookes Publishing Co.

Collins, P.H. (1998). *Fighting words: Black women and the search for justice.* Minneapolis: University of Minnesota.

Deering, P. (1996). An ethnographic study of norms of inclusion and cooperation in a multiethnic middle school. *Urban Review, 28*(1), 21–39.

Ewald, R.S. (1996). Principal's influence in facilitating inclusive schools. *Dissertation Abstracts International, 57*(05), 1924 (UMI No. 9625781).

Gilley, K. (1997). *Leading from the heart: Choosing courage over fear in the workplace.* Boston: Butterworth-Heinemann.

Gutierrez, G. (1988). *A theology of liberation: History, politics, and salvation.* Maryknoll, NY: Orbis Books.

Hawley, J. (1993). *Reawakening the spirit in work.* San Francisco: Berrett-Koehler Publishers.

Herman, S. (1994). *The Tao at work.* San Francisco: Jossey-Bass.

Janney, R.E., Snell, M.E., Beers, M.J., & Raynes, M. (1995). Integrating students with moderate and severe disabilities into general education classes. *Exceptional Child, 61*(5), 425–439.

Katsiyannis, A., Conderman, G., & Franks, D. (1996). Students with disabilities: Inclusionary programming and the school principal. *NASSP Bulletin, 80*(578), 81–86.

Keyes, M.W. (1996). *Intersections of vision and practice in an inclusive elementary school: An ethnography of a principal.* (Doctoral dissertation, University of Wisconsin–Madison). *Dissertation Abstracts International, 57*(09), 3891.

Keyes, M.W., Hanley-Maxwell, C.A., & Capper, C.A. (1999). "Spirituality? It's the core of my leadership": Empowering leadership in an inclusive elementary school. *Educational Administration Quarterly, 35*(2), 203–237.

Lakey, B.M., Lakey, G., Napier, R., & Robinson, J.M. (1995). *Grassroots and non-profit leadership: A guide for organizations in changing times.* Philadelphia: New Society Publishers.

Lipsky, D.K., & Gartner, A. (1997). *Inclusion and school reform: Transforming America's classrooms.* Baltimore: Paul H. Brookes Publishing Co.

Palmer, P.J. (1998). *The courage to teach: Exploring the inner landscape of a teacher's life.* San Francisco: Jossey-Bass.

Rankin, D. (1995). The high school principal and inclusive practices. *Dissertation Abstracts International, 56*(06), 2069 (UMI No. 9535794).

Rude, H.A., & Anderson, R.E. (1992). Administrator effectiveness in support of inclusive schools. *Case in Point, 8*(1), 31–35.

Schoeller, K. (1989, January). Good school principals are the key principle in integration. *Pacesetter.*

Stainback, S., Stainback, W., & Forest, M. (Eds.). (1989). *Educating all students in the mainstream of regular education.* Baltimore: Paul H. Brookes Publishing Co.

Stainback, W., & Stainback, S. (Eds.). (1990). *Support networks for inclusive schooling: Interdependent integrated education.* Baltimore: Paul H. Brookes Publishing Co.

Sykes, L. (2001, April 3). Desegregating: As Milwaukee's population diversifies, metro area still ranks among nation's most segregated. *The Milwaukee Journal Sentinel,* p. 1.

Udvari-Solner, A. (1996). Examining teacher thinking: Constructing a process to design curricular adaptations. *Remedial and Special Education, 17*(4), 245–254.

Udvari-Solner, A., Villa, R.A., & Thousand, J.S. (2002). Access to the general education curriculum for all: The universal design process. In J.S. Thousand, R.A. Villa, & A.I. Nevin (Eds.), *Creativity and collaborative learning: The practical guide to empowering students, teachers, and families* (2nd ed., pp. 85–103). Baltimore: Paul H. Brookes Publishing Co.

Van Horn, G.P., Burrello, L.C., & DeClue, L. (1992). An instructional leadership framework: The principal's leadership role in special education. *Special Education Leadership Review, 1*(1), 41–54.

Villa, R.A., & Thousand, J.A. (1990). Administrative supports to promote inclusive schooling. In W. Stainback & S. Stainback (Eds.), *Support networks for inclusive schooling: Interdependent integrated education* (pp. 201–218). Baltimore: Paul H. Brookes Publishing Co.

Wisniewski, L., & Alper, S. (1994). Including students with severe disabilities in general education settings. *Remedial and Special Education, 7*(2), 49–53.

Yoder, N.A. (1998). Inspired leadership: Exploring the spiritual dimension of educational administration. *Dissertation Abstracts International, 60*(05), 1418A (UMI No. 9911683).

commentary 5

THE ROLE OF VISIONING

Commentary on the Formation of a Spiritually Centered Community at Congress School

LEONARD C. BURRELLO

In Chapter 5, Keyes and colleagues capture the passion of a school's faculty and leadership in developing an inclusive community for staff, students, and families in a Milwaukee elementary school. Congress School also demonstrates the effect that building an inclusive culture has on student achievement and staff cohesiveness.

WHY ARE VISION AND PASSION IMPORTANT?

Architects of inclusive school movements would be wise to attend to the change process outlined in Chapter 5. This commentary focuses on why the perspective that members of this school community share is important. The selection of Palmer's (1998) framework for social movements informs others where one must start any change process. Palmer's four stages are certainly part of what must transpire in creating urgency for change—passion for the idea and the need for change—and established in conversations inside and outside a school. The role of need for change is somewhat obvious, but passion for the idea merits further discussion. Passion becomes the glue that links relationships between people as they try to make their personal passion or "personal mastery" (Senge,

Table 5C.1. Factors in professional community building

Social and human resources supporting school-based professional community	Structural conditions that support school-based professional community
Openness to improvement	Time to meet and talk
Trust and respect	Physical proximity
Access to expertise	Interdependent teaching roles
Supportive leadership	Communication structures
Socialization	Teacher empowerment and autonomy

From Louis, K.S., & Kruse, S.D. *Professionalism and community: Perspectives on reforming urban schools* (p. 25), copyright © 1995 by Corwin Press, Inc.; adapted by permission of Corwin Press, Inc.

2000) into a shared matter of concern. As Keyes et al. document, Congress School was able to transform this passion, through conversations, into something that translated into a shared vision. Teachers' individual, private dialogues became public and were tested—only to survive stronger for the challenge. Yet, having created and shared their vision, Keyes et al. also demonstrate the last stage of Palmer's framework. This is one of the most complex components of change reward structures. Palmer suggested that any new behavior requires a new incentive or, in scientific terms, a new attractor (see Zimmerman, Lindberg, & Plsek, 1998). New attractors are attracting forces that bring people to a new place or disposition toward the change embodied in the shared vision.

In these ways, the Chapter 5 description of Congress School demonstrates the community building necessary in urban schools (e.g., see Louis & Kruse, 1995). Both Palmer (1998) and Louis and Kruse start with very important first factors: trust and respect. In Louis and Kruse's view, trust and respect flow out of an openness to improvement. Table 5C.1 presents a number of additional conditions that they believe should be considered in developing a professional community.

Much like Palmer (1998) suggested in his four stages, Louis and Kruse (1995) noted a flow of relationships that lead to professional community (see Figure 5C.1). As Congress School demonstrates, shared values are related to collaboration, which is then related to the creation of a professional community. Figure 5C.1 and the evidence from Congress School also suggest that shared values and collaboration are related to reflective dialogue—a practice strongly encouraged by Keyes and colleagues in the professional development work discussed in Chapter 5.

WHAT CAN OTHER COMMUNITIES DO TO PROMOTE INCLUSION?

Each community comes to consider its position on an inclusive school philosophy in a number of ways. Many principals and teachers begin their work on inclusive schooling by listening to and observing the practice of other leaders who have made inclusion happen in their districts or school. Clearly, however, there is no formal way. The following two examples illustrate the different ways that administrators, teachers, parents, and community members might use the information provided by Keyes and colleagues in their own communities.

Consider, for instance, a district director of special education who attended a workshop and decided to send all of her principals a list of students being educated outside their neighborhood schools and the district at large. She followed up with an invitation to return students to their neighborhoods, with their funded support systems in place. Each school was then asked to create a plan to return students to their home schools. Naturally, the schools responded to this request in different ways, but each school understood the goals of the school district. This director had a vision of home schools for all students, convinced her

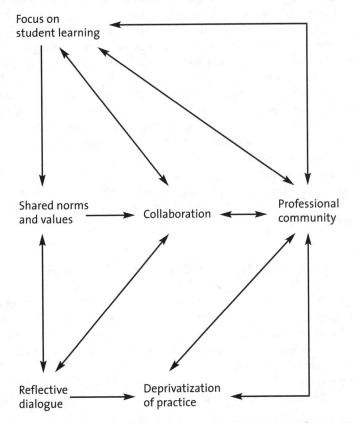

Figure 5C.1.   Relationships between dimensions of community. (From Louis, K.S., & Kruse, S.D. *Professionalism and community: Perspectives on reforming urban schools* [p. 242], copyright © 1995 by Corwin Press, Inc.; adapted by permission of Corwin Press, Inc.

staff and the principals of this vision's validity, and provided the alternative reward structure to ensure that students were included locally.

In another district, a principal was asked to include 10 students with severe disabilities in their neighborhood schools. He fought this vigorously until his superintendent said, "Do it!" His first change of heart occurred when a new student with multiple disabilities was brought into his office. Already standing next to the principal was a student named Jesse. Jesse was in the office because he had pulled a fire alarm the day before. The principal asked "fire-alarm Jesse," as he was called, to introduce the new student to the school. The first thing that Jesse did was push the boy in his wheelchair past the fire alarm. Jesse stopped, returned, and wheeled the student so that they both were directly in front of the alarm. Then Jesse said, "We never pull this alarm unless there is a fire." From that day forth, "fire-alarm Jesse" became just "Jesse." The principal realized that one student's seemingly intractable behavior problem improved because a student with disabilities was present and welcomed by the peer. As a result, the principal attended his first inclusion conference with several teachers from his school. Then, he attended and chaired the inclusion implementation meetings and supported the teachers and parents as they explored a feasible inclusion model. During the first year of change, students with severe disabilities started each day in the general education classroom, where teachers included them as much as possible. Teachers were specifically told that they could return students with severe disabilities to the special class at any time during the day. By the third year, the implementation team recommended the elimination of all special classes and resource rooms, and students with disabilities were fully included in general education classes.

In short, inclusive education is implemented in different ways. Regardless of how they get there, school staff must have a vision and understand how to create change.

WHAT THREE THINGS CAN WE DO TO GET STARTED?

Figure 5C.2 offers a change practice that incorporates Palmer's (1998) stages and extends them to answer the question "What three things can we do to get started?" First, the leader has to learn about the context of the school and district and, like the leadership at Congress, determine opportunities to enact the vision of a more inclusive school.

A second way to move ahead is to ask "wicked questions" or very difficult questions that require honest reflection. Examples include the following:

- Why are students with disabilities not included?
- Who are the second-class citizens in our school, and can we tolerate this?

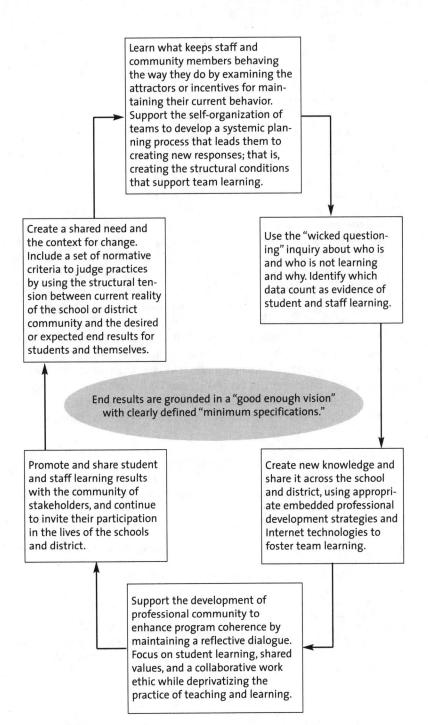

Learn what keeps staff and community members behaving the way they do by examining the attractors or incentives for maintaining their current behavior. Support the self-organization of teams to develop a systemic planning process that leads them to creating new responses; that is, creating the structural conditions that support team learning.

Create a shared need and the context for change. Include a set of normative criteria to judge practices by using the structural tension between current reality of the school or district community and the desired or expected end results for students and themselves.

Use the "wicked questioning" inquiry about who is and who is not learning and why. Identify which data count as evidence of student and staff learning.

End results are grounded in a "good enough vision" with clearly defined "minimum specifications."

Promote and share student and staff learning results with the community of stakeholders, and continue to invite their participation in the lives of the schools and district.

Create new knowledge and share it across the school and district, using appropriate embedded professional development strategies and Internet technologies to foster team learning.

Support the development of professional community to enhance program coherence by maintaining a reflective dialogue. Focus on student learning, shared values, and a collaborative work ethic while deprivatizing the practice of teaching and learning.

Figure 5C.2. The Burrello-Hoffman Change Cycle. (For more information on this cycle, see Burrello, L.C., Hoffman, L.P., & Murray, L. [2003]. *Stories of leadership transforming schools.* Manuscript submitted for publication.)

- What data do we have demonstrating that these students are learning what we want them to learn and be able to do?
- How much of what we do is different, and should it be?
- Who is benefiting from our current programs, and who wants to keep it that way?

A third important idea is to consider the question "How do schools move from a pilot program to the whole school and, eventually, make inclusion the norm of the district as a whole?" This question requires the full cycle around the change practice wheel. Generating new knowledge and sharing it goes a long way to creating the standard of practice by which a district tells its staff and community, "This is the way we do business around here." Elmore (1996) and Schlechty (2001) provided examples of standards that promote teaching and learning as authentic and a public process that ensures learning is occurring.

In closing, I commend the work of the Chapter 5 authors. Those associated with the university demonstrate their willingness to roll up their sleeves and get into the rhythm of a school to support this important work. The principal is also to be commended for using the context that she saw to create the kind of school she knew could energize her staff to build and create with her. I am thankful that this group took the time to write a chapter on Congress School. We all can learn a great deal from them about creating inclusive schools!

REFERENCES

Burrello, L.C., Hoffman, L.P., & Murray, L. (2003). *Stories of leadership transforming schools.* Manuscript submitted for publication.

Elmore, R.F. (1996). Getting to scale with good educational practice. *Harvard Educational Review, 66*(1), 1–26.

Louis, K.S., & Kruse, S.D. (1995). *Professionalism and community: Perspectives on reforming urban schools.* Thousand Oaks, CA: Corwin Press.

Palmer, P.J. (1998). *The courage to teach: Exploring the inner landscape of a teacher's life.* San Francisco: Jossey-Bass.

Schlechty, P.C. (2001). *Shaking up the school house: How to support and sustain educational innovation.* San Francisco: Jossey-Bass.

Senge, P. (2000). *Schools that learn: A fifth discipline fieldbook for educators, parents, and everyone who cares about education.* New York: Doubleday Broadway Publishing Group.

Zimmerman, B., Lindberg, C., & Plsek, P. (1998). *Edgeware: Insights from complexity science for health care leaders.* Irving, TX: VHA.

chapter **6**

Supporting One Another

Peer Tutoring in an Inclusive San Diego High School

REBECCA JEAN BOND AND ELIZABETH CASTAGNERA

WHEN ASKED in 1999 to consider the most important reasons for inclusive education, "Julia," a high school student, replied:

> I think students without disabilities benefit from it [inclusion] because it gives them a taste of the real world, where there are people with disabilities. In life, you can't separate yourself from them. They are people like us with feelings, too.

Julia was a peer tutor for students with disabilities at Kennedy High School (fictional school name) in San Diego, California. Prior to her years at Kennedy, she had not known students with disabilities in school. Such students always seemed to be in a "different" section of the school.

Special education has traveled an exciting and difficult journey since the early 1970s. This journey has afforded the education system with many challenges and celebrations. Some of the most celebrated achievements at Kennedy High School are its efforts and successes in becoming an inclusive school. This chapter describes how inclusion at Kennedy High School made its special education department an essential component of the school community. In their efforts to create an inclusive environment, the teachers at Kennedy designed and implemented a peer tutoring course. These peer tutors have had a tremendous effect on the inclusion of all students at their school.

This chapter first discusses the history and school reform at Kennedy High School. The development of inclusive practices, including the supports and necessary services, is described in detail. The primary focus is the school's peer tutoring course, and ideas on how to develop a peer tutor course at other schools are provided.

CONTEXT: HISTORY AND SCHOOL
REFORM AT KENNEDY HIGH SCHOOL

Kennedy High School is located in Southern California. Of the school's approximately 1,800 students, 86% are Caucasian, 9% are Hispanic/Latino, and 5% are from other ethnic groups. In this school, diversity in the classroom exists not so much in racial differences as in ability levels. In one classroom, there may be a student who has been labeled as having a "severe disability" as well as a student who is in line to be class valedictorian.

Since Kennedy's opening in 1965, several educational reforms have taken place. One such reform was block scheduling, with students attending three or four classes per day for 90 minutes each. The school year is divided into two terms, so students typically complete three classes the first half of the year, then take three additional classes during the second half of the year. Other changes at the school have included integrated science courses, writing across the curriculum, content area reading strategies, career pathways, and, most recently, a bridging program. The bridging program aids incoming freshmen who are achieving below average in the areas of reading and mathematics.

In 1992, inclusive education began its gradual reform of Kennedy High School. Prior to this time, students (ages 14–22) identified as having significant disabilities attended special day classes. The focus of these classes was community-based instruction, with students spending a significant portion of their day traveling in small groups to shopping malls, parks, vocational development sites, and grocery stores. The remainder of the day was spent in a self-contained classroom and included activities such as cooking, functional academics, social skills development, and job preparation.

The first change that occurred within this program was the division of students according to age. The special education teachers at the school site made this decision based on best practices. The older students (ages 18–22) continued to focus on much of the same community-based, traditional functional activities to prepare them to live and work in their community.

These classes became known as the transition program. The younger students (ages 14–18) were scheduled to spend more time performing school jobs and joining in extracurricular activities to increase their exposure to and involvement in the high school experience.

By January 1993, a team including faculty members from Kennedy High School and staff from San Diego State University began discussions regarding changes in the special education service delivery model. The plan was to begin by including one student in general education classes in September of that year. In March 1993, however, a new student named Sarah enrolled at Kennedy. Her parents requested that Sarah be enrolled in general education classes. Thus, inclusion began a little sooner than planned but still with methods and strategies in place to ensure success. Sarah's classes were chosen based on the positive attitudes of the general education teachers involved and the relationships formed between general and special educators.

Within weeks, the special education teacher received positive reports from Sarah's teachers. They saw benefits for Sarah as well as for the entire class. The only frustration was experienced by the special education teacher, who was trying to coordinate Sarah's support and curriculum at the same time that she taught her special day class. This prompted the teacher to move a bit faster with the rest of her caseload. By September 1993, instead of the initial one student, nine additional students with significant disabilities were scheduled for inclusion in general education classes.

Increasing numbers of general educators became involved with the inclusive efforts at Kennedy High School. During the summer of 1993, there were many planning meetings and in-services to prepare for inclusion in the upcoming school year. Individual schedules, reflecting typical grade-level courses, were developed for each of the nine students to be included in the 1993–1994 school year. None of the students attended the same class at the same time. However, several of the students reported to the special education teacher for one class period per day to complete homework assignments and receive individualized instruction when needed. Students attended a wide variety of academic and elective classes, including art, English, film as literature, Spanish, math, physical education, chemistry, biology, geography, chorus, band, algebra, social studies, earth science, and photography.

By the end of the following school year, another teacher in the special education department was able to have all of her students enrolled in general education classes. This resulted in all students with significant disabilities learning in general education classes with their peers. Students were scheduled to attend classes according to their grade level, not according to their disability, which remains the model at Kennedy High School.

MEETING STUDENT NEEDS WITHIN
THE GENERAL EDUCATION STANDARDS

Kennedy High School's standards of inclusive education continue to evolve alongside those of the districtwide standards. The focus of the high school education of students with disabilities remains consistent with the standards of the students without disabilities while focusing on individual needs. For example, the district in which Kennedy is located developed its own standards, which state that all graduates of this district will be effective readers, competent writers, articulate speakers, and quantitative problem solvers and will be prepared for lifelong learning. Students who do not meet the criteria of these standards, given the appropriate accommodations and modifications, will not receive a diploma. Rather, they will receive a certificate of completion. Thus, students with disabilities are held to high standards.

Individual student needs are considered when planning for a student's education. These needs are determined by the parents, teachers, service providers, and, most important, the student when the individualized education program (IEP) is developed. An Infused Skills Grid is a useful tool for determining how these needs can be met in an inclusive environment (see Figure 6.1). Listed across the top are skills that are determined to be important for the student. Listed down the side are the various environments and activities offered at the student's school where these skills can be developed. A check mark is then placed in the boxes indicating when and where the student can naturally address the skills deemed important by the IEP team.

Using the information obtained from the Infused Skills Grid, an individual student schedule is developed that reflects classes typical of students at the student's same grade level. It is important to keep students with their same-age peers when including them in general education classes. Therefore, student schedules are determined by the student's grade level, the place where his or her IEP goals and objectives can be met, and the students' personal interests. In addition, IEP goals are reflective of the district's standards, with individual student needs taken into consideration.

Using the information garnered from her Infused Skills Grid (Figure 6.1), the following IEP objectives were developed for Hannah:

> By Annual Review 2002, Hannah will work toward becoming a lifelong learner by completing a senior project on the career of her choice, as evidenced by presentation of her project.

> By Annual Review 2002, Hannah will become a more effective reader by recognizing selected sight words from a designated sight word list with 80% accuracy, per teacher evaluation.

	School name:	School year:	INFUSED SKILLS GRID
	Kennedy High	2002–2003	

Student name: Hannah McCoy
Age: 17
Grade: 12
Parent/Guardian: Mr. and Mrs. McCoy
Telephone: 555-1212
Advocate teacher: Sheila Treat

Class schedule	Room
Block 1:	
Senior English–Thompson	1003
Block 2:	
Math–Mitchell	106
Block 3:	
Aerobics–Joplin	Gym

INFUSED SKILLS

ACTIVITIES/SUBJECTS/ ENVIRONMENTS	Increase sight word recognition	Communicate using complete sentences	Be responsible for belongings	Decrease paraprofessional support	Cope with environmental changes	Make purchases	Dress independently	Complete assignments independently	Communicate effectively when frustrated
Arrival		X	X		X				X
Senior English	X	X	X	X	X			X	X
Break	X	X			X	X			X
Math		X	X	X	X	X		X	X
Lunch	X	X			X	X			X
Aerobics		X	X	X	X		X		X
Departure		X	X		X				X
Check here if the infused skill has been identified by: Family	X		X				X		X
Student			X			X	X		
Peers				X				X	X
School	X	X	X	X	X			X	X

Figure 6.1. Sample Infused Skills Grid. (From Castagnera, E., Fisher, D., Rodifer, K., & Sax, C. [1998]. *Deciding what to teach and how to teach it: Connecting students through curriculum and instruction* [pp. 28, 39]. Colorado Springs, CO: PEAK Parent Center; adapted by permission.)

123

Collaboration

Student success in an inclusive environment depends on professionals working together, communicating, and collaborating. General education teachers must have information about the student's strengths, learning needs, and goals to provide the best educational environment. At Kennedy High School, the special education teacher prepares a Student Profile for general education teachers prior to the inclusion of a student with a disability (Figure 6.2). The information provided on this form includes specific objectives for the student in the class (e.g., how he or she can meet IEP objectives in the class), areas of strengths and interests, and strategies for learning. Communication strategies and behavior techniques are also included, as well as grading accommodations and any health concerns.

Once the general education teacher has the necessary information, the special education teacher should be made aware of assignments and activities in the student's general education classes. A Teacher Assignments sheet (Figure 6.3) is used by many faculty members at Kennedy High to communicate their weekly lesson plans. The general educator completes this form once per week (on Thursday or Friday)—listing assignments, activities, and tests that will occur during the following week—and returns the form to the special educator. The special educator then provides any accommodations or modified assignments to the general educator at the beginning of the week. Another useful tool is the Academic Unit Lesson Plan (Figure 6.4) which is completed collaboratively by the general educator and the special educator. Together, they use the information on the Student Profile, the Infused Skills Grid, and the standards and objectives for that teacher's particular unit to develop a modified unit for the student.

Another important aspect of the collaboration between general and special educators is sharing information regarding IEPs. A Teacher Input into Individualized Education Program form (Figure 6.5) is utilized to receive information and ideas from each student's general educator and is then shared at the student's IEP meeting. Most general educators are able to attend IEP meetings and personally share information due to the block schedule system at Kennedy High School. When a general educator is not able to attend an IEP, the special educator shares the information that was provided on the form.

Additional professionals, such as speech-language pathologists and occupational therapists, look for opportune times to provide services and support in inclusive environments. For example, some occupational therapy can be provided in a weight training class and, with a little creativity, speech-language therapy can occur during an English class or even during a biology lab. If it is not possible to provide specialized services in class, services are provided at a time that is least disruptive to instruction.

School name: *Kennedy High*	School year: *2002–2003*	**STUDENT PROFILE**

Student name: *Hannah McCoy*

Age: *17*

Grade: *12*

Parent/Guardian: *Mr. and Mrs. McCoy*

Telephone: *555-1212*

Advocate teacher: *Sheila Treat*

Classroom teacher: *Karri Thompson*

Class schedule	Room
Block 1:	
Senior English-Thompson	*1003*
Block 2:	
Math-Mitchell	*106*
Block 3:	
Aerobics-Joplin	*Gym*
Complete copy of IEP available in room 704.	

SPECIFIC OBJECTIVES FOR THIS CLASS:

1. Broaden knowledge of English curriculum
2. Increase social interactions with peers
3. Work on the following IEP goals:
- *Interacting appropriately with others*
- *Learning functional sight words*
- *Following directions*
- *Decreasing the need for paraprofessional support*

AREAS OF STRENGTH/INTEREST:

Hannah likes to draw, write, and put things together. She wants to help others.

SUCCESSFUL LEARNING STRATEGIES/MODIFICATIONS/ACCOMMODATIONS NEEDED:

Hannah will be supported by a paraprofessional and a peer tutor. With time, the staff support will be faded out, and a peer tutor will provide necessary support.

Hannah likes to copy and print words. She likes to read and is starting to read some sight words. Successful curricular modifications can include the use of pictures for essays, matching, and assignments requiring her to answer questions in complete sentences.

COMMUNICATION STRATEGIES:

Hannah is verbal. She will use gestures to help people further understand what she is saying.

POSITIVE BEHAVIORAL SUPPORT STRATEGIES:

When upset, Hannah gets red in the face. It is best to be explicit in giving her directions. Review the directions step by step with her. Giving her choices helps. She may grab others when she does not get her way. Paraprofessionals and peer tutors have been provided with strategies on how to diffuse such situations. See attached Behavior Support Plan.

GRADING ACCOMMODATIONS:

Hannah receives credit on the grade roster. She can receive letter grades on her assignments. A portfolio of completed classroom assignments will be reviewed quarterly and at Hannah's IEP meeting.

IMPORTANT FAMILY/HEALTH INFORMATION:

Hannah can become very sleepy at times. When this happens, it is best to have her go outside for a brief walk with a paraprofessional or her peer tutor.

Figure 6.2. Sample Student Profile. (From Castagnera, E., Fisher, D., Rodifer, K., & Sax, C. [1998]. *Deciding what to teach and how to teach it: Connecting students through curriculum and instruction* [pp. 29, 41]. Colorado Springs, CO: PEAK Parent Center; adapted by permission.)

TEACHER ASSIGNMENTS

Teacher's name: *Karri Thompson*   Week of: *2/10/03*
Student's name: *Hannah McCoy*

	Tests	Worksheets	Projects	Other	
Monday			X		*Learning stations*
Tuesday				X	*Essays*
Wednesday				X	*Peer reviews*
Thursday	X				*Great Expectations*
Friday				X	*Watch movie*

Comments: _____

_____

_____

Please return to ___*Sheila Treat's*___ box. Thanks!

Figure 6.3. Sample Teacher Assignments sheet. (From Rodifer, K., Castagnera, E., Fisher, D., & Sax, C. [1999]. Kennedy High School: From case-by-case to whole school inclusion. In D. Fisher, C. Sax, & I. Pumpian, *Inclusive high schools: Learning from contemporary classrooms* [p. 70]. Baltimore: Paul H. Brookes Publishing Co.; adapted by permission.)

The role of the special education teacher at Kennedy High School has become very different from that of the traditional special educator. Rather than teaching a special day class with all students with disabilities in one classroom, special educators coordinate the services and supports needed for the students to be successful in their general education classes. The special educator supports general educators and serves as an inclusion support teacher. He or she modifies the curriculum, supervises and trains people working with students with disabilities, and collaborates with general education teachers on how to best meet student needs.

Support for Inclusive Education

Inclusive education has a greater chance of being successful if the proper supports and services are in place. At Kennedy High School, support is provided in a variety of ways. These include accommodations, modified curricula, instructional and assistive technology, and personal support. An accommodation is a change made to the teaching or testing procedure that gives a student access to information and the ability to demonstrate knowledge and skills. Accommodations do not change the instructional level, content, or performance criteria for meeting the standards; rather, accommodations make it possible for students to gain access to and demonstrate knowledge of the same information. Examples of accommodations include enlarged print, oral versions of tests, books on audiotape, and calculators.

Although modifications to the curriculum are not always necessary, as is the case when teachers provide multilevel instruction, there are times when altering the assignment in some way benefits the student. There are four basic techniques used when modifying an assignment. The first technique, *same only less*, involves keeping the assignment the same except for reducing the number of items. An example of this technique is requiring a student to write only one paragraph when a five-paragraph essay is assigned. Writing assignments can also be completed with pictures, depending on the student's needs and ability levels. *Streamlining the curriculum* is a technique that reduces the assignment in size, emphasizing key points. For example, Hannah is required to focus on the main plot of a novel as opposed to the supporting details. A technique that ensures that IEP objectives are being addressed within the curriculum is using the *same activity with infused objective*. With this technique, the assignment remains the same, but an additional component, such as an IEP objective, is incorporated. For example, in Hannah's English class, students create a word wall by selecting words of their choice. Hannah selects her words from a sight word list to meet her IEP objective of increasing sight word recognition. With the final technique, *curriculum overlapping*, the assignment from one class can be completed in another class, such as completing requirements for a word processing class by typing assignments for other classes (Castagnera, Fisher, Rodifer, & Sax, 1998).

These four techniques can be used alone, used in combination, or not used at all. One assignment may only need to be reduced in size for the student to be successful, whereas another may lend itself easily toward infusing an important objective. Each technique should be considered for different situations. Additional examples of curricular modifications can be found in Castagnera and colleagues (1998).

Students may require personal support. This means that a paraprofessional, peer tutor, teacher, or therapist provides some sort of assistance to the student during the class. Personal support can include helping a student locate a classroom, assisting a student with the curriculum, helping a student keep assignments organized, and facilitating the student's social interactions with the rest of the class. Paraprofessionals often provide support

School name:	School year:	Class:	Unit:
Kennedy High	2002–2003	Senior English	Victorian Literature

Student name: Hannah McCoy
Age: 17
Grade: 12
Parent/Guardian: Mr. and Mrs. McCoy
Telephone: 555-1212
Advocate teacher: Sheila Treat
Classroom teacher: Karri Thompson

Class schedule	Room
Block 1:	
Senior English-Thompson	1003
Block 2:	
Math-Mitchell	106
Block 3:	
Aerobics-Joplin	Gym

MAJOR STANDARDS, OBJECTIVES, AND EXPECTATIONS FOR THE UNIT:

1. Students will learn about the Victorian time period.
2. Students will evaluate the theme of the Charles Dickens novel _Great Expectations_: judge a person by his or her character, not wealth.
3. Students will study three Victorian poets: Alfred, Lord Tennyson; Robert Browning; and Elizabeth Barrett Browning.

MATERIALS, BOOKS, MEDIA, WORKSHEETS, SOFTWARE, AND SO FORTH:

1. Copies of Victorian poems
2. The novel _Great Expectations_
3. All handouts and worksheets
4. Videotape of the movie _Great Expectations_
5. Learning stations for Victorian poets
6. Packet for essay

INSTRUCTIONAL ARRANGEMENTS (TIME AND OPPORTUNITIES FOR LARGE GROUP, SMALL GROUP, OR CO-OP GROUP PARTICIPATION; LEARNING CENTERS; INDIVIDUAL ACTIVITIES; NONCLASSROOM INSTRUCTION; EXPLAIN IF ANY OF THESE CHANGE FROM DAY TO DAY):

1. Learning stations for Victorian poets and learning about the time period
2. Large-group discussion when receiving the chapters assigned for homework
3. Think, pair, share method when discussing students' "expectations" and theme of the novel
4. Completion of individual assignments along the way

MATERIALS REQUIRING ADAPTATIONS AND/OR MODIFICATIONS:

1. Hannah will be given poems written in easier text and accompanied by pictures.
2. An audiotape version of _Great Expectations_ and a tape player will be available for Hannah.
3. A one-paragraph summary of each chapter, with comprehension questions requiring three- to four-word verbal answers, will be provided.
4. Hannah will complete a pictorial essay (collage).

INSTRUCTIONAL ITEMS REQUIRING ADAPTATIONS AND/OR MODIFICATIONS:

1. Provide Hannah with pictures representing the answers. She will verbally describe the pictures to her group, using three- to four-word sentences.

Figure 6.4. Sample Academic Unit Lesson Plan. (From Castagnera, E., Fisher, D., Rodifer, K., & Sax, C. [1998]. *Deciding what to teach and how to teach it: Connecting students through curriculum and instruction* [pp. 30–33, 43]. Colorado Springs, CO: PEAK Parent Center; adapted by permission.)

PROJECTS, SUPPLEMENTAL ACTIVITIES, AND HOMEWORK:

1. Individual poetry projects completed at each Victorian learning station
2. Worksheet on students' own "expectations" (i.e., goals in life)
3. Daily reading assignments of 20–30 pages of Great Expectations
4. Essay evaluating Pip

ITEMS REQUIRING ADAPTATIONS AND/OR MODIFICATIONS:

1. Hannah will be provided with simple poems to type on the computer.
2. Hannah will create a poster of personal goals, using magazine pictures and photographs.
3. Hannah will listen to the audiotape. A peer tutor will read one-paragraph chapter summaries and write down Hannah's answers (three- to four-word verbal responses) to the comprehension questions.
4. Hannah will complete a pictorial essay (collage).

ASSESSMENT(S) AND FINAL PRODUCTS (SUMMARIZE STUDENT PERFORMANCE ON THE REVERSE OF THIS PAGE; ATTACH EXAMPLES AS APPROPRIATE):

1. Poetry projects from the learning stations
2. Daily quizzes on the previous night's reading
3. Test once the novel is completed
4. Essay
5. Handouts to complete

ITEMS REQUIRING ADAPTATIONS AND/OR MODIFICATIONS:

1. Hannah will be given pictorial matching quizzes on the characters, main plot, and vocabulary words.
2. Hannah's test will be in a modified multiple-choice format (2 choices), will focus on the novel's main points, and will be read to Hannah.
3. Hannah will complete a pictorial essay (collage).

---

for students who present challenging behavior or when the course content is difficult.

DISTINGUISHING FEATURE: PEER TUTORING AT ITS BEST

Discussions regarding peer tutoring fall on a continuum from very ineffective to tremendously successful. Peer tutoring without the support and supervision from both special and general educators can result in a negative experience for everyone involved. However, when adequate support and knowledge of how to implement a peer tutoring course are combined, success can result. Numerous strategies allow a peer tutoring course to ascend to great heights. The following section provides detailed information of the peer tutoring course at Kennedy High School and the benefits experienced when a successful peer tutoring course is implemented.

Peer Tutoring Course

The peer tutoring course at Kennedy High is offered as an elective and provides graduation credit. The course consists of students in grades 9–12 assisting students with moderate and severe disabilities in general educa-

TEACHER INPUT INTO INDIVIDUALIZED EDUCATION PROGRAM

Teacher's name: *Karri Thompson*   Student's name: *Hannah McCoy*

Class: *English*   Block: *1*   Date: *3/3/03*

> IEP meeting is on *3/12/03* at *10 a.m.* Please let me know whether
> you can attend and whether you need a substitute. Thanks!
>
> *X* I can attend.   *X* I need a substitute.   ___ I cannot attend.

> Please return this form to ___*Sheila Treat's*___ mailbox. Thanks!

When completing the following items, please consider the relevant social, organizational, communication/language, and other areas in addition to academic/skill areas specific to your class and class activities.

1. Please list a few of the student's strengths demonstrated in your class
   (examples may include participation in group/class activities, presentations,
   social interactions with peers, and coming to class prepared):

   > *Hannah is very friendly toward other students. She wants to
   > participate in activities with other students. She is a joy to have
   > in class.*

2. Please list what you consider the most important skills that the student is
   learning in your class:

   > *Hannah's sight word reading has improved. She remains on task
   > for a longer period of time. She has been completing some
   > assignments independently.*

3. Please list the areas of need that you think are the most critical to the
   student's success in your class:

   > *Hannah needs to continue completing her assignments independently
   > and to remain on task.*

Figure 6.5.   Sample Teacher Input into Individualized Education Program. (From Rodifer, K., Castagnara, E., Fisher, D., & Sax, C. [1999]. Kennedy High School: From case-by-case to whole school inclusion. In D. Fisher, C. Sax, & I. Pumpian, *Inclusive high schools: Learning from Contemporary Classrooms* [p. 71]. Baltimore: Paul H. Brookes Publishing Co., adapted by permission.)

tion courses. Each peer tutor is paired with a student who has a disability. The tutor attends the general education class in which the student with a disability is enrolled, with the sole responsibility of supporting the student with the disability both academically and socially.

The focus of the peer tutor course is to provide more support to students with disabilities included in general education courses. Because of the support that peer tutors provide, the general school population experiences increased opportunities to be exposed to people with a variety of ability levels. This course also allows peer tutors to discover commonalities with people who have disabilities.

Peer tutors are taught how to assist students to be more actively involved in their classes, how to help these students complete their assignments, and how to facilitate communication and friendships with other students in the class. They receive instruction and assistance from the special educators. These teachers provide daily, ongoing training and support. Peer tutors also receive support and direction from paraeducators, specialists (e.g., speech-language pathologists), and general education teachers.

Peer tutors participate in formal training sessions provided by the special education teachers. These trainings focus on information pertaining to inclusion, curriculum modification, support strategies, the use of person-first language (e.g., "person with a disability" instead of "disabled person"), forms of communication, and a variety of learning disabilities. A major emphasis of the training is respect for and empowerment of the student being supported. These training sessions teach students to strive for social justice for people with disabilities and to celebrate human diversity. Learning and teaching strategies are practiced during these times, and the role and responsibilities of a peer tutor are explained in detail.

Peer tutors attend training sessions five times during an 18-week term. They do not go to class with the student whom they support on training days. While the peer tutors are receiving instruction, special education teachers work with the general education teachers to ensure that natural supports (e.g., students who are enrolled in the content class) are in place. This allows the peer tutors to meet as a group with the special education inclusion teachers for a training session.

These training sessions encourage peer tutors to develop an understanding of people with disabilities, which results in better support for students. The training sessions consist of short lectures, activities, homework assignments, and group discussions. There is a phenomenal response from the peer tutors during these group discussions. They truly recognize that the students whom they are assisting are individuals just like them and are their peers. The training sessions are specifically designed to encourage and guide peer tutors to independently formulate this sense of equality.

How Peer Tutoring Works

Peer tutors check in with the special education teacher at the beginning and end of the class. They briefly discuss the day's lesson plan, and the peer tutor shares what happened that day. They then decide what type of support, materials, and modifications will be needed.

The peer tutor is given a Weekly Assignments sheet (Figure 6.6) to be completed daily and to share with the special education teacher. The student with a disability fills out the calendar to the best of his or her ability, with the peer tutor assisting as necessary. The eventual goal is that the student with a disability will learn how to complete the Weekly Assignment sheet independently. This calendar provides information about what occurred in class, which assignments and topics are upcoming, and when tests and projects are due. The peer tutor also informs the special education teacher of any behavioral issues that are occurring in class and any of his or her own needs as a peer tutor.

Peer tutor grades are determined collaboratively by the special education teacher and the general education teacher. Information from a Peer Tutor Self-Evaluation (Figure 6.7) can also be utilized. Grades are based on attendance, the quality of support provided, and the completion of assignments.

Levels of Support

Often, peer tutors quickly become independent in providing appropriate support and adapting in-class assignments. Simple modification techniques are taught to the peer tutors during the training sessions. These include the strategies mentioned in the Support for Inclusive Education section, such as *same only less* and *streamlining the curriculum*. Peer tutors are also taught a variety of learning strategies such as note taking, paraphrasing, and color coding important information.

Peer tutors may provide physical assistance as needed. For example, they may write for a student who is unable to do so. Peer tutors are trained to utilize a variety of assistive technology devices, such as AlphaSmarts (portable keyboards), which are sent with students to their general education classes to aid in taking notes or completing written assignments. Peer tutors also become familiar and often assist students with using books on audiotape and augmentative and alternative communication devices, such as the BIGmack, which is a large push-button switch that can communicate a single message that is approximately 30 seconds long.

The peer tutor's ultimate goal is to have the student become as independent as possible and utilize the natural supports that are available in the

WEEKLY ASSIGNMENTS

Student name: _Hannah McCoy_   Subject: _English_

Monday	Tuesday	Wednesday	Thursday	Friday
Date: _2/10/03_	Date: _2/11/03_	Date: _2/12/03_	Date: _2/13/03_	Date: _2/14/03_
List class activities: _Learning stations on poetry_	List class activities: _Writing essays_	List class activities: _Editing peer essays_	List class activities: _Test_	List class activities: _Watch the movie_ _Great Expectations_
Homework assigned: _Work on poem_	Homework assigned: _Work on poem and essay_	Homework assigned: _Study for test_	Homework assigned: _Finish essay_	Homework assigned:
Upcoming assignments, projects, and tests: _Poems due Wednesday_	Upcoming assignments, projects, and tests: _Test on Thursday_ _Essay due Friday_	Upcoming assignments, projects, and tests:	Upcoming assignments, projects, and tests:	Upcoming assignments, projects, and tests:

Figure 6.6.   Sample Weekly Assignments sheet.

133

PEER TUTOR SELF-EVALUATION

Name of tutor: _____   Date: _____

Name of student supporting: _____

Directions: Complete the following evaluation form to grade yourself as a peer tutor. This can help you better understand the quality of your work.

1. How do you rate your attendance?	Great	Okay	Needs improvement
2. How flexible are you in responding to the needs of the student you are supporting?	Great	Okay	Needs improvement
3. How effective do you think you are as a peer tutor?	Great	Okay	Needs improvement
4. How positive are you as a role model?	Great	Okay	Needs improvement
5. How are you doing as a peer tutor?	Great	Okay	Needs improvement
6. How comfortable are you in your assigned general education class?	Great	Okay	Needs improvement
7. How do you use your time when working with the student you support?	Great	Okay	Needs improvement
8. How actively do you involve the student you support in class discussions, group work, and projects?	Great	Okay	Needs improvement

Figure 6.7.   Blank Peer Tutor Self-Evaluation. (From Villalobos, P.J., Tweit-Hull, D., & Wong, A. [2002]. Creating and supporting peer tutor partnerships in secondary schools. In J.S. Thousand, R.A. Villa, & A.I. Nevin [Eds.], *Creativity and collaborative learning: The practical guide to empowering students, teachers, and families* [2nd ed., p. 396]. Baltimore: Paul H. Brookes Publishing Co.; adapted by permission.)

classroom. During the training sessions, peer tutors are shown how to fade their support and facilitate interactions with other students in the class. With the help of general educators and peer tutors, other students can support students with disabilities when it is not disruptive to their own learning. For instance, peer tutors are taught to slowly fade their support during group projects when opportunities arise for natural support by the other students. Often, students in the class volunteer when they see that another student needs help. Peer tutors are not meant to foster dependency. Rather, they are to teach students with disabilities to be as independent as possible.

Not all students with disabilities require personal support in all classes. The level of support that an individual requires depends on many things, such as student behavior, course content, the classroom teacher, and the environment. Depending on student needs and the classroom environment, students with disabilities can utilize natural supports. Other students in the class volunteer to help by taking notes on carbon paper, recording homework assignments, reviewing course content for clarity, and involving students with disabilities in group activities. This sort of natural support occurs when students have friends in the class who are willing to help or when a general education teacher can orchestrate the support. Natural supports are essential. Not only do they provide a more natural learning environment for students with disabilities, they also allow support to be provided continuously, even in the peer tutor's absence.

Everyone Benefits

Students with disabilities, peer tutors, general and special educators, and the entire school community benefit from an effective peer tutor course. Students with disabilities are given numerous opportunities to build relationships with their peers. They are able to fully participate in a typical high school experience and to have peers without disabilities as models for learning. They receive greater academic support and have one-to-one assistance as needed. They are exposed to a greater number of academic and elective courses and are more involved in on-campus activities and clubs.

Peer tutoring has also been shown to be substantially beneficial to peer tutors. They increase their understanding and respect for individual differences. A sense of responsibility is developed, and valuable teaching techniques are gained. Peer tutors improve their communication and social skills. Friendships form that otherwise may have not have done so without a peer tutor course. Peer tutors also are exposed to a review of academic content and, as a result, increase their academic skills. A study conducted by Bond (2001) at Kennedy High School revealed the growth that peer tutors experienced in their academic classes as a result of being a peer tutor.

It was shown that peer tutors' knowledge increased in the subject areas in which they tutored. A large percentage of these peer tutors also stated in self-reflection questionnaires that they learned more about a subject area after tutoring in that class and that it affected their academic learning (Bond, 2001).

Research indicates that peer tutoring can be beneficial for all students involved. A correlation exists between the social development of students with disabilities and peer tutoring (Hughes et al., 1999; Staub & Hunt, 1993). Staub and Hunt also believed that peer tutoring enhances interactions and the development of prosocial behaviors and communications skills for students with disabilities. In addition, peer tutoring has been shown to be an effective strategy for teaching academics to students with moderate and severe disabilities (Longwill & Kleinert, 1998; Staub, Spaulding, Peck, Gallucci, & Schwartz, 1996).

Research also supports benefits for the peer tutors of students with moderate and severe disabilities. Peer tutors experience positive changes in attitude, increased appreciation of self-worth, and increased comfort levels around people with disabilities (Gartner & Lipsky, 1990; Staub et al., 1996). Furthermore, peer tutors of students with moderate and severe disabilities demonstrated increased academic performance in regard to personal responsibility and study skills (Cushing & Kennedy, 1997; Longwill & Kleinert, 1998).

Peer tutoring also provides additional support for both general and special education teachers. Peer tutors not only assist the students who require additional help, but also aid in curriculum modifications and adaptations. The school community is positively affected as well. All students and staff take an active role in recognizing the needs of each other, thereby creating a supportive atmosphere that will carry into the future. Those same students who have been in inclusive classrooms will become the lawmakers, teachers, business owners, voters, and citizens who will make community and business decisions that support people with disabilities.

The following statement by a Kennedy High School senior who graduated in 2001 is evidence of the far-reaching benefits of a peer tutoring program:

> In tenth grade, I needed an elective, so I enrolled in the peer tutor course. I didn't want to be a special education teacher at this time. I only wanted to get involved because my nephew has a disability. My experience as a peer tutor has had a positive influence on my life. I have learned that all students with disabilities are not the same. I have also learned how to modify work to make it easier for others. I didn't know we had so many

things to help kids, like assistive technology devices. I didn't even know what inclusion meant and how important it was until I became a peer tutor. I think peer tutoring and inclusion is really good. It gets people involved—it's not just a bunch of kids in a separate room. They get to learn with other people. Working with students with disabilities has been one of the best experiences of my life, so much that I want to further my schooling and major in special education. Working with students around my age is great, and I get to practice what I love to do! The friends that I have made are phenomenal and will be lifelong friends.

PRACTICAL IDEAS FOR IMPLEMENTING PEER TUTORING

As noted in the previous section, peer tutoring benefits all students. Any school can develop an effective peer tutoring course given the appropriate resources. The following section provides suggestions for developing a peer tutoring course, implementing peer tutor training sessions, and planning for the success of all students.

Make it a Graduation-Credit Class

The best way to implement a peer tutoring course is to make it a class for which students receive graduation credit. Before setting up any new course, administrative approval must be obtained. Be prepared to tell administrators about the benefits for students both with and without disabilities. Prepare a course description and meet with the personnel who are responsible for student scheduling, such as counselors. The rest of the faculty should be made aware of the new course and the rationale for using peers as support for students in their classes. Again, faculty must be made aware of the benefits experienced by all students. Having buy-in from the faculty increases the chance of success.

Once the faculty members are aware of the course, it should be advertised in any way possible. For example, a description of the course should be included in the school's catalog, and attractive flyers could be posted in the guidance office. At Kennedy High School, the peer tutoring course is even included as a suggested elective under the health and human services career pathway. It is also important to talk about the program with incoming freshman classes, as students who are new to the school may be unaware that such a course exists.

Many logistical matters must be determined when establishing a peer tutoring course, such as developing a training program and setting up systems for attendance, communication between peer tutors and teachers, and evaluation of peer tutors. At Kennedy, peer tutors report daily to the inclusion resource room at the beginning of each block. They sign the attendance sheet, then discuss with the inclusion support teacher what will occur in the classroom with the student whom they support. Modified curriculum and support strategies are provided to the peer tutor at this time. Then, the peer tutors either meet the student whom they support in the general education classroom or walk over to the classroom with him or her. Peer tutors should be given formal training as a group and information and training regarding the individual whom they are supporting.

Teach Peer Tutors the Necessary Skills

As part of the peer tutoring course, trainings should be designed to fit the needs of the peer tutors, as well as the needs of the students they will be supporting. At Kennedy High School, the peer tutor training sessions expose students to the philosophy of inclusive education and explain how to support students with a wide variety of disabilities. The five training topics are divided as follows: 1) introduction (e.g., inclusion, modifications, support and behavior, people first language, and respect), 2) modifying curriculum and teaching strategies, 3) support and behavior, 4) communication and learning disabilities, and 5) culminating activity and commentary. These training sessions are an integral part of the peer tutoring course.

Integrated into the trainings are hands-on activities that allow students to practice and demonstrate the concepts being taught. These activities allow the students to come to conclusions regarding person-first language, labeling, respect, and the differences and similarities between themselves and people with disabilities. One activity involves having the tutors compare their own circle of friends to that of someone with a disability. They discover that some people with disabilities have a circle of friends that consist primarily of paid professionals. Students' original assumptions about people with disabilities should then be discussed.

Students are asked to brainstorm possibilities for modifying a curriculum and to share their ideas with each other. They are taught numerous ways to adapt a curriculum. They are given case studies and are asked to creatively design ways to adapt the curriculum to ensure the success of their peers.

Opportunities are provided for the students to engage in a variety of activities. They practice active listening techniques to improve their skills when working with others. They complete a celebrity quiz, through which they learn about celebrities with a variety of learning disabilities (e.g., Winston Churchill, Tom Cruise, Walt Disney, Thomas Edison, Albert Einstein). Students participate in activities that allow them to experience what it is like to have a variety of challenges. For example, they are assigned a statement that they must communicate to one another without using verbal communication. In another activity, they are assigned a disability— such as a hearing loss, poor eyesight, reading or math learning disabilities, or a physical impairment—and asked to complete various activities. Their personal experiences are then discussed.

The culminating project for the term consists of tutors maintaining a portfolio that consists of items representing what the student whom they support has learned or accomplished. These items can include work samples, photographs, projects, positive remarks from teachers and other students, personal reflections on the student's success, and anything else that demonstrates student progress or achievement. These portfolios are often shared at IEP meetings and given to the students whom the tutors supported.

Plan for Success

Some simple strategies can make a difference in the success of a peer tutoring course. When implementing such a course, it is important to consider the needs of the peer tutor as well as the needs of the student with a disability. On the first day of class, peer tutors are asked to complete a Peer Tutor Survey (Figure 6.8). This survey provides special education inclusion teachers with pertinent information needed to pair the peer tutors with the students with disabilities. It is important to know the grade level of peer tutors and what classes they have taken. It is essential to try to the keep the peer tutors and students with disabilities close to the same grade level, as it is more comfortable for the students with disabilities. Seniors usually do not want freshman tutors helping them—typical teenagers! It is also useful if peer tutors have already taken or are currently enrolled in a similar course. This way, the peer tutors are knowledgeable about the subject area. Taking into account peer tutors' strengths and interests is also a key factor in making decisions about pairing students.

There are times when, for whatever reason, a peer tutor is not successful in certain situations. It may be a personality conflict between the two students, or there may even be something about the class that the peer tutor finds difficult or uncomfortable. In these cases, the peer tutors are reassigned to support a different student. Occasionally, a peer tutor finds that he or she is not happy or successful supporting *any* student in a class. In this situation, the tutor can be a classroom assistant to a special educator. He or she can be taught how to make modifications to the curriculum and can perform various office work, such as typing, filing, and making copies.

Peer Tutor Survey

Tutor name:_____ Date: _____

Block: _____ Year (circle): Freshman Sophomore Junior Senior

___

1. Please list your current schedule for this semester.

   Block   Class   Teacher

2. Please list any extracurricular activities in which you are involved, including clubs, sports teams, student government, and so forth.

3. Please list your favorite classes. Why do you enjoy these classes? Be specific.

4. What are your interests?

5. Do you have any hobbies and/or special skills? Please list.

6. Why did you sign up to become a peer tutor?

7. What type of help do you think you will need from the teachers to be more successful as a peer tutor?

If you need more space to respond to any of these questions, feel free to write on the back of this page.

Figure 6.8.   Blank Peer Tutor Survey. (From Villalobos, P.J., Tweit-Hull, D., & Wong, A. [2002]. Creating and supporting peer tutor partnerships in secondary schools. In J.S. Thousand, R.A. Villa, & A.I. Nevin [Eds.], *Creativity and collaborative learning: The practical guide to empowering students, teachers, and families* [2nd ed., p. 388]. Baltimore: Paul H. Brookes Publishing Co.; adapted by permission.)

CONCLUSION

Since the early 1990s, Kennedy High School has achieved success in implementing many school reforms. The school has an educational system that not only benefits students, but also sets an example for other schools. With the implementation of the Individuals with Disabilities Education Act (IDEA) Amendments of 1997 (PL 105-17), many schools struggle to provide an education for students with disabilities in general education environments. The many benefits of inclusive education are well known; however, inclusion can only be successful with the proper supports in place. Peer tutoring offers a way to provide support, with the added value of benefiting the person providing the support—the peer tutor. Designing a peer tutoring course initially takes a great deal of time, but once in place, it offers a way to successfully include students with disabilities in general education environments.

The peer tutoring course at Kennedy High School has been tremendously successful and is popular among students. This is evidenced by students enrolling in the course for more than one term. The peer tutoring course has been useful in providing the necessary supports to meet the diverse needs of students with disabilities. Due to the great success of Kennedy's peer tutoring course, a number of neighboring schools and nearby districts have visited the school and have implemented similar peer tutoring courses.

Kennedy High School has shown that with proper supports and resources, a peer tutoring course can be achieved successfully and with ease. It is important to note that the inclusion of all students with disabilities and the development of a peer tutoring course did not occur at once. Attempting to achieve too much at one time can sometimes lead to unexpected failures. Successful change happens little by little.

REFERENCES

Bond, R.J. (2001). *Peer tutors of students with moderate and severe disabilities in general education high school settings.* Unpublished master's thesis, San Diego State University, CA.

Castagnera, E., Fisher, D., Rodifer, K., & Sax, C. (1998). *Deciding what to teach and how to teach it: Connecting students through curriculum and instruction.* Colorado Springs, CO: PEAK Parent Center.

Cushing, L.S., & Kennedy, C.H. (1997). Academic effects of providing peer tutor support in general education classrooms on students without disabilities. *Journal of Applied Behavior Analysis, 30,* 139–151.

Gartner, A., & Lipsky, D.K. (1990). Students as instructional agents. In W. Stainback & S. Stainback (Eds.), *Support networks for inclusive schooling: Interdependent integrated education* (pp. 81–93). Baltimore: Paul H. Brookes Publishing Co.

Hughes, C., Guth, C., Hall, S., Presley, J., Dye, M., & Byers, C. (1999). They are my best friends: Peer buddies promote inclusion in high school. *Teaching Exceptional Children, 31*(5), 32–37.

Individuals with Disabilities Education Act (IDEA) Amendments of 1997, PL 105-17, 20 U.S.C. §§ 1400 *et seq.*

Longwill, A.W., & Kleinert, H.L. (1998). The unexpected benefits of high school peer tutoring. *Teaching Exceptional Children, 30*(4), 60–65.

Rodifer, K., Castagnera, E., Fisher, D., & Sax, C. (1999). Kennedy High School: From case-by-case to whole school inclusion. In D. Fisher, C. Sax, & I. Pumpian, *Inclusive high schools: Learning from contemporary classrooms* (pp. 53–74). Baltimore: Paul H. Brookes Publishing Co.

Staub, D., & Hunt, P. (1993). The effects of social interaction training on high school peer tutors of schoolmates with severe disabilities. *Exceptional Children, 60*, 41–57.

Staub, D., Spaulding, M., Peck, C.A., Gallucci, C., & Schwartz, E.S. (1996). Using nondisabled peers to support the inclusion of students with disabilities at the junior high school level. *The Journal of The Association for Persons with Severe Handicaps, 21*, 194–205.

Villalobos, P.J., Tweit-Hull, D., & Wong, A. (2002). Creating and supporting peer tutor partnerships in secondary schools. In J.S. Thousand, R.A. Villa, & A.I. Nevin (Eds.), *Creativity and collaborative learning: The practical guide to empowering students, teachers, and families* (2nd ed., pp. 379–403). Baltimore: Paul H. Brookes Publishing Co.

PEER-TO-PEER RELATIONSHIPS AS A FOUNDATION FOR INCLUSIVE EDUCATION

CRAIG H. KENNEDY

One explicit goal of inclusive education is facilitating social relationships between students with and without disabilities. Judging from the existing research base, this goal is being accomplished more effectively each year (see Fisher & Ryndak, 2001). However, researchers are learning that for inclusive education to be meaningful and effective, peer-to-peer relationships are more than an outcome—they are a critical component of the process of inclusive education.

Without well-developed peer-to-peer relationships, inclusive education cannot exist. Developing those relationships, however, is a challenging part of the process of inclusion. This commentary highlights a few key points that reflect on Chapter 6 and the importance of peer-to-peer relationships in developing inclusive educational practices. Throughout this commentary, I refer to approaches for facilitating peer-to-peer relationships using the generic term *peer support strategies* (see Kennedy, in press).

WHY ARE PEER SUPPORT STRATEGIES IMPORTANT?

Peer support strategies produce at least three important outcomes for students with and without disabilities in inclusive educational environments: 1) belonging, 2) equality, and 3) social support.

Belonging

Belonging means being a valued part of a classroom and school. When a student, with or without disabilities, feels like he or she belongs to a classroom, that student identifies him- or herself as a member of that environment and a contributor to its success. Similarly, belonging implies a certain level of reciprocity. Not only does a student feel like he or she is part of a classroom, but others in the classroom also view that student as an important member of the class.

Equality

Another benefit of inclusion is increasing a particular student's equality among his or her peers. *Equality* refers to being perceived as the same as others. Like belonging, it suggests an "embeddedness" within a social milieu, but it also implies that a person is viewed as similar to others. For example, a student with disabilities who is perceived as being the equal of his or her peers without disabilities is considered to have similar status, power, and prestige. This does not mean that others ignore or are unaware of the student's disability, only that they see beyond the disability and appreciate the person for his or her abilities.

Social Support

Along with belonging and equality is the more tangible idea of social support. Typically, *social support* refers to behaviors that people engage in to help each other in some way. For example, people might share information about current events at school, loan someone a pencil to take a test, or provide assistance to someone when he or she is transferring from a wheelchair. These exchanged behaviors provide a person with supports that he or she might not otherwise obtain. Such behaviors form a basis for why social interaction contributes so significantly to a person's sense of happiness and well-being.

Again, for the outcomes of belonging, equality, and social support to occur, peer support strategies seem to be a necessary part of the inclusion process. This is because peer-to-peer relationships provide the context for social relationships to develop and beneficial outcomes to emerge. It has been repeatedly shown that inclusive school environments provide these benefits to students with and without disabilities to a far greater degree than more traditional educational arrangements (e.g., self-contained or resource classrooms) (Fryxell & Kennedy, 1995; Kennedy, Shukla, & Fryxell, 1997).

HOW DO SCHOOLS FACILITATE PEER SUPPORTS?

As is reflected in the many chapters in this book, inclusion is not based on a single student or teacher; it is a schoolwide effort. So if peer support strategies are a foundation for inclusive practices, how do schools facilitate peer supports? The following subsections detail three ways in which schoolwide efforts enable effective peer support programs.

Creating Interdisciplinary Teams

Administrators usually structure the planning activities of educational professionals in their school buildings using education teams (Fisher, Sax, & Pumpian, 1999; Kennedy & Fisher, 2001). Unlike traditional approaches to school structure, school teams focus on groups of students across academic disciplines. This is a radical departure from traditional arrangements based on a particular discipline (e.g., the math team).

Interdisciplinary teams are composed of a group of teachers from the same grade level, each with a different area of expertise, working together to focus on a specific group of students. Often, teams are composed of teachers from the following disciplines: English/language arts, health, math, science, social studies, and special education. The students who are the focus of the team's efforts are heterogeneous. The students then attend classes in their different content areas with the teachers from the interdisciplinary teams.

Such arrangements allow teachers across disciplines to coordinate the curriculum. Interdisciplinary teams also allow coordination efforts to focus on a specific group of students. Because each student takes classes with each team member, the teachers (as a group) get to know the students in their team much better than in traditional arrangements. In addition, school teams embed special education services within the context of other academic disciplines. This means that special educators are involved from the beginning in curriculum planning and the development of curricular modifications or adaptations for students. The benefits of interdisciplinary teams create a structure that is conducive to meeting the needs of a broad range of students within the general education classroom.

Providing Access to the General Education Curriculum

A significant barrier to inclusive educational practices has been that students with and without disabilities are learning different curricula. This limits inclusion when students with and without disabilities are in the same educational environments but are required to learn different material. Schoolwide efforts to coordinate curriculum for students with differing abilities has been an important component of effective school inclusion.

Referred to as "aligning with the general education curriculum," this strategy facilitates access for students with disabilities to what students without disabilities learn in general education classes (Ryndak & Billingsley, in press).

Typically, the goals from a student's individualized education program (IEP) are assessed to see which goals could be learned in a general education class. For IEP goals to be taught in general education classes, special education teachers and paraprofessionals focus on ensuring that the student's goals are met within the framework of the classroom curriculum. Material can be modified or adapted as required, but the student 1) has contact with the same material as other students in the class and 2) meets the goals specified on his or her IEP as being important skills/knowledge to acquire.

There are multiple positive outcomes of providing equal access to the general education curriculum. First, general education teachers are provided with a context within which to understand what the student with disabilities needs to learn. Second, special educators are provided with specific materials that they need to incorporate into a student's instructional activities. Finally, students with and without disabilities are able to work on the same class materials and themes, reducing the possibility of isolation as a result of curricular differences.

Rethinking the Role of Paraprofessionals

Clearly, in an inclusive school, teachers who specialize in teaching students with a particular type of disability cannot be in every classroom with every student each period. (Otherwise, the school would not be inclusive.) The challenge of needing to be in several school environments simultaneously is causing a rethinking of the roles and responsibilities of paraprofessionals.

When students with a specific disability were taught in a single classroom (e.g., a self-contained classroom), who did what with whom was clear. For example, paraprofessionals directly worked with students with disabilities and were supervised by the special educator who was the "classroom teacher." However, in inclusive environments, the student with disabilities is part of the general education class and special educators are consultants to those multiple classrooms.

The need to have special educators in multiple environments has prompted researchers to reconsider what paraprofessionals do (Giangreco, Broer, & Edelman, 2002). During initial efforts to include students with disabilities into general education classes, paraprofessionals were assigned as direct support providers to those students. However, two problems have arisen. First, there are not enough paraprofessionals to match to students with disabilities on a one-to-one basis. Second, directly assigning paraprofessionals to particular students with disabilities often creates barriers to interaction for students with and without disabilities.

Work regarding paraprofessionals' roles in inclusive schools is focusing on having these individuals serve as indirect support providers who are under the dual supervision of the general education teacher and the special education consultant. Within the context of peer-to-peer relationships, this arrangement allows paraprofessionals to supervise peer support programs to facilitate appropriate social interactions. In addition, it provides the general education teacher with additional assistance in the classroom. Such an arrangement also provides the special educator with the opportunity to move among multiple general education classrooms.

HOW CAN OTHER SCHOOLS FACILITATE PEER SUPPORTS?

In Chapter 6, Bond and Castegnera do a wonderful job of identifying what needs to be done to facilitate peer supports. Establishing peer support programs at a school is a nonlinear endeavor that requires time and effort (Kennedy & Fisher, 2001). The three topics discussed in the preceding section are essential for a schoolwide effort to support inclusive education by using peer support programs. However, the following subsections discuss three steps that educators can take to begin developing peer support programs like those described by Bond and Castegnera.

Identify General Education Classes and Peers

Most efforts to develop peer support programs end before they ever start. This is because the task of identifying when, where, and who to use as peer supports is very different from the traditional activities in which special educators have been taught to engage. This requires effective communication and interaction with administrators, parents, general education teachers, and students without disabilities.

A necessary first step in developing peer support programs is to identify which general education classes a student will attend. The literature on peer support programs suggests that there are numerous ways of going about this task, including 1) administrative recommendations, 2) personal contacts, 3) expressions of interest by other school personnel, and 4) school building announcements. An important issue when looking to establish collaborative relationships in general education environments is to be clear and honest about expectations, roles, and responsibilities for everyone involved.

Similarly, peers without disabilities who can serve as peer supports in general education classrooms need to be identified. Effective strategies for recruiting peer supports include 1) using members of a student's current friendship network, 2) contacting friends of friends, 3) making classroom announcements, and 4) making school building announcements. As with adult-to-adult relationships, it is important to clearly specify with peers what is expected of the various parties involved in the peer support groups.

Identify Curricular Content and Instructional Strategies

Allowing students with disabilities to learn new skills and ideas within the context of the general education curriculum greatly facilitates belonging and membership in a classroom. Using an IEP Matrix to find opportunities to embed IEP objectives within specific general education classes has emerged as an effective means of aligning general and special education curricula (Ryndak & Billingsley, in press).

In addition, rethinking the curricular needs of a student with disabilities within the context of each subject area (e.g., math, science) facilitates curricular integration. When curricular content issues are resolved, instructional strategies—long the strength of special educators—can be identified and matched to the needs of the student and learning context.

Use Special Educators as a Classroom-Wide Resource

Most educators initially react to inclusion by placing the special education paraprofessional next to the student with disabilities. Such an arrangement at first seems intuitive, efficient, and able to ensure a high level of adult supervision. Yet, Giangreco and colleagues (2002) clearly showed the negative effects of using a paraprofessional as the primary support person in a general education classroom. If part of the goal of being in general education environments is the development of peer-to-peer relationships, then using paraprofessionals in this traditional arrangement is counterproductive.

By adopting peer support strategies, paraprofessionals become classroom-wide resources for the teacher and the students, and the facilitation of peer-to-peer interactions becomes easier to accomplish. Although this approach requires educators to rethink some of their assumptions regarding the use of paraprofessionals and may require additional training and supervision, the improved social and academic outcomes are well worth the effort involved.

CONCLUSION

This commentary briefly summarizes some of my thoughts on the benefits of peer support programs and issues related to effectively implementing these strategies. Chapter 6 is an excellent blueprint and reflection on how one school has established programs for facilitating peer-to-peer relationships. For educators interested in establishing peer support programs, Bond and Castagnera's chapter is an outstanding resource. In addition, the reference section that follows this commentary lists some additional resources that readers may find useful in facilitating social relationships in inclusive schools. Regarding peer-to-peer relationships, it is important to remember that although they are not tradition-ally considered part of a student's IEP, social relationships are at the heart of what an inclusive school is and what it hopes to achieve. Incorporating active efforts to facilitate social interactions and friendships among students with and without disabilities has numerous short- and long-term benefits for all involved.

REFERENCES

Fisher, D., & Ryndak, D. (2001). *The foundations of inclusive education.* Baltimore: TASH.

Fisher, D., Sax, C., & Pumpian, I. (1999). *Inclusive high schools: Learning from contemporary classrooms.* Baltimore: Paul H. Brookes Publishing Co.

Fryxell, D., & Kennedy, C.H. (1995). Placement along the continuum of services and its impact on students' social relationships. *Journal of The Association for Persons with Severe Handicaps, 20,* 259–269.

Giangreco, M.F., Broer, S.M., & Edelman, S.W. (2002). "That was then, this is now!" Parapro-fessional supports for students with disabilities in general education classrooms. *Exceptionality, 10*(1), 47–64.

Kennedy, C.H. (in press). Social relationships. In C.H. Kennedy & E. Horn (Eds.), *Including students with severe disabilities.* Boston: Allyn & Bacon.

Kennedy, C.H., & Fisher, D. (2001). *Inclusive middle schools.* Baltimore: Paul H. Brookes Publishing Co.

Kennedy, C.H., Shukla, S., & Fryxell, D. (1997). Comparing the effects of educational place-ment on the social relationships of intermediate school students with severe disabili-ties. *Exceptional Children, 64,* 31–47.

Ryndak, D., & Billingsley, F. (in press). Accessing the general education curriculum. In C.H. Kennedy & E. Horn (Eds.), *Including students with severe disabilities.* Boston: Allyn & Bacon.

chapter 7

How-To High

Analyses and Processes in Chicago High Schools

MARK W. DOYLE AND LAURA OWENS

SCHOOLS DIFFER depending on their leadership and school culture; however, high schools typically function in ways that tend to exclude students with disabilities from participating in general education environments. For students and staff, the culture of high schools tends to be impersonal, hurried, and competitive. Teachers tend to work in isolation, seldom interacting with other professionals to problem solve or share strategies. In addition, the curricula and instructional strategies are generally dictated by district or state guidelines, limiting the amount of interdisciplinary instruction and collaboration among colleagues (Bauer & Brown, 2001). Segregation of students with disabilities is considered necessary due to the belief that student success is based on performance in subject-specific knowledge. The idea that all students must perform equally also affects instructional practices, course content, and student placement (Roach, 1999). Another factor that affects inclusive educational practices in high schools is the structure of the school day. Although some schools are moving toward block scheduling (versus the 48-minute class period), too often instruc-

We acknowledge two individuals who have journeyed with us in our quest to make schools a better place for *all* students: Peter Zimmerman at Stephen Tyng Mather High School and Diane Jackson at Englewood High School.

tional practices are essentially the same. Teachers who must teach using the traditional 48-minute class period report that they do not have the time to individualize instruction or to utilize varied instructional arrangements such as cooperative group activities.

The goal of education is to teach students the skills necessary to live, work, and recreate in America's diverse society. The U.S. Department of Labor (1991), in its watershed Secretary's Commission on Necessary Skills (SCANS) report, identified eight categories of skills needed for success in life:

1. Identify, organize, plan, and allocate resources

2. Work with others

3. Acquire and use information

4. Understand complex relationships

5. Work with a variety of technologies

6. Perform basic skills (e.g., read, write, perform arithmetic and mathematical operations, listen, speak)

7. Perform thinking skills (e.g., think creatively, make decisions, solve problems, visualize, know how to learn, reason)

8. Display certain personal qualities (e.g., responsibility, self-esteem, sociability, self-management, integrity, honesty).

These skills can and should be taught within the context of the general education curriculum. For example, in a geometry class, students are taught the core academic content for the class. In addition, students learn several skills necessary for success in adult life, including basic reading and writing; understanding the complexities of relationships; organizing thoughts about theories; and displaying personal qualities such as responsibility, sociability, and self-management. In other words, academic classes provide students with both content knowledge and life skills.

These opportunities are also necessary for students with disabilities. Too often, however, the task of supporting students in inclusive high schools is seen as overwhelming or unnecessary. Students with disabilities are then provided an "alternative" or "functional" curriculum in which they do not acquire content knowledge or the necessary social skills to be successful as adults (Wagner, Blackorby, Cameto, Hebbeler, & Newman, 1993). As a result, the lack of student success is often blamed on the student and his or her disability rather than on the system of support being offered. Lawsuits, parent grievances, and state compliance reports suggest that school districts are using the wrong approach for educating students with disabilities.

Getting it right, however, is not a simple task. In general, high schools are complex systems that make supporting students with disabilities a chal-

Table 7.1. Challenges facing urban high schools

Student issues	Educator issues	Staffing, building, and policy issues
Student performance below ninth-grade level	Major emphasis on outcomes/standards versus good instructional strategies	Overrepresentation of students with disabilities
English as a second language and multiculturalism	Focus on content-driven instruction	Shortages of both special educators and general educators, particularly in math and science
Admission criteria that discriminate	Multiple initiatives competing for time and resources	Difficulty in securing substitutes for teacher planning time, staff development, and basic classroom coverage
Use of grades for assessing student classroom performance	Lack of planning time	
	Exclusive use traditional support models (i.e., self-contained classrooms or resource rooms)	Safety and security
High mobility rate of students		Size of the building and number of students
Frequent discipline referrals leading to lost time in the classroom	Lack of proven processes (e.g., planning, staff development)	Declining student enrollment
	Lack of data-driven decisions by the educational team	Policies that dictate class selection (e.g., all students must take trigonometry)
	Poor parent involvement	
	Insufficient orientation and training regarding inclusion	

lenging, but not impossible, proposition (McLeskey & Waldron, 2000). In Chapter 10 of this book, Villa, Falvey, and Schrag identify several of the challenges that personnel face in urban schools. A summary of the challenges we have encountered is presented in Table 7.1.

Many of these challenges require a simultaneous and focused effort and a great deal of resources to address. This chapter first focuses on the importance of analyzing the special education service delivery system and other systems operating in the high school that influence the support of students in general education classrooms. Then, the chapter outlines various processes that may help high schools address each of these challenges. Stressed throughout the chapter is the importance of implementing effective resource management, gathering critical information and data, establishing customized processes, teaming and collaborating, using meaningful instruction, using differentiated and effective instructional strategies, and supporting diversity in classrooms rather than labeling diversity as a cause for separation.

CONTEXT: THE CHICAGO PUBLIC SCHOOL EXPERIENCE

Our experience in supporting students with disabilities is drawn from more than 65 Chicago public schools, half of which are high schools. The Chicago Public School (CPS) district is the third largest in the United States. In 596 schools, the district serves 435,470 students, of whom 52% are African American, 35% are Hispanic/Latino, 9.6% are Caucasian, 3.9% are Asian/ Pacific Islander, and 0.2% are Native American. Nearly 85% of the students are from low-income families, and 13.8% have limited English proficiency. Approximately 57,500 (10%) of CPS students have been identified as being eligible for special education. CPS employs 26,348 teachers. There are 92 secondary schools (including 48 schools that are general, technical, or academic preparatory), 13 specialty schools, 16 magnet schools, 8 community academies, 7 vocational schools, and 6 secondary charter schools.

Much of this chapter's information comes from the initial experience of working with two CPS high schools: Stephen Tyng Mather High School and Roberto Clemente Community Academy High School. These schools taught us a great deal about urban high schools and were environments that offered opportunities to try out change processes. Over the past several years, these processes have been expanded on, fine tuned, and customized for several additional high schools in CPS, including Englewood Technical Preparatory, Roosevelt, Taft, Bogan, and Juarez, among others. These processes have proven to be successful in supporting the schools' efforts to educate students with disabilities as part of the diversity experienced in urban high school classrooms.

It is important to note that these schools began working toward a more inclusive schooling because of a class action lawsuit, *Corey H. v. Board of Education of the City of Chicago, et al.* This case mandated that all Chicago public schools develop a plan to include students with disabilities in the least restrictive environment (LRE), in accordance with the Individuals with Disabilities Education Act (IDEA) and its amendments. The following section provides a brief overview of the lawsuit and the response of CPS before focusing on the processes that have been used to facilitate inclusive educational opportunities.

Class Action Lawsuit

CPS, similar to the Los Angeles Unified School District, was out of compliance with both federal and state laws. On May 22, 1992, Corey and three other students with disabilities, along with their parents, filed a class-action lawsuit in federal court on behalf of all students with disabilities receiving services from CPS. Plaintiffs alleged that the Board of Education of the City of Chicago (or the Chicago Board) and the Illinois State Board of

Education (ISBE) were not educating students with disabilities in the CPS district in the LRE. The plaintiffs sought to have CPS and ISBE correct the alleged systematic failures by educating children with disabilities in the LRE.

Under the court-approved settlement agreement in 1998, the district must, over an 8-year period, ensure that (at a total cost of approximately $24 million) between one third and one half of its 553 schools become compliant with IDEA's LRE mandate. A monitor was appointed to oversee the implementation of the agreement. ISBE decided not to settle this matter, so the case proceeded to trial on October 22, 1997. After a week-long trial and a review of extensive evidence, the judge found in favor of the plaintiffs. Judge Gettleman stated that ISBE continued to "defend the undefendable and deny the undeniable."

The Response of the Chicago Public School District

Resulting from the lawsuit and settlement agreement, one of CPS's actions was to create "Education Connection—School-Based LRE Plans and Staff Development Project." Education Connection is a 3-year process during which each school receives an average of $110,000 to assist in devising a staff development process to enhance the ability to educate students with and without disabilities together. Through a school-based planning process, schools that are selected for the Education Connection review the way in which services are provided to students with disabilities and design a plan that will enable students with disabilities to be educated, with appropriate supports and services, in the general education classroom. The following section provides an overview of 2 of the 28 schools selected for participation in the Education Connection. Each year, 30 additional schools are selected. Schools can use their grant funds for professional development, technical assistance, and teacher release days to implement the plan.

Both schools profiled, Stephen Tyng Mather High School and Roberto Clemente Community Academy High School, have committed to moving toward an inclusive delivery model outlined in their plans. Mather was one of the first high schools to participate in the Education Connection project, whereas Clemente joined later. Each school brings a completely different set of resources, structures, and students. Each school has been a wealth of opportunity to improve the process of supporting students with disabilities in the LRE.

Stephen Tyng Mather High School

Mather is a general high school that serves a diverse population of more than 1,950 students. It is a multilingual, multicultural school. Seventy-five percent of Mather students speak a language other than English at home, and more than 50% of the students have been in an English as a Second Language (ESL) program at some time during their school years. Students' home languages include Romanian, Greek, Filipino, Korean, Arabic, Bulgarian, Hindi, Vietnamese, Korean, Malay, Polish, or one of the other 50 languages of the school community. Students are served by teachers of ESL classes in language arts, social studies, and computer science. Mather serves 211 students (11%) who have been identified as having a disability.

Mather High School has been a member of the Coalition of Essential Schools (CES) since 1990. CES, a school reform movement conceptualized by Theodore R. Sizer, has provided the faculty with a common philosophy of the Ten Principles of Essential Schools. These Ten Principles, adapted by the faculty at Mather, are included in Table 7.2.

Because Mather is a CES member, its faculty have focused on authentic student assignments and assessment, integrated curriculum, personalization, and the creation of strong learning communities to avoid problems caused by teacher and student isolation. These teachers acknowledge that school reform and restructuring are easily developed on paper. Actual change in their school and classrooms has been slow but steady. There have been moments of great frustration and moments of breathtaking success. Students are engaged and active, searching for answers to interesting questions. Students are comfortable in class, and they feel important and respected. There is a tone of decency in the school, and the ideas of all members of the school community are respected.

Mather, built in the 1950s, is a single-story building designed to support 1,200 students. To accommodate its 1,950 students, Mather has five different start times for students. Given these space limitations, Mather has not had space for self-contained special education classrooms. As a result, students with disabilities are usually educated in general education classes. Thus, space limitations, coupled with a CES philosophy and the ethnic diversity of Mather's students, has led to a culture of respect for diversity and inclusion over the years. Mather staff provide specialized instructional services for students with disabilities in a variety of ways, including special education teacher consultation with general educators; resource room homework support; team-teaching and co-teaching between general and special educators; and self-contained classes for a few students. When the faculty at Mather wrote their original plan, most of the students with disabilities were educated in resource rooms. The goal established by the Mather staff was to expand the number of students supported in general education classes through the use of collaborative teaching and team-teaching. Within 2 years Mather staff and administration increased the number of team-taught classes from 6 to 27. In observing the Mather faculty expand the collaborative teaching and team-teaching models, we have

Table 7.2. Ten Principles of Essential Schools

1. The school should focus on helping adolescents learn to use their minds well. A school should not attempt to be "comprehensive" if such a claim is made at the expense of the school's central intellectual purpose.

2. The school's goal should be simple: that each student master a limited number of essential skills and areas of knowledge. Although these skills and areas will, to varying degrees, reflect the traditional academic disciplines, the program's design should be shaped by the intellectual and imaginative powers and competencies that students need rather than by conventionally defined subjects. The aphorism "less is more" should dominate: Curricular decisions should be guided by the aim of thorough student mastery and achievement rather than by an effort to cover content.

3. The school's goal should apply to all students, whereas the means to this goal will vary as students themselves vary. School practice should be tailor made to meet the needs of every group or class of adolescents.

4. Teaching and learning should be personalized to the maximum feasible extent. Efforts should be directed toward a goal of no teacher having direct responsibility for more than 80 students. To capitalize on this personalization, decisions about the details of the course of study, the use of students' and teachers' time, and the choice of teaching materials and specific pedagogies must be unreservedly placed in the hands of the principal and staff.

5. The governing practical concept of the school should be "student as worker" rather than the more familiar one of "teacher as deliverer of instructional services." Accordingly, coaching will be a prominent pedagogy to provoke students to "learn how to learn" and, thus, to teach themselves.

6. Students who enter secondary school studies are those who show competence in language and elementary mathematics. Students of traditional high school age who are not yet at appropriate levels of competence to enter secondary school studies will be provided intensive remedial work to assist them to meet these standards quickly. A diploma should be awarded upon successful final demonstration of mastery for graduation, or an "exhibition." A student's exhibition of his or her grasp of the central skills and knowledge of the schools' program may be jointly administered by the faculty and by higher authorities. Because the diploma is awarded when earned, the school's program proceeds with no strict age grading and with no system of credits earned by time spent in class. The emphasis is on student demonstration of possessing important skills.

7. The tone of the school should explicitly and self-consciously stress values of "unanxious expectation" ("I won't threaten you but I expect much of you."), trust (until abused), and decency (the values of fairness, generosity, and tolerance). Incentives appropriate to the school's particular students and teachers should be emphasized, and parents should be treated as essential collaborators.

8. The principal and teachers should perceive themselves as generalists first (teachers and scholars in general education) and specialists second (experts in but one particular discipline). Staff should expect multiple obligations (teacher, counselor, manager) and a sense of commitment to the entire school.

9. Ultimate administrative and budget targets should include (in addition to total student loads per teacher of 80 or fewer pupils) substantial time for collective planning by teachers, competitive salaries for staff, and an ultimate per-pupil cost not to exceed that at traditional schools by more than 10%. To accomplish this, administrative plans may have to show the phased reduction or elimination of some services now provided students in many traditional comprehensive secondary schools.

10. The school should demonstrate nondiscriminatory and inclusive policies, practices, and pedagogies. It should model democratic practices that involve all who are directly affected by the school. The school should honor diversity and build on the strengths of its communities, deliberately and explicitly challenging all forms of inequity.

learned a great deal about the efficient use of resources. This information, which is useful for other high schools, is discussed later in this chapter.

Roberto Clemente Community Academy High School

Clemente High School serves approximately 1,783 students. Eighty-nine percent of students live at the poverty level and qualify for free or reduced-price lunches. More than 86% of Clemente's students are Hispanic/Latino; 11% of students are African American; 2% are Caucasian, and 0.4% are Asian (primarily Vietnamese). These percentages have remained fairly stable (i.e., the percentage of Hispanic/Latino students was 85.2 in 1995 and 86.2 in 2001). Twenty-three percent of students have limited English proficiency. The majority of the students' parents did not complete high school. Clemente High School serves 343 students with disabilities (19%).

Clemente serves the area of West Town, where unemployment is high. Signs of community vitality include the Wilbur Wright Vocational Technical Center, the New Humboldt Park Library Branch, and a new sports complex. The community's assets include several physical and mental health care providers, active and stable community social agencies, and vibrant social and cultural institutions.

Clemente is structured into two academies: the Junior Academy, made up of ninth- and tenth-grade students, and the Senior Academy, made up of eleventh- and twelfth-grade students. The Junior Academy is organized into units (cores) of approximately 100 students and 8 teachers each. Of these 100 students, approximately 20 have disabilities. This structure ensures that students with disabilities are not grouped together for classes and that they accrue the benefits of these smaller learning communities. Each teacher within the core is responsible for the basic curriculum and related subjects. The structuring of Clemente staff is based on student needs and includes a bilingual and/or ESL teacher when needed. There are four cores of 100 freshmen. Each core has clerical, supervisory, and resource staff. This particular structure is similar to a "school within a school" model.

In the Senior Academy, teachers provide instruction in the career pathways or college preparatory areas such as the Legal Careers Pathway, which includes courses in social studies and English, field experiences, and internships in local legal or government offices. The Architecture and Building career pathway includes courses in math, science, and drafting, as well as internships in the community (e.g., with Habitat for Humanity).

Twice per week, the staff from the cores at the Junior Academy attend staff development meetings, or learning community meetings. Once per week, these staff work with teachers from two different cores to support instructional activities. The other weekly meeting is used to share lesson plans, discuss strategies for improving student performance, and generate solutions for specific student's academic, behavior, or attendance problems.

The faculty from Clemente focused on their instructional strategies for supporting students with disabilities in their improvement plans. As they have implemented these plans, students with disabilities have experienced greater access to the core curriculum and have needed fewer paraprofessional supports. Again, we have had the opportunity to learn from this school's faculty as we have developed processes for school change. The next section focuses on the distinguishing features of Mather and Clemente and the many other Chicago public schools that have worked to make inclusive education a reality.

DISTINGUISHING FEATURES

This section highlights the importance of self-assessment as a way for high schools to move toward more inclusive school communities. Historically, students with high-incidence disabilities (i.e., learning disabilities) were supported in high school general education classes through the concept *mainstreaming*. Mainstreaming gave students with mild disabilities access to general education classes only when they could "keep up" with the curriculum. Students were segregated when they required additional assistance or individualized instruction to be successful. However, since the 1990s, students with more significant support needs have been included in high school general education classrooms (Jorgensen, 1998). Advocates of this service delivery system known as *inclusion* believe that supports can and should be brought to the students in their general education classroom rather than requiring students to leave the classroom to receive needed supports. School personnel often confuse the two terms and their philosophical differences. Too often, special education is seen as a place within the school and not a set of unique supports and services that can be transported throughout the school. Unfortunately, many school staff and administrators say they provide inclusive environments for all students with disabilities but their schools still operate numerous segregated, self-contained classrooms. Thankfully, increasing numbers of teachers and administrators have created inclusive schools. We have learned from them that self-analysis is a powerful tool for creating inclusive schools.

Self-Analysis of Current Systems

A critical ingredient to successful school reform is making a commitment to understanding the culture of a school and customizing processes to that particular school's needs. As a result, a constant expansion of the scope of processes is necessary to be responsive to the variety of needs encountered. For example, in the early stages of the CPS Education Connection project, it was assumed schools would see the need to and know how to engage in self-analysis of their special education service delivery system. Some schools were able to self-analyze, others relied on an external consultant to assist them, and still others attempted to move forward without completing a self-analysis. The schools in the last group had the most difficulty getting their plans approved by the regional offices and court monitors. These schools had even more difficulty successfully supporting students with disabilities in general education classrooms.

The process of self-analysis has evolved since the late 1990s. Many schools, as well as the district itself, relied on an external consultant who had experience with the special education service delivery system to assist with the self-analysis. In the initial year of the Education Connection (1997), the selected planning sites were given a seven-page template that contained format and content tips for school teams to use when drafting their plans. The original analysis required teams to attend specific focus areas, including the following:

1. The extent to which students residing in the school's attendance area are or are not attending the school

2. The extent to which students with disabilities are participating in all aspects of the school, including academic and nonacademic classes, extracurricular activities, and testing

3. The support models employed when students with disabilities participate with peers who do not have disabilities

4. The number and type of school-based intervention and behavior management strategies utilized within the last year

In addition, magnet, gifted, charter, and vocational schools were asked to include information regarding their general admission criteria, recruiting methods, admissions tests, and accommodations provided to students with disabilities.

As we worked with schools in gathering this information, additional questions arose, and further information was necessary to better analyze each school's needs. This additional information included items such as planning and collaboration efforts, the type of instruction provided in general education classrooms, the ways in which progress is documented, the interventions available to students and teachers prior to individualized education program (IEP) referral, staff stability, and professional development opportunities.

As the plans were reviewed by various constituent groups and compared with the settlement agreements from the Corey H. class action suit, a revised Self-Analysis Survey was created. Thus, in addition to the previously identified factors, school applicants for Education Connection funding complete the Self-Analysis Survey.[1]

The Self-Analysis Survey consists of two parts, a staff survey and an IEP Review Survey. School staff are to review seven randomly selected IEPs, and interview the case manager, as well as a minimum of three special educators, three general educators, any appropriate related service providers, and, if possible, one or two parents. A minimum of 10 interviews must be completed.

Although the revised Self-Analysis Survey is an improvement considering its predecessor, it can be improved further. Disagregation of the students with disabilities by division or grade level is necessary. The student breakdown is important for planning purposes, allowing staff to see the buildings' overall and grade-level incidence of disability. This is particularly important when working with staff who schedule both students and teachers in classes. For example, Table 7.3 reflects the breakdown by division of Clemente High School. As the data indicate, this school had a higher enrollment of students with disabilities than the CPS standard of 13%. The table also shows the number of students with specific disabilities by grade level. This information is valuable in determining resource allocation (i.e., number of co-taught classes, educator assignments, and so forth) and where to prioritize and focus efforts.

Another area on the Self-Analysis Survey that requires expansion is the team's ability to analyze the current models of support provided to students with disabilities. Determining the number of students with disabilities supported in each school's support model provides staff a snapshot in time of how various resources (e.g., space, staff) are being used. For example, if a particular school defined *collaborative team-teaching* in the following manner, more detail would be required:

> General and special education teachers plan, design, and deliver instructional services together in a classroom that includes students with and without disabilities. Teachers work with students, parents, and related services providers to implement IEP goals and objectives and to monitor academics progress as well as behavioral progress.

---

[1]A copy of the Self-Analysis Survey can be obtained by contacting the Assistant Director, Office of Specialized Services, Chicago Public Schools, 125 South Clark Street, Suite 800, Chicago, IL 60603.

Table 7.3. Student breakdown, by grade level (September 2000), of the 343 students at Roberto Clemente Academy High School identified as having a disability

Grade	Total number of students	Students without IEPs	Students with IEPs							Percent of students with IEPs
			LD	EBD	EMH	TMH	SPL	TBI	VI	
9	714	541	137	28	5	0	2	1	0	24.23
10	488	419	59	5	4	0	0	0	1	14.14
11	356	283	59	2	9	1	0	1	1	20.50
12	225	197	22	2	4	0	0	0	0	12.44
Total students in school	**1,783**	**1,440**	**274**	**37**	**22**	**1**	**2**	**2**	**2**	**19.24**

Key for disabilities under the fourth column: LD = learning disability; EBD = emotional/behavioral disabilities; EMH = "educable mentally handicapped"; TMH = "trainable mentally handicapped"; SPL = speech and language impairments; TBI = traumatic brain injury; VI = visual impairments.

It would also be beneficial to determine how many classes are co-taught, by whom, and in what content areas. These data may reveal that the special educator is supporting four different general educators, across three grade levels, in three content areas. Clearly, this would be a difficult job for anyone.

PRACTICAL IDEAS: LESSONS LEARNED

We have learned and are still learning many things about supporting students with disabilities in large urban high schools. It would take more than a chapter to detail much of what we have learned. However, we would like to share a few processes that have made a difference in support of students with disabilities in general education classrooms. It is our hope that these processes may assist others in their reform efforts.

Determine the Area of Focus and a Prioritization Process

Schools from which we have had the opportunity to learn begin inclusion reform by identifying the students with disabilities who will participate in specific general education classes. As previously noted, targeting the students with disabilities with whom the team of school personnel will focus their efforts is critical. In determining where to begin, expand, or—depending on resources—scale back efforts, we suggest that the team analyze, by grade level and primary disability, where students with disabilities are in the school. This chapter has already addressed the importance (for planning purposes) of knowing which grade levels and what types of supports students require.

Using a chart similar to the chart in Table 7.3, it is suggested that the team gather information on how many incoming freshmen come from feeder schools. This helps building staff determine whether a feeder school is sending a disproportionate number of students with disabilities as compared with other local high schools. Next, the team should analyze the current models of support available at the school site. Determining the models used, the way those models are being implemented, and the numbers of students with disabilities supported by the different models provides information about the ways in which various resources (e.g., space, staff) are currently being used and whether the resources are being used effectively and efficiently.

Once the team knows the numbers of students, their support needs, and the current models available within the school, it is ready to analyze the school's current resources (e.g., space, staff, materials). Most urban high schools would benefit from additional resources. Unfortunately, new resources are hard to find and are not readily available. Therefore, the team must look critically at the ways in which its school's existing resources are being deployed. As one of our principal colleagues says, "Doing more with less has allowed me to innovate." Look at the various existing initiatives; determine which ones complement each other and could share resources. At Clemente High School, the team was able to piggyback efforts on inclusion with the restructuring initiatives that were already funded. This collaboration provided additional ideas and resources that supported both efforts.

At this point, with knowledge of the student numbers, the models of support available, and resources, the team is ready to plan for students to gain access to general education classes. Of course, these steps are not enough to ensure success, but they are a necessary beginning. The next component in moving toward inclusive schooling involves the professional development of teachers.

Implement a Staff Development Process

A key variable to success to supporting students with disabilities in general education classes is having properly trained team members. Identifying professional development needs is critical to the success of students (Villa & Thousand, 1995). Given that team members are asked to spend their time in many different and new ways, professional development should be ongoing, accessible, and based on best practices. Team members should receive professional development on a wide range of topics, including collaboration, curriculum modification, behavioral support, and the use of paraprofessionals to name a few. These professional development events should be available to all team members, including administrators, general educators, special educators, paraeducators, related services providers, and parents.

A note of caution is necessary here. Too often, schools immediately require all building staff to attend "inclusion workshops." Unless the school is small or has a wealth of resources, beginning with the entire staff is extremely difficult. In addition, unless some of the teachers have experience with inclusion and can discuss it with their peers, the questions and concerns are great. Furthermore, the number of dates on which all school staff would be available are limited. Finally, the format and audience size make it difficult to personalize and customize the information to the needs of the participants. Thus, begin with the team members who will first be invited to partake in the inclusive educational experience. These individuals can then share their success stories with the colleagues and build a "bottom-up" need for additional professional development.

One way that schools in Chicago determined the needed professional development topics was to conduct regular needs assessments. Readers are cautioned not to make assumptions about the knowledge base of any of their team members. Often, general educator team members assume that special educators have the skills to support students with disabilities in general education classes. Many do not, as their training and experience are related to the support of students with disabilities in a resource room or self-contained classroom. The skills and experiences necessary to support students in the general education classroom are very different from those used in segregated classes. This is why it is critical to inventory each team member who will be involved. Figure 7.1 provides a sample Professional Development Inventory that can be used to survey professional development needs. The assessment focuses on instructional strategies, organizational management techniques, communication, proactive and reactive behavioral strategies, and roles and responsibilities. This tool is interesting in that it allows team members to use a Likert-type scale to indicate whether a particular item is a strength or an area for future professional growth. Tallying these findings across team members will identify group areas of professional development as well as individuals who can assist in delivering training. It is suggested that team members schedule time at the end of a staff meeting for individuals to complete the survey. We often use the survey as the exit ticket or pass out of the meeting, which ensures a high percentage of returned surveys.

Once the team has collected the Professional Development Inventory information, the team is ready to plan professional development events. The "size" and complexity of the learning required, as well as the desired learning outcomes, will aid in determining the formats for professional development. For example, one team may want to form a book club and read a professional book together, such as *Inclusive Schools in Action: Making Differences Ordinary* (McLeskey & Waldron, 2000) or *Inclusive High Schools: Learning From Contemporary Classrooms* (Fisher, Sax, & Pumpian, 1999). Other teams may want to have "make it–take it" workshops in which they engage in hands-on curriculum development and modification activities. Still other teams may need large-group, facilitated discussions about the "whys" of inclusion before they move to the "hows" of inclusion working in their school.

To ensure that each team member can assess the variety of professional development opportunities provided by the school or district, creating Professional Development Master Schedule is recommended (see Figure 7.2). Schedule users should plot the dates for internal and external professional development activities that correspond to each listed instructional strategy, organizational management technique, communication strategy, and proactive and reactive behavioral strategy. The master schedule will help in planning substitute coverage, registration processing, meeting space, and other logistical activities necessary for successful implementation of the professional development activities.

In addition to the site-based professional development opportunities available for team members, external workshops and conferences should be considered. Although it is far more cost-effective to conduct internal professional development activities, individuals from the outside can often push conversations and beliefs further. Sending a few team members to external experiences will assist schools in identifying topics and presenters for future internal development events. Conference attendees often report significantly changed beliefs about inclusion (e.g., Grove & Fisher, 1999). In addition, external experience can serve as "perks" for those who have demonstrated leadership supporting students with disabilities.

In addition to professional development activities, it is useful to expand the professional library available for team members' use. Professional libraries should include professional books, videotapes, software, and other materials that relate to the goals of inclusive education and school reform. Many teachers have spoken about a book, an article, or a videotape that allowed them to "get it" and changed their beliefs about inclusion. Peak Parent Center (http://www.peakparent.org) is an excellent resource for accessible materials on inclusion.

PROFESSIONAL DEVELOPMENT INVENTORY

School name: _____ School year: _____

Grade taught: _____

Directions: Please rank your skill in each of the following areas on a 1 to 5 scale, with 1 being an area that requires growth and 5 being an area of strength.

INSTRUCTIONAL STRATEGIES			
Alternative assessment strategies		Computer-assisted instruction	
Structured daily schedule		Differentiated instruction	
Adapting curriculum		Language and literacy	
Thematic instruction		Flexible/creative grading	
Core content instruction to all students		Integrated curriculum	
Co-planning		Learning styles	
Co-teaching		Learning centers	
Collaborative teaching		Understanding learning strengths and needs	
Visual organizers		Problem solving	
Comprehensive strategies		Multilevel instruction	

ORGANIZATION MANAGEMENT			
Observing and assessing general education teaching styles		Incorporating individualized education program (IEP) goals throughout the curriculum	
Observing and assessing general education physical environment		Lesson preparation	
Coordinating related services		Using humor with students as a classroom management technique	
Cooperative lesson plan design		Organizational strategies	
Progress assessment		Portfolio assessment	
Building rapport with families		Time management	
Coordinating information from specialists		Working knowledge of the Individuals with Disabilities Act (IDEA)	
Developing IEPs			

Figure 7.1. Blank Professional Development Inventory.

COMMUNICATION		
Communication with teachers	Communication with paraeducators	
Communication with parents	Communication with students	

PROACTIVE STRATEGIES TO ADDRESS CHALLENGING BEHAVIOR		
Alternatives to punishments	Discipline with dignity	
Arrangement of the physical environment	Identifying individual motivators	
Conflict-resolution strategies	Problem-solving procedures	
Creating a democratic classroom		

REACTIVE STRATEGIES TO ADDRESS CHALLENGING BEHAVIOR		
Active listening	Diffusing tension	
Cuing and monitoring	Redirection	

PERSONAL ATTRIBUTES/ROLES AND RESPONSIBILITIES		
Flexibility with role release	Flexibility and openness to new ideas	
Personal confidence	Effective organizational skills	
Professional competence	Experience in teaming with others	
Professional enthusiasm	Willingness to invest extra time in processes as needed	
Respect for colleagues	Commitment to planning weekly	
Good teaming skills	Experience in supporting general education curriculum	
Personal interest in professional growth		

How would you like to obtain information about specific strategies? Check all that apply.

___ Printed materials/handouts

___ Classroom demonstration with coaching

___ Classroom demonstration without coaching

___ Discussion

___ Observation of another teacher

___ Teacher interest centers

___ In-service, day-long, or half-day programs

___ Others (list below)

_____

(continued)

Figure 7.1.   *(continued)*

Would you be willing to use *one* preparation period or *one*
grade level meeting to learn about a particular strategy?

___ Yes   ___ No

Would you be willing to meet before or after school to
learn about a particular strategy?

___ Yes   ___ No

Do you have other suggestions about how to obtain information you need?
If so, please list them below.

Are there any immediate concerns/issues that you would like the least
restrictive environment (LRE) consultant to address?

Would you like the LRE consultant to observe and provide feedback about any
aspects of your classroom environment or students? If so, please indicate
which class period room number.

PROFESSIONAL DEVELOPMENT MASTER SCHEDULE

School name: *Washington High School*   School semester: *Fall 2003*

Directions: Fill in the date(s) under the appropriate month(s) and indicate whether the professional development session is internal (I) or external (E).

Instructional Strategies	July	August	September	October	November	December
Alternative assessment strategies			*19(I)*			
Structured daily schedule						
Adapting curriculum		*22(I)*		*14(I)*		*5(I)*
Thematic instruction						
Core content instruction to all students						
Co-planning	*10(E)*				*10(E)*	
Co-teaching						
Collaborative teaching						
Visual organizers						
Comprehensive strategies						
Computer-assisted instruction						
Differentiated instruction					*17(E)*	
Language and literacy						
Flexible/creative grading						
Integrated curriculum						
Learning styles						
Learning centers						
Understanding learning strengths and needs						
Problem solving						
Multilevel instruction						
Organization Management	July	August	September	October	November	December
Observing and assessing general education teaching styles						
Observing and assessing the general education physical environment						
Coordinating related services						

(continued)

Figure 7.2.   Filled-in Professional Development Master Schedule.

Figure 7.2. *(continued)*

Incorporating individualized education program (IEP) goals throughout the curriculum						
Lesson preparation						
Using humor with students as a classroom technique						
Organizational strategies						
Progress assessment						
Building rapport with families						
Coordinating information from specialists						
Developing IEPs						
Portfolio assessment						
Time management						
Working knowledge of the Individuals with Disabilities Education Act (IDEA)						
Communication	July	August	September	October	November	December
Communication with teachers			*10(I)*	*14(I)*	*8(I)*	*12(I)*
Communication with parents		*19(E)*				
Communication with paraeducators						
Communication with students						
Proactive Strategies to Address Challenging Behavior	July	August	September	October	November	December
Alternatives to punishments						
Arrangement of the physical environment						
Conflict-resolution strategies						
Creating a democratic classroom						
Discipline with dignity						
Identifying individual motivators						
Problem-solving procedures				*17(I)*		

Figure 7.2. *(continued)*

Reactive Strategies to Address Challenging Behavior	July	August	September	October	November	December
Active listening						
Cuing and monitoring						
Diffusing tension	*30(E)*					
Redirection						
Personal Attributes/Roles and Responsibilities	July	August	September	October	November	December
Flexibility with role release						
Personal confidence						
Professional competence						
Professional enthusiasm						
Respect for colleagues						
Good teaming skills						
Personal interest in professional growth						
Flexibility and openness to new ideas						
Effective organizational skills						
Experience in teaming with others						
Willingness to invest extra time in processes as needed						
Commitment to weekly planning						
Experience in supporting general education curriculum						

Provide Communication and Support for the General Educator

Countless general education teachers have reported that they receive no information, too much information, or useless information regarding efforts to support students with disabilities in general education classrooms. Finding the right balance of information content, amount, and timing can make a huge difference in efforts to support general educators.

Copies of IEPs often are not very useful for the general educators. Although these documents contain a great deal of information, general educators indicate that they need up-to-date information that is relevant to them, their class, and their teaching. We recommend providing a general educator with the following critical pieces of information prior to the first day of class for a students with a disability (e.g., Fisher et al., 1999):

- IEP summary: A summary that contains the most important and relevant information on the IEP

- Infused skills grid: A grid that indicates when and where IEP goals, objectives, and benchmarks are addressed during the course of the day

- Adaptation/modification/support grid: A grid that outlines the organizational, motivational/behavioral, curriculum/presentation, testing/assessment, and homework supports that the student needs in each content area, as well as their frequency of use

- Student profile: A profile that provides the teacher with specific information about the student (e.g., learning style, successful instructional formats, adaptations that have worked)

- Behavior intervention plan (when applicable): A plan that outlines positive intervention strategies for improving the student's behavior

There are several formats for each type of information available for a variety of sources. We have gathered many of them to share the best ones with team members. After team members have had time to review each version of a tool, we ask them to select the forms that best meet their needs.

Providing critical student information to the general educator is a significant first step for acquainting him or her with the needs of specific students with disabilities. A more formal orientation process could be developed within each school, such as the following:

- Determine what the general educator already knows and what he or she will need to know about the specific needs of students with disabilities.

- Develop and/or gather accessible orientation materials.

- Identify orientation formats that are flexible to meet the needs of the targeted general educator.

- Develop an evaluation/feedback mechanism for the general educator to provide valuable information about the effectiveness of the orientation process.
- Adjust the orientation process based on this feedback and as new orientation information and materials become available.

CONCLUSION

There are no simple solutions to the complex task of supporting students with disabilities in general education classrooms. This is especially true in urban high schools. Efficient and effective management of existing resources certainly makes the task more manageable. Creating simple and flexible processes to analyze the existing special education service delivery system, determining the areas of focus and prioritization, addressing professional development, and offering communication and support for general educators are just a few of several processes that schools have developed and used to support students with disabilities in inclusive schools. The school staff with which we have had the privilege to work say that in hindsight, the growth that they have seen by the students with disabilities in inclusive environments has made it worth the effort put forth. As one teacher colleague says, "Trust the process and you'll see the benefits!"

REFERENCES

Bauer, A.M., & Brown, G.M. (2001). *Adolescents and inclusion: Transforming secondary schools.* Baltimore: Paul H. Brookes Publishing Co.

Corey H. v. Board of Education of the City of Chicago, et al. Case No. 92 C 3409.

Fisher, D., Sax, C., & Pumpian, I. (1999). *Inclusive high schools: Learning from contemporary classrooms.* Baltimore: Paul H. Brookes Publishing Co.

Grove, K., & Fisher, D. (1999). Entrepreneurs of meaning: Parents and the process of inclusive education. *Remedial and Special Education, 20,* 208–215.

Individuals with Disabilities Education Act (IDEA) Amendments of 1997, PL 105-17, 20 U.S.C. §§ 1400 *et seq.*

Individuals with Disabilities Education Act (IDEA) of 1990, PL 101-476, 20 U.S.C. §§ 1400 *et seq.*

Jorgensen, C.M. (1998). *Restructuring high schools for all students: Taking inclusion to the next level.* Baltimore: Paul H. Brookes Publishing Co.

McLeskey, J., & Waldron, N.L. (2000). *Inclusive schools in action: Making differences ordinary.* Alexandria, VA: Association for Supervision and Curriculum Development.

Roach, V.R. (1999). Reflecting on least restrictive environment policy: Curriculum, instruction, placement: Three legs of the achievement stool. In D. Fisher, C. Sax,

& I. Pumpian, *Inclusive high schools: Learning from contemporary classrooms* (pp. 145–156). Baltimore: Paul H. Brookes Publishing Co.

Sizer, T. (1992). *Horace's compromise: Redesigning the American high school.* Boston: Houghton Mifflin.

U.S. Department of Labor. (1991). *What work requires of schools.* Washington, DC: Author.

Villa, R.A., & Thousand, J.S. (Eds.). (1995). *Creating an inclusive school.* Alexandria, VA: Association for Supervision and Curriculum Development.

Wagner, M., Blackorby, J., Cameto, R., Hebbeler, K., & Newman, L. (1993). *The transition experiences of young people with disabilities: A summary of findings form the National Longitudinal Transition Study of Special Education Students.* Menlo Park, NJ: SRI International. (ERIC Document Reproduction Service No. ED365086).

Education Connection

Reflections on Descriptions
of Inclusive High Schools in Chicago

James McLeskey and Nancy L. Waldron

In the quest to "leave no child behind," perhaps the most difficult task educators in U.S. public schools face is to provide a high-quality education for students who live in poverty and attend school in large urban school districts. In these areas, schools are often poorly funded, teacher turnover is abysmally high, many teachers are teaching "out of field," and bureaucracy is frequently a major impediment to school improvement (Fullan, 2001; Hill & Celio, 1998; McLeskey, Smith, Tyler, & Saunders, 2002). Add to these obstacles the rarity of inclusive high schools, coupled with the difficulty in changing any high school, and the nature of the change process described by Doyle and Owens in Chapter 7 is significant.

In Chapter 7, the authors provide a description of the catalyst for change (a court order), the context for the change (Chicago Public Schools, or CPS), the framework for change (CPS's Education Connection project), and two high schools that participated in Education Connection. The following paragraphs reflect on this change process, beginning with comments regarding the court order that mandated changes in CPS and how CPS administration responded to this court order. This commentary is followed by reflections on how the two high schools responded to these changes.

THE CHICAGO PUBLIC SCHOOL SYSTEM'S RESPONSE TO A COURT-ORDERED MANDATE FOR MORE INCLUSIVE SCHOOL PROGRAMS

A critical factor influencing any school improvement effort is the context within which the activity occurs. As Doyle and Owens note in their chapter, the CPS district is very large and diverse. A vast majority of its students come from families with low incomes, and many students speak English as a second language. Furthermore, the district, as well as the state of Illinois, had made little progress toward developing inclusive programs prior to the advent of the Education Connection project. It is noteworthy that based on the U.S. Department of Education data from *Reports to Congress*, Illinois is one of nine states with the most restrictive placement practices in the United States (McLeskey & Henry, 1999).

The stimulus for moving CPS toward more inclusive practices was a class-action lawsuit, which resulted in a finding against the Illinois Board of Education and CPS. The lawsuit outcome noted that students were not being educated in the least restrictive environment (LRE). The court ordered schools in Chicago to move toward educating students with disabilities in less restrictive, and thus more inclusive, environments.

A court order to provide students with improved schooling—or any top-down mandate, for that matter—often fails to achieve the desired results (Fullan, 2001). However, the CPS response to this court order seems prudent, which could help to blunt the potentially negative effects of the coercive court order. To address the court order, the school district developed a project called Education Connection—School Based LRE Plans and Staff Development Project. This project provides local schools with funding (on average, $110,000 per school) for 3 years. This funding is meant to help the schools engage in a systematic approach to school change as they examine their school, develop a plan for delivering more inclusive services, provide needed professional development for teachers, and subsequently implement the plan.

There are many benefits to a systematic approach to school change, and CPS seems to be attempting such an approach. First, although schools in CPS clearly have top-down support for developing inclusive schools, they also have been provided the time and autonomy to develop inclusive programs that will meet their particular school needs. This empowerment of the local school to make decisions regarding school change should result in more buy-in from local stakeholders and bottom-up support for the change effort. Thus, the framework developed by CPS to support change in local schools facilitates the movement of the change effort from a mandate to a change effort that is more of a balance between top-down and bottom-up support. This strategy should significantly increase the probability of success of the change efforts in local schools (Fullan, 2001; McLeskey & Waldron, 2002a).

A second benefit of the plan that is used by CPS is that the 3-year period for making changes will not only provide schools the opportunity to plan major changes, but also bring coherence to the changes that they propose (Fullan, 2001). School change frequently proceeds too quickly, without time for stakeholders to examine their school, ruminate regarding proposed changes, gain buy-in to any proposed changes, and so forth. This often results in superficial change, or what Goodman called "change without difference" (1995, p. 2). The approach to school change being used by CPS has the potential to avoid this pitfall and to create changes in many schools that are substantial and sustainable.

Third, the systematic approach to school change that is employed in local schools—progressing from an examination of the local school to interviews with stakeholders, developing a plan, and implementing the plan—will provide participants with the opportunity to develop the necessary skills to work together successfully. This process will also provide stakeholders the opportunity to obtain much useful information about their school. These qualities of the school change process serve to increase the odds for the improvement effort's success (McLeskey & Waldron, 2002a).

Finally, funds are provided to support teachers in developing the new skills they need to successfully implement the inclusive program. This need for professional learning as an integral part of the development of any inclusive program is indispensable (McLeskey & Waldron, 2002b), as teachers are asked to perform different tasks and to serve in roles that require the use of skills that differ from the skills they have typically used.

In sum, CPS administration has made a significant effort to turn a potentially bad situation into an opportunity. Based on the description provided by Doyle and Owens, the school system avoided what Fullan (2001) called the bureaucratic mentality of many local schools and school systems, which often results in adding on "changes" or mandates without careful thought. In contrast, CPS has taken a problem-solving approach (Fullan, 2001), as it has carefully examined the issues that face the school system and has used current information on supporting school improvement efforts to guide their plans for school change. This framework should lead to much success as schools in CPS work to develop more inclusive school programs.

REFLECTIONS ON THE CHANGES MADE IN THE HIGH SCHOOLS

In reflecting on changes made in the two high schools described in Chapter 7, it is important to note that one of the schools, Roberto Clemente Community Academy High School, had just begun its changes as the chapter was written. Thus, we have limited information to which we can respond regarding the school's accomplishments. In contrast, Stephen Tyng Mather High School has been engaged in developing more inclusive programs for several years as part of the Education Connection. As a consequence, reflections primarily address the changes made at Mather High School.

In most high schools, a foundation for effective inclusive programs is team-teaching (Cole & McLeskey, 1997; Fisher, Sax, & Pumpian, 1999; Jorgensen, 1998). As Doyle and Owens note, Mather High School increased the number of team-taught classes from 6 to 27 within 2 years. Although the previously described change process was important in helping the stakeholders at Mather, at least two other factors seemed to contribute to the development of co-teaching arrangements.

First, a lack of space at Mather very likely contributed to the rapid changes that occurred as more inclusive environments were developed and implemented. We know from a long history in special education that if a separate class is available for students with disabilities, it will be filled (Shepard & Smith, 1983; Taylor, 1988). Simply not having space available for separate classes thus led the stakeholders at Mather to seek opportunities to educate students with disabilities alongside their peers in general education classrooms.

Second, a major factor that seems to have set the stage for success at Mather is the previous work that the school faculty and administration had completed as participants in Sizer's Coalition of Essential Schools (CES; for more information, go to http://www.essentialschools.org). Our experience indicates that the probability of success in any school change endeavor increases if a school has already been engaged in a high-quality change effort. Furthermore, most high schools that we have seen develop successful inclusive programs were already good schools that did much to meet the needs of all students. An examination of the Ten Principles of Essential Schools (see Table 7.2 in Chapter 7) reveals that many of these principles align with principles that might be used to develop a more inclusive school. For example, the school's goal should be simple: that each student master a limited number of essential skills and areas of knowledge (Principle 2). This principle contrasts with practice in many high schools, in which large-group instruction with similar or identical requirements for all students is the norm. In contrast, Principle 2 suggests that teachers differentiate their expectations by examining the curriculum and determining what every student needs to learn. This goal is reflected in the Degrees of Learning pyramid that Vaughn, Bos, and Schumm (2000) have used in working with schools to develop inclusive programs. This principle clearly provides a foundation for the development of inclusive programs. Furthermore, throughout the Ten Principles of Essential Schools, there are allusions to ideas that are supportive of inclusive practices:

- The school's goals should apply to all students (Principle 3).
- Teaching and learning should be personalized (Principle 4).

- Coaching will be a prominent pedagogy to provoke students to "learn how to learn" (Principle 5).
- The principal and teachers should perceive themselves as generalists first and specialists second (Principle 8).
- The school should demonstrate nondiscriminatory and inclusive policies (Principle 10).
- The school should honor diversity and build on the strengths of its communities (Principle 10).

Thus, these principles guided Mather High School's change efforts prior to the advent of the Education Connection project and provided a firm foundation for the subsequent development of better educational programs for all students through team-taught inclusive classes.

WHY IS WORK IN THE CHICAGO PUBLIC SCHOOLS SYSTEM IMPORTANT?

Chapter 7 is important for many reasons. When considering the difficulty in developing an inclusive high school, coupled with the added complexities of working in an urban environment, one is tempted to paraphrase a well-known song lyric: "If you can do it here, you can do it anywhere." Yet, we already know that inclusive high school programs *can* be developed in any environment, as scores of schools have aptly illustrated since the mid-1980s (Biklen, 1985; Cole & McLeskey, 1997; Fisher et al., 1999; Jorgensen, 1998). However, there is little doubt that fewer inclusive programs have been developed in high schools than in elementary schools. Furthermore, some evidence suggests that school improvement efforts have been less successful in schools with large numbers of students who live in households with low socioeconomic status (Fullan, 2001; Hill & Celio, 1998). Thus, Chapter 7 is important because it provides further evidence that inclusive programs can be developed in urban high schools.

A second reason that the information presented in Chapter 7 is important is that it provides an example of how schools can be improved when what is known about school change is used in practice. As noted previously, the framework that has been developed by CPS to support this school change effort applies many of the critical principles of school change (e.g., see Fullan, 2001; McLeskey & Waldron, 2000). Related to this issue, one aspect of CPS's response to the court mandate is particularly important. That is, CPS provides an example of how a large, urban school system can respond effectively to an outside mandate for change. Such mandates come in many forms and from many sources (primarily from courts, state laws, and federal laws). Responses by school systems—urban, suburban, and rural alike—to such mandates are all too often heavy handed and highly prescriptive. CPS did not take this route. The school system used much of what is known about effective school change to develop a framework for change, then provided support for local schools in figuring out how to address the mandate. The district's central administration shared responsibility for changes by empowering local schools to make the changes that best met their needs, thereby increasing the likelihood of buy-in by the local schools and the potential for the school change effort's success.

WHAT CAN OTHER COMMUNITIES DO TO PROMOTE INCLUSION?

Unfortunately, in many states with poor records for promoting the development of inclusive programs (see McLeskey & Henry, 1999), litigation may be necessary to move state and local bureaucracies toward the development of more inclusive programs—as was the case in CPS and the state of Illinois. Indeed, with the many demands placed on school systems for meeting high standards, the development of inclusive programs often takes a back seat to other school improvement efforts. However, other things can be done in local communities to increase momentum toward developing more inclusive programs.

First, stakeholders must work to convince policy makers that inclusion is not just about students with disabilities; rather, it is about making schools better, more supportive places for *all* students (McLeskey & Waldron, 2000, 2002a). For example, much evidence reveals that students who are not labeled with disabilities do better on academic measures when they are educated in inclusive environments (Staub, 1996; Waldron, 1997). Thus, inclusion can and often should form the foundation of a coherent, schoolwide improvement effort and not just focus on the needs of a small group of students (McLeskey & Waldron, 2000, 2002a).

Second, any worthwhile school improvement effort should improve the delivery of services for students with disabilities and should make these services more inclusive. The CES movement is a good example of this effort. As noted previously, the principles of the CES movement have many qualities that should lead to improved, more inclusive services for students with disabilities. What stakeholders must do in our local communities is ensure that students with disabilities are included and given full consideration in any school improvement effort. This is not always the case. Indeed, all too often, the needs of these students are completely ignored and relegated to the special education office, with the assumption that reform in special education involves only a small group of students and other stakeholders.

Third, stakeholders must educate local school board members about the needs of students with disabilities. As many are painfully aware, the needs of students who are labeled gifted and talented often carry the day when it comes to school board elections and controversial school issues (Kohn, 1998). This will continue to occur, especially if these officials do not understand that the needs of students with disabilities are not appreciably different from or less important than the needs of other children. Stakeholders must ensure that this message is clearly articulated and understood by decision makers in local schools.

Finally, stakeholders must cultivate a view of the broader landscape of general education. It is not enough to articulate, however well, the compelling reasons for creating inclusive environments for students with disabilities. A common justification for inclusive schooling is based on the rights of students with IEPs to participate in the full range of human experiences. It then follows that these same students must be considered contributors to the human experience. In other words, it is vital to keep the experience of school for all students in mind when constructing inclusive supports. For instance, at Mather High School, inclusive educators considered the potential benefits to the entire school when designing supports and services for students with disabilities. When space issues were a concern, educators designed an educational approach that alleviated facility problems. They also used the common reform vocabulary of the school, in this case the CES, to deepen and extend the school's commitment to these principles. It can be argued that some of Mather's success is due to educators' attention to the contributions that inclusive education has made to the school environment. To be made full partners in school design and programming, stakeholders must be willing to consider the needs of the entire school population, not only students with IEPs.

CONCLUSION

Since the early 1970s (Fullan, 2001; Sarason, 1971), a great deal has been learned about how to more effectively change and improve schools. The process is not easy. It is time consuming; involves risk, frustration, and anxiety (Fullan, 2001); and, even with the best efforts, often leads to very limited success. As more is learned about the school change process, it is critically important that stakeholders employ this knowledge in practice and that these efforts are richly described in the professional literature. The work of CPS, as reported by Doyle and Owen-Johnson in Chapter 7, provides an important example of how urban schools can use what is known about school change to successfully develop inclusive programs. Indeed, CPS has done an admirable job of taking a mandated change and using it as a catalyst for developing a collaborative change process with local school personnel. It would be very useful to have a more detailed description of how CPS developed the process of change that was employed in the Education Connection projects. Furthermore, a long-term evaluation of the project's effectiveness (e.g., how many schools successfully developed inclusive

programs, how many programs were maintained) would add significant information to the professional literature on school change. It is through such efforts
that more will be learned about how schools can be changed, even under less
than ideal circumstances, and how inclusive programs can be developed to better serve the needs of students with disabilities in *all* schools.

REFERENCES

Biklen, D. (1985). *Achieving the complete school: Strategies for effective mainstreaming*. New
   York: Teachers College Press.
Cole, C., & McLeskey, J. (1997). Secondary inclusive programs for students with mild disabili-
   ties: Developing curricular alternatives through teaching partnerships. *Focus on Excep-
   tional Children, 29*(6), 1–15.
Fisher, D., Sax, C., & Pumpian, I. (1999). *Inclusive high schools: Learning from contemporary
   classrooms*. Baltimore: Paul H. Brookes Publishing Co.
Fullan, M. (2001). *The new meaning of educational change* (3rd ed.). New York: Teachers Col-
   lege Press.
Goodman, J. (1995). Change without difference. *Harvard Educational Review, 65*, 1–29.
Hill, P., & Celio, M. (1998). *Fixing urban schools*. Washington, DC: Brookings Institution Press.
Jorgensen, C.M. (1998). *Restructuring high schools for all students: Taking inclusion to the
   next level*. Baltimore: Paul H. Brookes Publishing Co.
Kohn, A. (1998). Only for my kid: How privileged parents undermine school reform. *Phi Delta
   Kappan, 79*, 569–577.
McLeskey, J., & Henry, D. (1999). Inclusion: What progress is being made across states?
   Teaching Exceptional Children, 31(5), 56–62.
McLeskey, J., Smith, D., Tyler, N., & Saunders, S. (2002). *The supply of and demand for special
   education teachers. A review of research regarding the nature of the chronic shortage of
   special education teachers*. Gainesville, FL: Center on Personnel Studies in Special Educa-
   tion, University of Florida.
McLeskey, J., & Waldron, N. (2000). *Inclusive schools in action: Making differences ordinary*.
   Alexandria, VA: Association for Supervision and Curriculum Development.
McLeskey, J., & Waldron, N. (2002a). School change and inclusive schools: Lessons learned
   from practice. *Phi Delta Kappan, 84*(1), 65–72.
McLeskey, J., & Waldron, N. (2002b). Professional development and inclusive schools: Reflec-
   tions on effective practice. *Teacher Educator, 37*(3), 159–172.
Sarason, S. (1971). *The culture of school and the problem of change*. Boston: Allyn & Bacon.
Shepard, L., & Smith, M. (1983). An evaluation of the identification of learning disabled stu-
   dents in Colorado. *Learning Disability Quarterly, 6*(2), 115–127.
Staub, D. (1996). *On inclusion and the other kids*. Denver, CO: National Institute for Urban
   School Improvement.
Taylor, S. (1988). Caught in the continuum: A critical analysis of the principle of the least
   restrictive environment. *Journal of The Association of Persons with Severe Handicaps, 13*,
   41–53.
Vaughn, S., Bos, C., & Schumm, J. (2000). *Teaching mainstreamed, diverse, and at-risk stu-
   dents in the general education classroom* (2nd ed.). Boston: Allyn & Bacon.
Waldron, N. (1997). Inclusion. In G. Bear, K. Minke, & A. Thomas (Eds.), *Children's needs II:
   Development, problems and alternatives* (pp. 501–510). Washington, DC: National Association of School Psychologists.

chapter **8**

Pathfinders

Making a Way from Segregation to Community Life in New York

CONNIE LYLE O'BRIEN, BETH MOUNT, JOHN O'BRIEN, AND FREDDA ROSEN

Pathfinders has made a world of difference for my granddaughter, Shunelle, and for me, too. After the meetings, I feel so much more informed and enlightened in terms of understanding that possibilities exist in our communities for people with disabilities. I never thought that Shunelle would be able to do the things she's doing right now. I didn't know that I could trust myself to allow her to negotiate the world on her own. But in

Preparation of this chapter was partially supported through a subcontract to Responsive Systems Associates from the Center on Human Policy, Syracuse University, for the Research and Training Center on Community Living. The Research and Training Center on Community Living is supported through a cooperative agreement (No. H133B980047) between the National Institute on Disability and Rehabilitation Research (NIDRR) and the University of Minnesota's Institute on Community Integration. Members of the Center on Human Policy are encouraged to express their opinions; these do not necessarily represent the official position of NIDRR.

Thanks to Pathfinders' staff, Carolann Granata and Debbie Lamothe, and the students and family members who inspire us with their vision, courage, and determination. Special thanks to Spencer Browne and his mother, Vaulda Kendall Browne, and Cristina Rodriguez and her parents, Ramon and Lucia Rodriguez, for sharing their stories.

the last few months, Shunelle has begun traveling to work, to therapy, the beauty salon, a favorite Chinese restaurant and my office on her own. She seems to be happy about her accomplishments and newfound independence. (Jeffery, 1999)

Pathfinders helped us put the emphasis on who Josh is, what he can do, not what he can't do, and his own particular loves, interests, values, and strengths. We began seeing him differently and thus with more hope and less despair over what he can't do. . . . Person-centered planning helped us to focus on creating a community for Josh. I can't emphasize that enough. As we think about Josh's future, there's nothing more important that we can do for him than to help build a community around him because one of our concerns and fears has been his isolation and lack of friends. (Wolf, 2000/2001)

Shunelle and Josh are among a small group of young New Yorkers finding their own paths into community life from segregated school experiences. Instead of spending their final 2 years of eligibility for special education services looking forward to catching special busses to day activity centers or sheltered workshops, these Pathfinders have rolled and walked from their homes to experience new connections and opportunities in their own neighborhoods and in the vibrant cultural and economic life that is a bus or subway ride away. These young adults have been accompanied on their way by small teams made up of family members and allies from their schools and adult services. The work of their teams has been supported by Pathfinders, a project initiated and implemented by Job Path, an adult service provider committed to innovation in services to people with developmental disabilities, with co-sponsorship from New York State's Office of Mental Retardation and Developmental Disabilities (OMRDD), New York State's Developmental Disabilities Council, and New York City's special education department.

THE FOCUS OF PATHFINDERS

A relentless search to discover and mobilize hidden capacity threads through the whole fabric of Pathfinders. In relationship to the city's special education and adult service systems, Pathfinders as a whole is designed as a person-centered development project (Mount, 1994). In relation to each student and team, Pathfinders focuses on generating actions that challenge a deficiency view of a person, family, neighborhood, and city (Mount, 2000a, 2000b).

It is reasonable to ask why Shunelle and Josh and their fellow Path-finders are discussed in a book about inclusive urban schools. New York City's public schools enroll approximately 1,100,000 students. Approximately 85,000 of these students receive special education services, and 20,000 of these students are served by District 75, a separate administrative unit that among other programs, operates 60 special education schools at more than 300 program sites. Some sites and schools are co-located with another of the city's more than 1,000 general education schools, but most high school students spend the majority of their time in a combination of self-contained classwork and community-based instruction near their schools. Because schools specialize in particular disabilities or program purposes (e.g., transition), most students are transported out of their local areas (New York City Board of Education, 2001). The individualized education programs (IEPs) for all 97 of Pathfinders participants identify a District 75 school as the least restrictive environment for them.

Like most systems, New York City's special education and adult services systems aspire to seamless transitions for special education graduates. However, the design of the city's adult services system for people with developmental disabilities makes continuing segregation the most likely outcome for District 75 graduates. Very large agencies operate a range of large, Medicaid-funded day programs that are backed up by clinics and specialized transport arrangements. Those who considered for their children the future after special education came to Pathfinders with the unquestioned assumption that a slot in an existing program represented the best possible alternative. They asked how to marshal the necessary resources to avoid long waits for adult services and how to select a suitable day program from the range offered.

Perhaps a fitting way to describe Pathfinders is by stating first what it is not. Pathfinders is not a program or placement option. Rather, it is affiliated with Job Path, a service provider established as a demonstration project in 1978 through the Vera Institute of Justice in New York City. The mission of Job Path is to develop innovative approaches for people with developmental disabilities. Pathfinders simultaneously builds the capacity of young adults with disabilities and the capacity of the community to develop natural supports that are available but unused.

The seed of Pathfinders was planted in 1993. Teachers and administrators from nine District 75 schools joined District 75 Transition Coordinators to learn person-centered planning by joining teams with 12 students and family members from their schools. Initially, a training course provided the necessary shelter from routine to allow new possibilities to emerge. School staff and family members were able to give themselves sufficient time and space outside ordinary requirements to produce exciting results and important learning. The energy from this initial effort stimulated the development of a project to carry the work forward.

Pathfinders coordinates workshops and forums for people with developmental disabilities as well as their families and friends. In addition, agency representatives, teachers, and other service providers join to listen, brainstorm, solve problems, and, at times, commiserate. A series of workshops is organized to focus on developing and implementing person-centered development. Forums serve as committed times to identify barriers and to share resources and information with one another. At all times, celebration of successes remains central to this community-building project.

WHY THE COMMUNITY NEEDS PATHFINDERS

Many participants have spent their entire educational careers in segregated settings. Without interventions like Pathfinders, the most likely outcome for them would be to spend their adult lives in segregated settings—sheltered workshops, institutional living, or jail (Wagner, Blackorby, Cameto, Hebbeler, & Newman, 1993). The approach of adulthood and subsequent ending of special education services at age 22 creates a further challenge for these young adults whose educational experiences have prepared them only for future life in exclusionary settings. Thus, the mission of the Pathfinders project is to rapidly expand participants' experiences to increase the range of options available to them.

Because they have not been beneficiaries of inclusive school experiences, Pathfinders participants cannot testify to the benefits or efficacy of major system change efforts. However, Pathfinders students and their families belong in this book as witnesses to the deep wells of capacity that can be tapped even in enormous systems bound to large-scale, lifelong segregation. This is possible even in a city that prides itself on being the nation's biggest, densest, most fast paced, most competitive, and most aggressive; even among families who struggle with poverty, language and cultural barriers, and a history of poor relationships with schools and professionals; and even with students who most people have defined as "too disabled" to face the demands and experience the rewards of ordinary life. Almost all Pathfinders participants have gained at least five things: 1) new neighborhood connections; 2) a clear vision of their interests and gifts, which is shared with family members and some of the staff that assist them; 3) a plan for developing opportunities; 4) membership in a supportive network of other people with disabilities and their family members; and 5) better informed expectations for the adult services system, which should provide them with individualized support to work and participate in community life.

Pathfinders is not a repair kit for mitigating the limitations created by years in segregated settings. It is a means of altering the trajectory of future life experiences that were set into motion years before. As its name connotes, this organization seeks to establish new paths for its participants using a person-centered planning approach. Although it is impossible (and undesirable) to predetermine the journey, it is recognized that the end depends on the beginning. Pathfinders, therefore, is about beginnings.

WHY TRANSITION IS BEING DISCUSSED
IN A BOOK ABOUT INCLUSIVE SCHOOLING

Pathfinders participants belong in this book as witnesses to the stickiness of segregated services. Despite good person-centered plans and an adult services system commitment to fund and deliver individualized supports for inclusive lives, almost two thirds of Pathfinders graduates remain hostages to segregated adult services or remain at home without day services because more individualized supports have proven too hard for adult services providers to arrange or sustain. Many who attend segregated adult programs do maintain the local connections initiated during Pathfinders, but their own energy and the support of families and community members make this happen.

Change in this area is not the result of billion-dollar systems throwing their full weight into new paradigms of special education and individualized supports. Change has happened because a small group of teachers, school administrators, and adult services managers decided to work together, with leadership from New York City's smallest adult service provider, to seek possibilities for a few students with disabilities and their families willing to explore new paths. Some people who have invested in and learned from Pathfinders hold key positions in their organizations as managers, administrators, and transition coordinators, so its effects slowly multiply as these people work to realign the systems in which they work. This painstaking work is slow to shift an enormous system's inertia. Reports can only be made on the way to small, fragile, and significant changes in a very big and complex place.

Finally, a book about inclusive schooling innovations would be incomplete without acknowledging two very important realities: 1) not all children with disabilities in the United States reap the benefits of inclusive schooling and 2) the transition from special education services to adult services is rocky and replete with unexpected twists and turns. Sharing the Pathfinders experiences will provoke questions and offer possible solutions for those who consider the future of the children and adolescents with disabilities.

THE CHALLENGE OF CAPACITY THINKING IN NEW YORK CITY

Capacity thinking is the art of first discovering the qualities that a person with a developmental disability can contribute to community life and then discovering people and places that value that contribution. In a sprawling and complex place like New York City, imagining the capacity of the community also is a unique challenge.

Gaining a Sense of Scale

The city's scale and variety challenge the imagination and organizing skills of any reformer. There is the challenge of demographics. If New York City's 309 square miles were a state, its more than 8 million inhabitants would make it the nation's 12th largest state. Almost a million immigrants established themselves in the city during the 1990s, adding to a mix of racial and ethnic identities that counts 35% of the population as Caucasian, 27% as Hispanic/Latino, 25% as African American, and 10% as Asian (New York City Department of City Planning, 2002). In 1990, Manhattan had the highest level of income inequality of any county in the United States: people in the top income quintile made 33 times more money than the bottom quintile. The average 1990 family income in a census tract between 85th and 91st Streets was $301,000; the average 1990 family income in a census tract between 145th and 150th Streets was $6,000 (Beverage, 1996).

Students in the city's public school system speak 140 languages at home. Sixteen percent of public school students identify themselves as Caucasian. More than half of the students are eligible for free lunches (New York City Board of Education, 2001), and 62% live in areas of concentrated poverty (Campaign for Fiscal Equity, 2001).

In addition, there is the challenge of political and administrative complexity. Since the city's consolidation in 1898, borough governments have been in constant conflict with mayors. For 200 years, the city has been in continued conflict with New York State's legislature. Most adult services to people with developmental disabilities are administered by New York State's OMRDD. Education is the city's affair, managed by a complex, decentralized bureaucracy that struggles to provide adequate buildings and sufficiently trained teachers to meet the demand for high-quality schooling. The administrators negotiating agreements around transition count their budgets in the tens and hundreds of millions and function as part of multibillion dollar systems responsible to different levels of government (New York City Board of Education, 2001). Everything around Pathfinders has a highly charged political dimension.

Expanding Capacity by Reducing Scale

Size, diversity, variety, complexity, and the special education and human services systems' attempts to respond to them all challenge capacity thinking. Many District 75 students travel long distances from their own neighborhoods to work with teachers who may also commute a long distance to pursue community-based instruction in a neighborhood where neither the teachers nor the students live. This matters because neighborhood matters to most New Yorkers. Neighborhood resources and relationships contribute significantly to many people's sense of identity and security.

Practicing capacity thinking in New York City requires looking closely at the blocks that surround where a person lives and being able to spot places and people that might welcome that person's contribution. Sometimes, this calls for people with the gift of seeing past obvious poverty, apparent differences, and even danger to find the local associations and places that make a good life possible. A systematic approach to person-centered planning is required to cultivate the art of finding the niches that escape the system's notice and assisting people with developmental disabilities to inhabit them along with their neighbors. Figure 8.1 describes the Pathfinders framework for discovering capacity in the social spaces that are too small for the big systems to notice.

HOW PATHFINDERS WORKS

The Pathfinders project offers students in their last 2 years of eligibility for special education two kinds of support: focused staff time and a person-centered planning process. When this support is successful, students have a team that includes members of their family, school staff, and adult services staff; a person-centered plan that guides their team in supporting their search for new possibilities; and the funding necessary to move smoothly to receiving individualized supports from an effective and well-informed adult services provider.

Five themes define the core of the Pathfinders process, guiding the work of each student's team and structuring each Pathfinders workshop:

1. Build a capacity view of the student and consequent expansive views of his or her positive future in community life.

2. Challenge deficiency thinking—old ways of thinking about what the student cannot do—and leave behind limiting views about the future.

3. Discover places, people, and associations in the student's local community and strengthen the student's involvement in the opportunities presented by each.

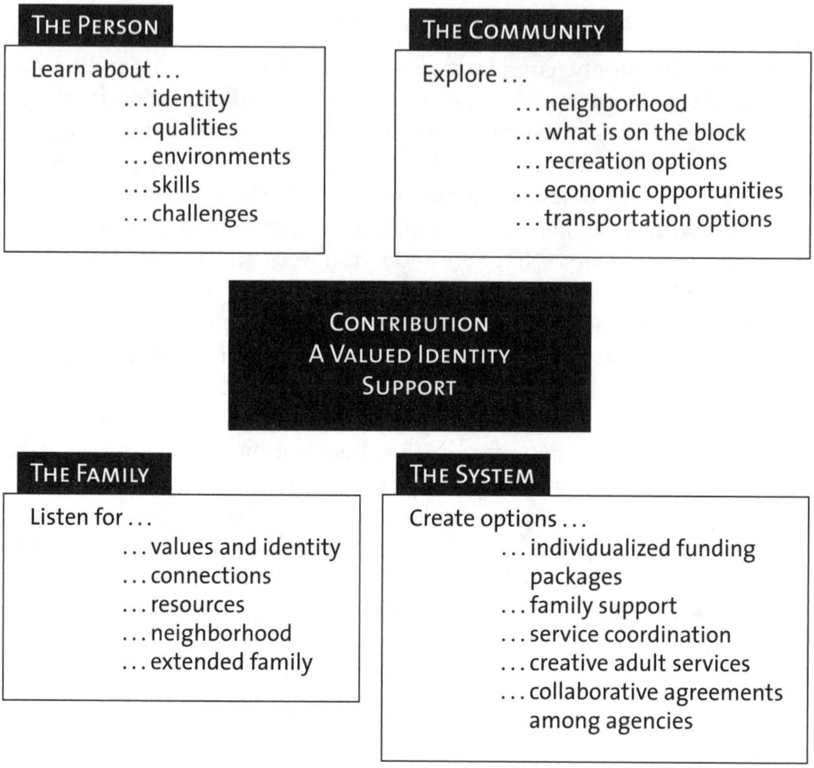

THE PERSON

Learn about ...
    ... identity
    ... qualities
    ... environments
    ... skills
    ... challenges

THE COMMUNITY

Explore ...
    ... neighborhood
    ... what is on the block
    ... recreation options
    ... economic opportunities
    ... transportation options

CONTRIBUTION
A VALUED IDENTITY
SUPPORT

THE FAMILY

Listen for ...
    ... values and identity
    ... connections
    ... resources
    ... neighborhood
    ... extended family

THE SYSTEM

Create options ...
    ... individualized funding
      packages
    ... family support
    ... service coordination
    ... creative adult services
    ... collaborative agreements
      among agencies

Figure 8.1. Pathfinders framework. (From Mount, B., Lyle O'Brien, C., & Rosen, F. [2000]. *The Pathfinders project* [p. 8]. New York: Job Path; reprinted by permission.)

4. Increase expectations of school programs and adult services agencies to provide individualized support for inclusive community experiences.

5. Join with others to advocate for resources and services that fit the student's vision.

Staff Support Through Pathfinders

Two skilled Pathfinders staff members support students and families by meeting them in their homes and helping them to arrange the assistance necessary to participate in the project, such as interpreters, transportation plans, and food preferences. In addition, support staff assemble and maintain a working team to assist participants in following through on plans and filling out forms that are printed in unfamiliar languages. The staff help the family negotiate eligibility for adult services funding, including locating and selecting an adult service provider. These individuals are also available on request to offer school and adult services system staff consultation, problem solving assistance, and links to help. The direct engagement with families on their own turf is one key to a much higher level of family and extended family participation in the Pathfinders process than predicted by school personnel. These staff members are employed by Job Path at 1.5 Full Time Equivalents, the unit of school funding generated by the participants through public school enrollment.

Pathfinders staff do not duplicate the efforts of system personnel. Instead, they partake in the relationship work that often goes undone by overloaded teachers, service coordinators, and case managers. It is up to them to discover ways to shift the system's inertia, opening up small cracks in walls of routine that allow people to wiggle through and experience new possibilities. They help teams find ways to offer each member real opportunities to contribute to the student's success. They also bear the frustration that often goes with high expectations for people they care about in a system that often does not know how to keep its agreements with the people and families it serves.

Person-Centered Development Through Pathfinders

Person-centered work holds both the worth of clear values and the reality of uncertainty. The worth of specialized supports is measured by their contribution to people's experience of five valued experiences: 1) having the respect that comes from playing a valued social role, 2) sharing ordinary places and activities, 3) participating in relationships and associations, 4) making choices, and 5) contributing to community life (O'Brien & Lyle O'Brien, 1987). These valued experiences specify the direction of each individual's search for a good life. Uncertainty derives from two sources. First, people differ gloriously in their heritage, their gifts, and their actual and potential relationships. Second, opportunities are unpredictable. Many people find their way to interesting and satisfying lives when preparation makes an unexpected connection. For most individuals, these events are regarded as serendipitous—unexpected but fortunate occurrences that serve as mileposts in their lives. They may take for granted, however, that a necessary antecedent of serendipity is the opportunity for multiple daily transactions with others. In other words, the unexpected opportunities that arise throughout many people's lives are unlikely to occur for those who spend their lives in isolation. Person-centered planning seeks to increase the circle of people known to and by Pathfinders participants to set into motion the unexpected opportunities that will naturally emerge.

Person-centered development projects have four aspects:

- Framing a Focus Question
- Developing Working Groups that Create Spaces to Explore New Methods
- Investing in Renewal
- Creating Forums

These elements develop recursively, like ripples in a pond. The energy and learning from an initial pattern of person-centered change generate interest and inform action among a wider circle of people. This wider circle revises and repeats the pattern in ways that energize and inform a still-wider circle.

Framing a Focus Question: The End Depends on the Beginning

Person-centered development projects hinge on a focus question that motivates a working group to learn together by changing the opportunities available to a growing number of people. For Pathfinders, the focus question is, "Could students whose current best option is placement in a segregated adult facility find paid and volunteer work in the community, become involved in social and recreational activities in their neighborhoods, and develop new friendships and associations in their workplaces and neighborhoods?"

This question invites broad participation because it can be grasped from at least two starting points. Some people, including the originators of the project, see this as a question about the education system's and adult services system's capacity to provide effective assistance. For them, the ability of people with developmental disabilities and their families and their neighborhoods is not in question. Other people, including many of the people with developmental disabilities and families and school staff who have been active and successful in Pathfinders, interpret it as a question about what is possible for people with developmental disabilities who live in New York City. Either serious consideration of the focus question gets people on the path with an attitude of experimentation. It is not necessary to convert to a belief in people's capacity before joining the work. It is only necessary to join with a genuine interest in discovering the limits and creative ways to push those limits.

Developing Working Groups
to Create Spaces that Explore New Methods

Because continuing segregation is the typical result of the special education and adult services systems (Wagner et al., 1993), people who take the focus question seriously have to create a work space that is outside the current system's habits and demands. It truly challenges everyone to "think outside the box." By working group members constantly challenging themselves and each other to envision possibilities, many of Pathfinder participants have established new connections to their neighborhood communities. Figure 8.2 summarizes some of the new roles and connections that students have developed in their own neighborhoods through their participation in Pathfinders. The logo in the center of the figure expresses the project's values.

Investing in Renewal

Pathfinders invests in renewal by creating habits and rituals among its participants. Participants share their dreams and visions. They devote regular time to celebrating good news. They routinely talk about what is working and what needs to be improved. They reflect on what they are learning from their efforts. They find occasions to tell others their stories and the lessons they have learned.

Five times in each school year, 12–20 Pathfinders students and their teams gather from across the city for a day-long workshop. Project participation and team membership are voluntary. Teams include District 75 students, school staff, and family members (usually one or two parents; sometimes grandparents, sisters, and brothers; and occasionally aunts, uncles, and cousins). As graduation approaches, adult services staff sometimes join the team.

The meeting space reflects the efforts of Pathfinders' staff to create a welcoming and stimulating environment for creative work. The variety of meals and snacks mirror the participants' diverse cultural identities, and provision has been made to accommodate different languages and modes of communication. There is a roving microphone to amplify each person's contribution to the large group's work. Poster paper, multicolored pens, and graphic aids are abundantly available for communicating positive visions for the future and people's capacities.

A team of experienced facilitators guides the process. The facilitators work to build a large group climate of trust and collaboration by making it safe and acceptable for every team member to share dreams, fears, achievements, reservations, discoveries, and uncertainties. They support people to talk from their hearts and not just from their heads. They encourage clear, ordinary language and discourage the jargon, acronyms, and labeling that can trap people's thinking and create distance between those who label and those who bear labels. They invent ways to invite people to move people beyond the roles of "teacher," "mother," "assistant principal," "transition coordinator," or "special ed student" and into creative thinking and action for real change. They actively support students in speaking out about what

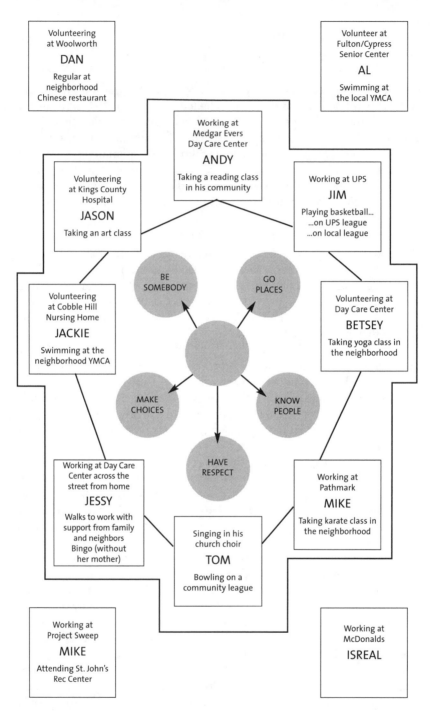

Figure 8.2. Some of the neighborhood connections and roles developed with Pathfinders participants. (From Mount, B., Lyle O'Brien, C., & Rosen, F. [2000]. *The Pathfinders project* [p. 11]. New York: Job Path; reprinted by permission.)

really matters to them, in whatever form allows them expression. They structure the work of the students' teams and the work of the whole group to encourage an active search for capacity and opportunity.

The purpose of each workshop is the same as the purpose of each team meeting: to encourage, guide, and actively support each student, family member, and staff person to connect with local opportunities to discover their capacities and make a positive contribution. From the first workshop, team members hear firsthand stories of students, parents, and staff who have gone before them.

Initial workshops support teams to construct personal profiles and a living account of a desirable future, as envisioned by the student and those who know and care about the student. (See Mount, 2000b, for the details of this process and the graphic formats that support it.) Later workshops provide information about the ways the system works; about the everyday work of community building; and, perhaps most important, from other teams regarding their discoveries, achievements, difficulties, and questions. The level of mutual support that develops among students and parents outweighs the problems of many teams working in the same time and space. Teams have the opportunity to follow up on partially completed tasks as they meet between workshops.

Over time, the ritual of sharing dreams and good news has had a powerful effect on many people with developmental disabilities. At large group workshops, a young woman who spent her first workshop in silence, with her head down, now demands her turn with the microphone. She says that hearing other students with disabilities speak inspired her to use her voice. A very shy young man without speech, overlooked in a previous year's final workshop because of his usual reluctance to share with a large group, brought forward the poster that expresses his dream and chose a team member to interpret it for the workshop. As the annual sequence of five workshops unfolds, each with its time and rituals for renewal, voices become more clear, signs become more emphatic, and shoulders become straighter. These changes in communication reflect changes in methods that people have tried and changes in the support that they experience from the people who love them and the people who teach them—changes that need to be given meaning by sharing them.

One father described how his family changed when it began attending Pathfinders workshops on person-centered planning:

> This journey toward community inclusion started the day we let ourselves brainstorm about community building. You won't believe what you will come up with if you ask yourself the same questions, and are open to new ideas!

We have learned that Cristina is in the center of her future, and we have become the source of encouragement for her to continue to become more independent. Cristina dreams about living in her own apartment in New York City. She talks about her mother, sister, and I coming to visit only!!! Given all that has happened in the past year, anything seems possible when we have faith, determination, and take one step at a time! (Rodriguez, 2000, p. 17).

Creating Forums

To managers of the systems that define the life chances of people with developmental disabilities, person-centered development projects can play the sort of role that Lewis and Clark played for Thomas Jefferson. They bring news of the way to previously uncharted destinations, appreciation of the good things to be found there, and estimates of the costs and risks of further development. The best medium for communicating a project's discovery is a forum. Forums allow face-to-face contact between those involved in a person-centered development project and those with authority over resources for continuing and disseminating the project's work. Forums bring people together for creative problem solving. They are not structured as reports to decision makers but as occasions to jointly design platforms for changes in the system's policies, practices, and programs that will multiply the lessons learned through the project.

Forums accentuate the strength of person-centered development projects, which change what the whole system does for a small number of people who are actively involved in designing the change. Their efforts demonstrate new possibilities and identify the exact system rules, routines, and structures that block important next steps or make it difficult for others to follow the path. Forums set the problem of adapting the system squarely in front of its managers so that growing numbers of people will benefit from what project participants demonstrate. Forums allow the kind of thinking that influences decision makers' agendas over time.

Some forums have a large-group format, but many consist of a few interested people thinking together about how the Pathfinders experience is relevant to their assigned tasks. Principals from District 75 schools, District 75 Transition Coordinators, regional OMRDD managers, and adult services agency managers have participated in forums that considered the implications of the Pathfinders experience for their work. District 75 personnel say that their participation in Pathfinders has influenced curriculum for 14- to 18-year-olds in at least one school, the ways in which several schools involve students and family members in IEPs, and portions of the district's transition planning process. OMRDD and adult service managers say that participation in Pathfinders has influenced the ways that they plan with people and families and has strengthened their commitment to individualized supports and to "day programs without walls" (an individualized alternative to activity centers). The complexity of the systems makes Pathfinders one influence among many competing forces. The purpose of forums is to make that influence as clear and strong as possible.

HOW THE PATHFINDERS PROJECT CHANGES LIVES

In addition to a bird's eye view of the Pathfinders project and its community, a close view of the Pathfinders experience is also in order. Each story is different, of course. An approach to transition and the integration of services, agencies, and people that is predicated on crafting uniquely individualized encounters cannot be reduced to a canned, one-size-fits-all curriculum. However, telling one story also serves to tell the Pathfinders story. One parent vividly expressed how this process developed in her son Spencer's life (Kendall Browne, 2000). Her account captures an important quality of the space necessary for Pathfinders to work. In this space, people collaborate outside their usual roles and boundaries. This involved school staff moving from familiar territory to explore the opportunities available in Spencer's physical world. It involved Spencer and his family calling on their personal networks in new ways. It meant suspending certainty that anyone, professional or parent, fully understood Spencer in looking for new ways to decode his responses to changes in his expanding world. This mother's account also shows how participation in the project accelerated a change that had already begun in Spencer's school.

> Spencer and I were very fortunate to be in a District 75 school, 373K, with a Principal and Assistant Principal who were willing to listen to us and think differently. As the result of many failures to get Spencer to "adjust" to the inside of the school, we began to brainstorm together how to support him to be out in the community with good support. We finally found the right match between Spencer and a paraprofessional who respected Spencer and understood instead of just trying to control him.
>
> As we were involved in this brainstorming, we attended a person-centered planning workshop sponsored by District 75. Wow! This was it! We discovered that other people were thinking positively about the lives of people with disabilities, and we developed even better ideas for jobs and other community

activities that Spencer might enjoy. Spencer's behavior did not just change over night just because we were thinking about creative options. However, we did find that we were more able to listen to and interpret his behavior and make better choices on his behalf.

Spencer got a job at the Barnes and Noble bookstore on the Pratt Institute campus. This was a good fit because we had connections there, Spencer loved the work, and he was able to dress beautifully which is part of his claim to fame. He worked alongside college students stocking the bookshelves. He loved it, and the students were very supportive of him.

We have learned that things do not just get better and stay better. Spencer's advocate, the store manager, left and was replaced by another manager who was not supportive of Spencer. Spencer picked up on the manager's negative attitude and engaged old tactics of acting out in his usual way, so we began to look for another job. Spencer was still having outbursts, but they were far less frequent as he began to be more independent and form his own life.

When things fell apart at the bookstore, Spencer had already graduated from high school and we were already involved with an adult service agency that provides individualized support for community experience. (Kendall Browne, 2000, pp. 7–9)

Spencer now works as a store associate in the shoe department of a discount store, where he has been employed for 3 years. His story is unique and yet typical of the experiences of many Pathfinders participants. His path has been marked by fortuitous and unexpected events. However, his capacity for meaningful and increasingly independent transactions with the community continues to grow. This growth does not occur overnight, and Job Path's investment in Spencer will continue for years to come. What is critical in Spencer's story lies in its genesis in a person-centered planning process initiated by his school. By focusing on Spencer as an individual rather than as a client to be processed by an enormous bureaucracy, the arc of his life experiences has been altered. School life had represented segregation; now, there is reason to believe that his adult life will contain more inclusive experiences.

CONCLUSION

Of course, there are some Pathfinders stories with fewer exclamation points. Segregation is sticky, and some families trade uncertainty about whether adult services providers can learn to deliver individualized supports in a timely and reliable way for the certainty of a day activity program slot. Some students have not had a team member with the energy and ability to pull things together and have lost their place in valued neighborhood activities. Some graduates remain in the training placements popular with New York City's supported employment providers instead of gaining status as full, paid employees of the businesses for which they work. These problems cannot be explained by individual disability or family troubles. They are clearly problems that the service systems have to solve. A consequence of Pathfinders is that people with developmental disabilities and their families know that the problem is not their fault and that positive change is possible.

Pathfinders participants—students, family members, school staff, and adult services staff—witness that searching for capacity works as a way to "make it" in New York. And, as one of the city's anthems has it, "If you can make it here, you can make it anywhere." It is just not a solo effort.

REFERENCES

Beverage, A. (1996). Five important New York metro area trends. *American Sociological Association Footnotes, 24*(1), 2–3.

Campaign for Fiscal Equity. (2001). *The state of learning in the New York City public schools.* Retrieved June 3, 2001, from http://www.cfequity.org/ns-sta-1.htm

Jeffrey, P. (1999, Spring). Letter from a grandmother. *Pathfinders, 1,* 4.

Kendall Browne, V. (2000). Spencer's story. In B. Mount. & C. Lyle O'Brien (Eds.), *Lives in transition* (pp. 7–9). New York: Job Path.

Mount, B. (1994). Benefits and limitations of personal futures planning. In V.J. Bradley, J.W. Ashbaugh, & B.C. Blaney (Eds.), *Creating individual supports for people with developmental disabilities: A mandate for change at many levels* (pp. 97–108). Baltimore: Paul H. Brookes Publishing Co.

Mount, B. (2000a). *Person-centered planning: Finding directions for change using personal futures planning.* Amenia, NY: Capacity Works.

Mount, B. (2000b). *Life building: Opening windows to change using person-centered planning.* Amenia, NY: Capacity Works.

Mount, B., & Lyle O'Brien, C. (Eds.). (2000). *Lives in transition.* New York: Job Path.

Mount, B., Lyle O'Brien, C., & Rosen, F. (2000). *The Pathfinders project.* New York: Job Path.

New York City Board of Education. (2001). *District 75 citywide programs: At a glance.* Retrieved January 31, 2003, from http://www.nycenet.edu/d75/home/atglance.html

New York City Department of City Planning. (2002). *Change in total population, 1990 and 2000: New York City and boroughs.* Retrieved January 31, 2003, from http://www.nyc.gov/html/dcp/html/census/pop2000.html#population

O'Brien, J., & Lyle O'Brien, C. (1987). *Framework for accomplishment.* Lithonia, GA: Responsive Systems Associates.

Rodriguez, R. (2000). Challenge deficiency thinking. In B. Mount & C. Lyle O'Brien (Eds.), *Lives in transition* (pp. 16–17). New York: Job Path.

Wagner, M., Blackorby, J., Cameto, R., Hebbeler, K., & Newman, L. (1993). *The transition experiences of young people with disabilities: A summary of findings from the National Longitudinal Transition Study of special education students.* Menlo Park: SRI International. (ERIC Document Reproduction Service No. ED365086)

Wolf, M. (2000/2001, Winter). Who is Josh? Developing a capacity view. *Pathfinders, 2,* 4.

LESSONS FROM
NEW YORK CITY'S PATHFINDERS PROJECT

It Is Never Too Late to Start Doing Good Work

CAREN L. SAX

The Chapter 8 description of Pathfinders is particularly fitting in a book on inclusive urban schools. As the authors explained, "Pathfinders students and their families belong in this book as witnesses to the deep well of capacity that can be tapped even in enormous systems bound to large-scale, lifelong segregation" (p. 186). Although it is generally true that segregated schooling during the K–12 years typically leads to segregated adult lives, Pathfinders demonstrates that even when the odds against them are monumental, positive outcomes are possible. For example, almost every Pathfinders participant described acquired new personal and professional connections, established goals and plans for achieving these goals that reflect their talents and interests, and became better equipped to gain access to the adult service system more effectively. These successes illustrate that it is never too late to begin the work of creating quality adult lives, regardless of the preceding quality of schooling.

Preparation of this commentary was supported in part by grants from the U.S. Department of Education, Office of Special Education Programs (Grant Nos. H078C60008 and H158Q70009) and the Rehabilitation Services Administration (Grant No. H235W70045). No official endorsement should be inferred.

A STARTING POINT

Examining the Pathfinders approach is important for a number of reasons. First, Pathfinders provides a starting point that everyone can understand. It is easy to become overwhelmed by the task of reforming schools. By describing the grass roots efforts of Pathfinders, other interested and dedicated families and professionals may be encouraged to try to make a difference, even if only a small number of people benefit. Changes occurred in New York City because of such grass roots efforts, not because millions of dollars in funding enabled people to break free from an existing paradigm. Too many professionals believe that answers lie only in acquiring more money. Although additional resources obviously help, the lack of them should not be used as an excuse for maintaining the status quo. As Pathfinders confirms, even small, fragile changes can be significant in a large, complex system.

This common starting point includes the use of person-centered work; in fact, Pathfinders "is designed as a person-centered development project . . . that challenge[s] a deficiency view of a person, family, neighborhood, and city" (p. 184). Person-centered planning, viewed as a value and process versus a program, requires equal participation, positive and clear communication, and active involvement of the focus individual. Embracing this philosophy and implementing it in ways that support the commitment of long-term relationships need not be dependent on external funding nor on inclusive high school experiences. As students with disabilities make the transition from the public school system to the adult world, their options will continue to be severely limited unless families and professionals are willing to think about new ways of planning and support. Listening to individuals to nurture the exploration of their own talents, skills, and interests goes a long way in focusing the actions of a larger group.

CAPACITY THINKING

Consideration of the Pathfinders approach is also important for demonstrating the use of capacity thinking. As the authors define it, "Capacity thinking is the art of first discovering the qualities that a person with a developmental disability can contribute to community life and then discovering people and places that value that contribution" (p. 188). Essentially, this takes the process of person-centered work to the community level. Facing the daunting challenges presented by New York City's diversity, poverty, political and administrative complexity, and sheer size and numbers, the education and human services system can best make an impact by "discovering capacity in the social spaces that are too small for the big systems to notice" (p. 189). Once again, this approach can be implemented in any geographical area, regardless of widespread or minimal support by the existing systems. The framework designed by Pathfinders targets the person, family, community, and adult services delivery systems to identify and create new options that result in quality adult lives. If it can happen in New York City, the likelihood is that it can happen anywhere, as few other cities have more potential and more real barriers.

COLLABORATION IN OTHER COMMUNITIES

Pathfinders is an example of collaboration that is essential to encouraging the interaction of huge service and educational systems. Although everyone talks about collaboration, it remains an elusive goal to actualize. However, efforts in California provide another encouraging example. A number of urban school districts in California use the Transition Service Integration Model (TSIM), which focuses on students with significant disabilities exiting the public school system who are interested in pursuing employment, postsecondary education, and other activities for community inclusion and a quality adult life. Initiated in 1997 with funding from the U.S. Department of Education, the project has been implemented in almost a dozen school districts across California, including urban districts in San Diego, San Francisco, and San Jose (Certo et al., 2003). When TSIM was first implemented, activities were executed on two levels: strategies for delivering services to students and collaboration among the participating service delivery systems.

On the first level, targeted school district transition programs were encouraged to reconceptualize the provision of options to students with significant disabilities during the students' last year of public school (i.e., at age 21). Students, families, and teachers held person-centered planning meetings during the summer or fall prior to the students' final school year. Families were encouraged to consider goals related to careers, postsecondary education, and community activities, as well as the supports necessary to attain those goals. To examine a range of postschool options, meetings were also arranged with representatives from the schools, the Department of Rehabilitation (DR) and the Department of Developmental Disabilities (DDS), and nonprofit adult services providers. The students involved in the TSIM model opened or reactivated cases with DDS and/or DR at least 10 months earlier than they would have in traditional programs. Students and their families became acquainted and comfortable with adult agency staff early on, and teachers shared cumulative records directly with these staff. Common planning documents and assessment tools also were used to minimize duplication of efforts by each of the departments or systems. (A detailed description of the model can be found in Certo et al., 2002.)

The second focus, service integration, required stakeholders (e.g., schools, DR, DDS, nonprofit adult agencies) to consider new ways of collaboration. The

stakeholders that were brought together to implement TSIM discussed possibilities for designing services that differed from traditional approaches, resulting in
a new way of doing business. One of the most significant innovations included a
plan for sharing costs across DDS and DR for the same students. Although some
nonprofit agencies have access to funding from both of these systems, they typically design separate programs categorically so that individuals receive funding
from either DDS or DR. However, the needs for these individuals are not that
easily separated. For example, a student who works 10–15 hours per week in a
supported employment position will likely need support in attaining nonwork
activities, such as joining classes at a community college or participating in
other community activities. This expense would be covered by DDS funding
rather than by DR funding. By splitting funding between the two systems, the
student is able to receive increasingly individualized services. More specifically,
during the last year of school, when a student identifies work and nonwork
activities, the supporting agency can receive funding through DR while collaborating with school personnel to design nonwork activities that complement the
work schedule. When the student exits the school system, nonwork support is
continued through DDS funding via the same nonprofit agency. Thus, seamless
transition occurs. That is, the student's schedule is maintained without interrup-
tion after he or she exits the school system. All partners benefit, providing the
momentum to continue collaboration and problem solving as new issues arise.

Elements of Collaboration

Certain elements of collaboration were instrumental both in the TSIM approach
implemented in California and in Pathfinders' efforts. Adapted from the work of
Lipnack and Stamps (1993), who studied "boundary crossing" (going outside
one's own organization to negotiate the exchange of resources), these elements
include a common, unifying purpose; committed stakeholders; voluntary links to
form relationships; participants who assume responsibilities/leadership; and
connections on many interactive levels. Applying these components to transition planning and implementation can aid recognition of the value in working
across boundaries that often keep organizations and systems operating in isolation. The following subsections describe the elements of collaboration as they
relate to innovative approaches such as TSIM and Pathfinders. By incorporating
these elements into change initiatives, a committed group of people in any community can be successful in improving the status quo.

Common, Unifying Purpose

Discovering the common goal of all participants is essential for collaboration to
occur. Legislation—including the Individuals with Disabilities Education Act
(IDEA) Amendments of 1997 (PL 105-17), the Rehabilitation Act Amendments of

1992 (PL 102-569), and the School-to-Work Opportunities Act of 1994 (PL 103-239)—mandates transition planning. Most students with disabilities and their families are interested in pursuing quality adult lives that include meaningful employment, continuing education, social opportunities, and independent or supported living options. In negotiating the initial phases of such efforts, spending time on identifying these common purposes lays a foundation for effective progress.

Committed Stakeholders

Everyone needs to have a voice in the process, leading to new and improved partnerships among all the participants. Setting up rules of engagement helps to begin establishing an environment of trust. The stakeholders involved in both Pathfinders and TSIM clearly demonstrated their commitment and modeled it effectively to their peers. Celebrating successes and working together to brainstorm and solve problems add to the shared history of overcoming challenges. Whether this is done on an individual basis regarding one person's attainment of a dream or on a larger level related to systemic change, such acknowledgment helps stakeholders remain committed for the long term.

Voluntary Links to Form Relationships

Building relationships is central to the process of person-centered development and to systems change. Capacity needs to be built within the system to create ownership and long-term maintenance of change efforts. One way that this was accomplished through TSIM was by creating new links among the school districts and community agencies that provided services to adults exiting the school system. Schools subcontracted directly with these agencies, enabling staff from each to work together more effectively. Communication improved, assessment and other background information was more easily shared, and the transition to a new system with new staff and new strategies was eased by those who already knew the student and family best (i.e., the school staff). External funding was used to support a percentage of existing staff in schools, agencies, and DR rather than to bring in outside people who would disappear at the end of a grant cycle. The relationships among the agencies improved as they began sharing information and working together to provide the best services for individuals.

Participants Who Assume Responsibilities/Leadership

Many individuals stepped up to the plate to take on new responsibilities and to model leadership. As described in Chapter 8, participants can make great strides in communication and self-determination skills, resulting in great changes in their lives. At the systems level, participants who are able to be proactive rather than reactive help keep the momentum going. Sometimes it takes a "critical friend" who is outside the immediate system to provide a different perspective and constructive feedback. Facilitating a person-centered planning session or an interagency planning meeting requires the ability to cross boundaries and negotiate ways to do business differently.

The progress made in the second and third years of TSIM led to an environment of trust and respect that was not even on the horizon when the meetings first began. Each participant had opportunities to demonstrate leadership in unique ways. In both TSIM and Pathfinders, students and their families shared their stories to help others through the difficult process of transition.

Connections on Many Interactive Levels

Just as the Pathfinders participants mentioned in Chapter 8 found connections on many levels to support new activities, transportation, support services, and ongoing workshops for communication, TSIM stakeholders found ways to expand and reinforce their abilities to support a seamless transition for students. For example, early on, meetings to discuss programming and policy issues were separated. Some meetings were held with certain stakeholders to discuss logistical, programmatic, and practical issues, whereas other meetings addressed the policy and funding barriers that prevented the practitioners from doing their jobs. One size could not fit all, so different approaches were required in different school districts and cities. This required connections on many levels across the schools, DDS, and DR, with relationships among the people doing the work being the key to success.

CONCLUSION: WHAT NEXT?

So where do families and professionals start? What can be done at a grass roots level? First, high expectations must be held for individuals with disabilities related to pursuing and maintaining a high quality of life as an adult. More important, individuals with disabilities must have high expectations for themselves. The statistics are bleak. *Executive Summary: 2000 National Organization on Disability/Harris Survey of Americans with Disabilities* reported that only 3 in 10 working-age (i.e., 18- to 64-year-old) people with disabilities are employed full or part time, compared with 8 in 10 working-age people without disabilities (32% versus 81%). People with disabilities are much more likely than people without disabilities to live in poverty, reporting household incomes of $15,000 or less. At the other end of the spectrum, people with disabilities are much less likely than people without disabilities to live in households that earn more than $50,000 annually. As a result of lower income levels and higher unemployment rates, people with disabilities are more than twice as likely as those without disabilities to postpone needed health care. Linked closely with these outcomes is the lack of basic education. More than 1 in 5 people with disabilities fail to complete high school, compared with less than 1 in 10 people without disabilities. Despite these numbers, we must maintain the belief—and the value—that all individuals have the same right to a quality life. To do this, we must question the status quo. Nothing changes without challenging what already exists.

Next, when accomplishments happen, such as those described by Pathfinders, we must share the knowledge and learn from one another. As an educator and trainer, I have taught about person-centered planning for many years, based on my own experiences of facilitating meetings with students and their families. I always encourage my audience to take the time to arrange a meeting for themselves or someone close to them to get a feel for the process. Those who do so begin to see the power of this approach. It empowers focus individuals to recognize not only the control that they can have over their own lives but also the influence that such a process can have on gaining access to the service delivery system. The promising and inspiring examples from Pathfinders demonstrate that it is never too late to start doing good work.

REFERENCES

Certo, N.J., Mautz, D., Pumpian, I., Sax, C., Smalley, K., Wade, H., Noyes, D., Luecking, R., Wechsler, J., & Batterman, N. (2003). A review and discussion of a model for seamless transition to adulthood. *Education and Training in Developmental Disabilities, 38*(1), 3–17.

Certo, N.J., Sax, C.L., Pumpian, I., Mautz, D., Smalley, K.A., Wade, H.A., & Noyes, D.A. (2002). Transition service integration model: Ensuring that the last day of school is no different than the day after. In C.L. Sax & C.A. Thoma, *Transition assessment: Wise practices for quality lives* (pp. 119–131). Baltimore: Paul H. Brookes Publishing Co.

Executive summary: 2000 National Organization on Disability/Harris Survey of Americans with Disabilities. (2000). Retrieved July 10, 2002, from http://www.nod.org

Individuals with Disabilities Education Act (IDEA) Amendments of 1997, PL 105-17, 20 U.S.C. §§ 1400 *et seq.*

Lipnack, J., & Stamps, J. (1993). *The TeamNet factor: Bringing the power of boundary crossing into the heart of your business.* Essex Junction, VT: Oliver Wight Publications.

Rehabilitation Act Amendments of 1992, PL 102-569, 29 U.S.C. §§ 701 *et seq.*

School-to-Work Opportunities Act of 1994, PL 103-239, 20 U.S.C. §§ 6101 *et seq.*

WHOLE SCHOOLING AND INCLUSION IN DETROIT

Lessons from the Motor City

J. MICHAEL PETERSON

A FRIEND OF MINE has often said, "Where Detroit goes, so goes the country" (Gibson, 2000, p. 3). He went on to write

> Detroit has often taken the lead in social movements. The depression of 1929 began when a bank at the corner of Griswold and Michigan in Detroit closed. Many of the first industrial unions were formed there. The collapse of industrial work in the U.S. began in Detroit. There are many reasons to suggest it is an important bellwether location for the country. (p. 3)

He may be correct. This chapter explores ongoing efforts to root inclusive schooling in the Detroit metropolitan area, the challenges and successes of which may presage hope and opportunity for many communities. The chapter first describes inclusive schooling in the Detroit metropolitan area, then discusses three specific schools that are working toward effective inclusive education practices and have formed a network with other schools for inclusive schooling support and leadership.

Practical lessons from this work are described that are linked to the foundation and formation of a school renewal model that places inclusive schooling at the center: Whole Schooling (Peterson, Beloin, & Gibson, 1997). The overall experience of those involved with Whole Schooling in Detroit provides a powerful example of the necessary link between urban school reform and inclusive education. As educators have worked toward inclusive education in the Detroit area, it has become clear how deeply schooling is embedded in broader social contexts and how important it is to connect inclusive schooling to these challenges and opportunities if it is to survive and thrive.

In 1997, university and school colleagues, initially in Michigan and Wisconsin, developed the Whole Schooling framework for school renewal, in which inclusive schooling is considered a centerpiece, not an add-on. Whole Schooling was founded by two groups who usually operate in a parallel manner: one primarily concerned with issues of democracy, power, and responsible citizenship; the other primarily concerned with inclusive education of students with disabilities.

FIVE PRINCIPLES OF WHOLE SCHOOLING

Whole Schooling is founded on Five Principles (see Table 9.1), which are the key elements for building a school culture in which children learn and thrive. These principles describe a process of education for helping students become thoughtful, knowledgeable citizens who can function effectively in a democratic society (Principle 1). To do so, democracy is an outcome but must also be embedded in the way that schools operate at all levels. For democracy to be real and for students to learn, Whole Schooling posits that schools must commit to including all stakeholders in learning together. By definition, democracy is not possible if some individuals are systematically excluded. To learn to participate in building democratic communities, people need experience as they grow and develop in working with diverse peers. However, for such education to work, schools cannot deliver the standard "one-size-fits-all" curriculum but must use authentic multilevel teaching that supports diverse students in learning together—with little to no pull-outs, clustering, or ability grouping. Students can work together on similar topics and projects at their own levels, using materials that challenge them to move to the next level with support. In such a school, the building of community among adults and with children is critical. Community is a powerful source by which the social and emotional needs of adults and children are met, helping to prevent behavioral difficulties and violence and providing an atmosphere conducive to deep levels of learning and supportive of individual needs. Support becomes an important practice as schools reconfigure how specialized staff—special education teachers, teachers for gifted

Table 9.1. The Five Principles of Whole Schooling

1. *Empower citizens in a democracy.* The goal of education is to help students learn to function as effective citizens in a democracy.

2. *Include all.* All children learn together across culture, ethnicity, language, ability, gender, and age.

3. *Use authentic, multilevel teaching for learners of diverse abilities.* Teachers design instruction for diverse learners that engages students in active learning through meaningful, real-world activities. Teachers also develop accommodations and adaptations for learners with diverse needs, interests, and abilities.

4. *Build community and support learning.* The school uses specialized school and community resources (special education, Title I funds, gifted education) to build support for students, parents, and teachers. All work together to build community and mutual support within the classroom and school and to provide proactive supports for students with behavioral challenges.

5. *Partner with families and the community.* Educators build genuine collaboration within the school and with families and the community; engage the school in strengthening the community; and provide guidance to engage students, parents, teachers, and others in decision making and the direction of learning and school activities.

From Peterson, M. (2001). *Key elements in building whole schools.* Detroit, MI: Renaissance Community Press, Wayne State University; adapted by permission.

For more information, go to http://www.coe.wayne.edu/CommunityBuilding/WSC.html

students, paraprofessionals, speech-language pathologists, and others—can enhance the quality of general education classes and help to strengthen multilevel teaching and community. Such specialists work with teachers to provide proactive responses to behavioral challenges and the socioemotional needs of students rather than to control or manage behavior. Finally, partnerships with stakeholders outside the school's structural bureaucracy are crucial, bringing in critical friends for reflection and growth, collaborating with community resources, and, most important, creating a genuine and respectful working relationship at multiple levels with the parents of the children whom schools serve. Whole Schooling, then, provides a framework for self-analysis based on a paradigm and view of excellence in schooling, what one principal described as the "culture" of the school.

Since the creation of this approach in 1997, university faculty and staff and school educators have been involved in many activities seeking to use and better understand the concepts and practices embedded in Whole Schooling. Involved faculty have engaged in qualitative research in each school by spending time in classrooms; talking with teachers, children, parents, and principals; and functioning as "critical friends" who assist schools in grappling with a variety of challenges and support their work to improve practice. Collaborative work is underway to develop Whole Schooling more extensively as a school renewal model. Interested parties are exploring use of the Whole Schooling framework throughout the United States and in several countries. The unique characteristics of the Detroit metropolitan area, however, have provided a fertile field in which to use and understand these principles and associated practices.

Members of a Whole Schooling research team collaborated with the leadership of several schools to develop a formal partnership for strengthening inclusive education in those schools and throughout Michigan. School staff visited one another to learn and explore alternatives for their own improvement, teachers met to share and create strategies for providing mutual support, and school staff have attended four conferences and seminars to share exemplary practices in their schools and learn from national experts. On February 28, 2001, at a meeting of representatives from seven schools representing four school districts, the Michigan Network for Inclusive Schooling was established to facilitate cross-school learning and growth and to promote the expansion of inclusive education in Michigan. The group is committed to working toward stronger inclusive schooling practices based on the Five Principles of Whole Schooling, with the expectation and anticipation that some schools will adopt Whole Schooling as a guiding framework for school reform (Michigan Network for Inclusive Schooling, 2001).

CONTEXT OF EDUCATIONAL ISSUES IN DETROIT

For many years, Detroit had a stellar international reputation. In the early 20th century, the city was known throughout the world for the quality of its schools. A boom of school construction created many of the school buildings in which children continue to learn at the beginning of the 21st century. Despite debates about cutting "frills" such as art and music classes, and the role of schools in "Americanizing" foreign immigrants, most Detroit schools were filled with active learning, building on the ideas of John Dewey and other progressive educators of the time (Mirel, 1993).

There were more individual homes in Detroit than in any major city in the country. Early on, Michigan developed a progressive trend for caring for people with challenges, enacting some of the most generous social service legislation in the country. In this context, it was not a surprise that the state passed legislation in the 1970s to educate individuals with disabilities ages 3–26, setting a standard of comprehensive services that would eventually be incorporated into federal legislation. Michigan residents have long been proud of this heritage (Gibson & Peterson, 2001; Henrickson, 1991).

Yet, underneath this veneer, ethnic and monetary issues simmered. While Detroit rose in prestige as the center of the burgeoning auto industry, it began dividing into ethnic enclaves, each fighting for its share of resources, predicting Detroit's current city–suburb divide (Henrickson,

1991). This divide emerged in earnest in the 1950s, as the flight from the city began and fiscal resources for city schools gradually dwindled. Federal policy provided funds to create highways, which brought people quickly in and out of cities and destroyed many viable neighborhoods. People of different ethnicities were geographically concentrated, their mobility was hindered, and they found few loans for home improvement in such "redlined" areas. In 1967, tensions tore the inner city apart in racial conflict that resulted in property destruction, several injuries and deaths, and the use of federal troops to restore and maintain order. After this event, movement out of the city exploded. The census reports taken from 1970 to 2000 show that Detroit lost almost half a million people to the suburbs. As of 2003, Detroit is one of the most ethnically diverse yet most segregated metropolitan areas in the United States. Driving on Interstate 696, the newly constructed loop around the northern part of the city, takes one through small communities that are grouped together by ethnicity (Chaffets, 1990; Gibson & Peterson, 2001; Henrickson, 1991; Kozol, 1991).

The Detroit metropolitan area is composed of three counties—each unique, each linked to the other. The city of Detroit is located in Wayne County. Running through the area is the Detroit River, long a carrier of major cargo freighters from Lake Michigan to Lake Erie and a chief source of the city's early growth. Major auto plants and other industries were once located in the Down River area, which is now home to working and lower middle class communities, with most residents being Caucasian. Oakland County, northwest of Detroit, is home to the most wealthy residents. It is also home to the city of Pontiac, which also experienced a suburban exodus and loss of industry similar to that of Detroit. Macomb County is home to many residents of Eastern European descent, who moved from Detroit in the 1960s (U.S. Census Bureau, 2000).

Detroit Schools

Between 1990 and 2002, Detroit had seven school superintendents, each with a major reform agenda that failed (Mirel, 1993). Detroit's school system has lost approximately 30,000 students since 1997, with middle-class African Americans moving to the suburbs or placing their children in newly formed charter schools. A lawsuit pushing for integration of the entire metropolitan area was lost. By 2000, approximately 85% of the student population of the Detroit Public Schools was African American, with concentrations of other ethnic groups in particular locations throughout the city (Detroit Public Schools, 2000).

Reform has come in waves with each superintendent, and with a political restructuring of the city's governance of education. In the early 1990s,

Deborah McGriff brought efforts to follow the Chicago model of local school empowerment, which allowed Chicago schools to control their own budgets and make decisions at a school level, typically governed at the central office. The teacher's union members largely fought against these efforts that were seen as ways of reducing adherence to union-negotiated contracts. Eddie Green later promoted numerous progressive reforms in his short stay as superintendent, putting in place a major federal grant to improve math and science and obtaining funds for a major school reform initiative. Starting in 1997, this 5-year reform initiative required schools to work in clusters and apply for grants of up to $4 million to support school reform. Most of Detroit's 300 schools sought the funds that were eventually awarded to 10 clusters of some 35 schools in 1999. (Gibson & Peterson, 2001).

Michigan's governor at the time, John Engler, ousted the elected school board and asked Dennis Archer, Mayor of Detroit, to appoint a "reform board." This board comprised primarily members of the elite who had no connection to Detroit schools. The first-year board meetings overflowed with outraged citizens, held in check by as many as 200 police; some meetings were interrupted as police arrested protesting parents and students (Gibson & Peterson, 2001). When the board hired David Adamany, retired President of Wayne State University, as acting Chief Executive Officer (CEO) for a year, Detroit teachers ignored the recommendations of union leadership and walked off the job in a surprise strike (Gibson & Peterson, 2001). In the summer of 2000, Kenneth Burnley was hired as CEO. He came from Colorado Springs—a city in which inclusive education had become well established (Gibson & Peterson, 2001). As of 2003, Burnley initiated a rapid series of changes—establishing executive director positions over clusters of schools, adopting Open Court as the mandated literacy program, developing new achievement tests, and increasing pressure to raise state standardized test scores.

MEAP Madness: Standardized Testing in Michigan

All of these events occurred in a state in which the standards movement and standardized testing have increasingly driven educational practice. This factor has had a particularly strong impact on schools with many students whose families have low incomes or are considered working class. Initially established in the 1960s to identify schools that needed support and assistance in improving their practice, Michigan's standardized test (the Michigan Educational Assessment Program, or MEAP) became the centerpiece of educational policy during the 1990s. Hundreds of teachers and administrators joined in developing standards and a revised test, and the state department of education promised that the test would never be used to rank schools, students, or teachers. As of 2002, such promises rang hollow. Each Fall, the major state papers rank schools by their MEAP scores. In turn, real estate agents post scores on house profiles and principals' jobs are threatened if scores do not increase. The takeover of the Detroit school board was justified, in part, based on MEAP scores—despite the fact that researchers have found a very high correlation between family income and standardized test scores (Gibson & Peterson, 2001; Nease, 1998).

There is growing evidence that the MEAP tests also lead to the exclusion of students with disabilities from general education classrooms. Special education directors have reported that referral rates go dramatically up in the 2 months prior to the administration of the MEAP. Many schools clearly seek to have students with disabilities excluded from general education classes in an effort to raise the average test scores. Furthermore, there is evidence that the focus on testing keeps some schools from engaging in instructional techniques that make inclusive education more possible (Kohn, 1999).

Inclusive Education Efforts in the Detroit Metropolitan Area

Inclusive education efforts in the Detroit metropolitan area reflect the state's pattern in that they are uneven—an enclave of work and movement here and there. In the late 1980s, many schools began to experiment with inclusive education. Michigan was awarded a statewide systems change initiative, the Michigan Inclusive Education Project (Michigan IEP), which was influenced by Marsha Forrest and her colleagues in Ontario, Canada. Nonetheless, Michigan's state department has been ambivalent in its leadership, continuing to publish state regulations for special education that read as a catalog of segregated schooling options. In 1990, a committee developed a definition for inclusive education, and in 1994, a task force made recommendations for revising the special education rules promoting unification of general and special education (Peterson, 1997). However, these rule changes were never implemented. Efforts to finally change the rules were highly resisted by parents and shifted leadership from the state to counties. In 2002, Tom Watkins, newly named Superintendent of Education, issued rules that largely maintained existing rules with only minor technical changes.

It is not surprising that inclusion of children with disabilities is more frequent in schools in wealthier areas, particularly in several Oakland County districts. Southfield Public Schools also passed a board-level commitment to inclusion in 1996, and Birmingham schools engaged in an initiative to return students from center programs to local schools with increasingly inclusive options. Farmington Public Schools (1994) developed a comprehensive 10-year strategic plan for elementary schools, which commits all schools to implementing inclusive education. These shifts reflect much dialogue and learning. Many highly educated parents have insisted on inclusive education for their children, with success, in these districts. In addition, numerous educational leaders in these districts connect inclusive education and improved school experiences for all students.

In Wayne County, which is located outside Detroit and Macomb County (both largely populated by working-class families), segregated services are strongly supported. In Macomb County, the Intermediate School District directly operates large, well-funded special education schools. Some districts, such as Wyandotte Public Schools, have led the way. This district has had co-teaching models for students with mild disabilities in place since the late 1980s, has made substantive inclusive efforts for students with moderate disabilities, and has placed classrooms for students with severe disabilities in a prominent place in the local high school (Peterson, Tamor, Feen, & Silagy, 2002). Despite these positive efforts, most services remain largely segregated.

Moving Toward Inclusion in Detroit

Detroit schools are highly segregated, maintaining historic patterns and showing little movement toward inclusive education. The system operates 13 segregated schools for students with moderate to severe disabilities. A small number of programs for students with cognitive impairments have self-contained classes in general education schools. In almost all schools, students labeled as "learning disabled" or "cognitively impaired" are educated in self-contained classes (Detroit Public Schools, 2001b). Until 2000, some schools contained no students identified as having disabilities. Students were transferred to other schools if they were identified as having a disability.

Inclusion has occurred in some Detroit schools, typically for very short periods of time. In some schools, outdated models in which students are "mainstreamed" into classes that match their presumed mental age are used. Thus, in two schools, 13-year-old students with mental retardation were mainstreamed for a partial day into a third-grade class (Peterson, Gibson, & Feen, 1999).

Since the early 1990s, some dialogue and work toward inclusive education has occurred. In 1994, the Detroit district established a study group for inclusive education and identified the move toward more "inclusionary options" as part of the special education strategic plan (Detroit Public

Schools, 1994). This goal, however, was virtually unknown to rank-and-file special education teachers and school principals (Peterson et al., 1999). A short-term project funded by the Michigan Developmental Disabilities Council sought to work in schools where parents were insisting on inclusion for children with more severe disabilities. However, this project was abandoned by the district prior to its completion, as a new special education director brought new priorities. During this time, some resource rooms were established, moving away from full-time, self-contained placement for students with mild learning disabilities—an effort seen as a major reform in an otherwise totally segregated system (Peterson, 1997).

Inclusion in Head Start has been a high point in establishing inclusive education. In the 1997–1998 school year, 205 children with diagnosed disabilities were enrolled in Detroit's Head Start program, a number slightly higher than the federally mandated 10% of enrollment. These children were included in general Head Start classes with support services. Transition efforts for inclusive placements have been fraught with difficulty and met with resistance by school staff, despite efforts by Head Start staff to develop collaborative programs with special-education funded, preprimary impaired, self-contained classes in Detroit elementary schools (Office of Early Childhood Education, 1999). Typically, children with moderate to severe disabilities are sent automatically to segregated special education schools.

During the 1990s, there were a few unsuccessful efforts at local schools to establish inclusive education through collaborative work between local school staff and university faculty of the Whole Schooling Consortium. As part of the 21st Century Schools initiative, Whole Schooling Consortium faculty provided substantial assistance to a cluster of three schools, called the Eastside Detroit Whole Schooling Cluster. This cluster adopted the Five Principles of Whole Schooling to guide reform efforts. Ultimately, however, as schools were awarded money to implement school renewal efforts, they backed away from the commitment to implement inclusive education as part of the renewal efforts (Peterson, 2000).

As of this writing, the direction of the administration of Detroit Public Schools is not clear. A special education director with a reputation for promoting unification of general and special education has been hired. In Fall 2000, special education students who were previously bussed across town were returned to their neighborhood schools. In April 2001, reform and change efforts to improve the schools were announced that included a commitment to "move towards full compliance with federal law by relocating special education students from self-contained settings to least restrictive environments" (Burnley, 2001). A district newsletter published on the same date announced a commitment to "improve service to special education students" and "enhance the district's ability to use inclusion and mainstreaming to benefit regular and special education students" (Detroit Public Schools, 2001a, p. 7). The comprehensive study of the schools on which this initiative is based articulated key problems with segregation and the need to establish pilot inclusive education programs while moving all schools toward effective inclusive options (Detroit Public Schools, 2001a). As part of the implementation of the district's restructuring plan, several special education schools were closed and students were transferred in groups to particular wings in local high schools (Detroit Public Schools, 2001a). In some schools, special education teachers began providing in-class support for students with mild disabilities. However, in most schools, special education has remained segregated.

SNAPSHOTS OF THREE INCLUSIVE SCHOOLS

In this complex context, we briefly explore the work of three schools: Beard Elementary in Detroit, MacArthur Elementary in Southfield, and Hillside Elementary in Farmington. Each school has made a commitment to move toward inclusive schooling practices. We have studied each of these schools as part of the Whole Schooling Research Project, and two of the schools have utilized Whole Schooling to assist their planning for school improvement efforts. The information below draws from the final report of the Whole Schooling Research Project (Peterson, Tamor, Feen & Silagy, 2002).

Beard Elementary School: Detroit's First Inclusive School

Beard Elementary is located in Southwest Detroit, which is home to many Hispanic/Latino families. Beard Elementary was housed in Detroit's oldest school building until the 2001–2002 school year, when staff and children moved to one of four new schools constructed in Detroit. The proposed location for the new facility was a former industrial waste site, but district officials successfully assured residents that areas of contamination would be effectively sealed off. The combined staff and students from Beard and Montrose Elementary Schools filled the completed building.

Beard has been acclaimed for its efforts to implement several interrelated school improvement efforts. The Comer School Development Program, a school reform model that emphasizes parent participation and social supports for all children, has provided a foundational philosophy. Beard has a long history working to build a sense of community. Whereas many schools in Detroit have high degrees of teacher turnover, many teachers have remained with Beard for much of their careers and have a sense of school ownership. Guests at the school are greeted with "hellos" and usually see parents meeting with teachers in offices and talking with children in the halls. Meetings are held with and for parents weekly, and programs for parents and their children are run at night and on the weekend.

At Beard, 85% of the students receive free or reduced-price lunches. Poverty brings daily, concrete, and often draining problems—from head lice to accusations of child abuse by parents to behavior problems. Yet, the connection of families and the sense of community are palpable (Peterson, 2001).

In August 2000, Beard's principal was asked to open a special education classroom because students were being transferred back to their neighborhood schools. However, he told central office officials that the school did not have space for such a classroom and that he would only support inclusive education for these students. He himself had been in segregated bilingual education and special education classes and remembered their negative impact. He suggested that Beard be the first school to model inclusive education in Detroit.

During the 2002–2003 school year, Beard started its journey toward inclusive education by 1) including students with mild disabilities who were previously being transported across the city to other schools and 2) seeking to keep all students in the school who are subsequently identified as having disabilities. (Students with moderate to severe disabilities have been served in separate schools and have not yet returned to Beard.) For Detroit's first inclusion specialist, the principal selected a teacher who had deep roots in the local community and experience with young children and art therapy. She partnered with the school social worker and has pulled in additional resource staff: a teacher consultant, a school psychologist, and a social worker in the local community mental health center program that provides collaborative school-based services. This teacher and faculty of Wayne State University—who specialize in bilingual education, literacy, and inclusive education—met as a support team. The team selected the Five Principles of Whole Schooling as a vision for the school.

Teachers were initially concerned about children (some labeled as having disabilities) causing behavior problems, particularly at lunchtime. To address this issue, a "lunch club" was developed. During the lunch club, the inclusion specialist and these children did fun, special activities. Suddenly, the lunch club became the place to be rather than a place of punishment, and other students were invited to participate.

In general, developing a systematic working process was difficult. The inclusion specialist developed a collaborative teaching schedule in eight general education classes once or twice per week. She helped adapt lessons, provided teaching suggestions, and assisted with students with behavior challenges. However, because this individual provided emergency assistance when students had difficulties such as behavior outbursts, she was often drawn off her assigned schedule.

Some of Beard's teachers were involved in a Clinical Staff Development Program with faculty from Wayne State University. The program addressed exemplary second language learning, literacy, and inclusive teaching practices. Every 2 weeks, a group of volunteer teachers met with a supporting faculty member for an hour-long study and dialogue session about inclusive education. Much conversation focused on making inclusion work, developing community in the school, and understanding needs of children. A series of in-service workshops on attention-deficit/hyperactivity disorder, differentiated instruction, and other topics were held to heighten conversation and thinking about inclusive teaching practices. In turn, linkages have been made with other schools that are working toward inclusion.

As the district's first school with a goal of full inclusion, the school has been watched carefully. Beard Elementary has shown a strong beginning, but it also has a long way to go. However, it has a solid foundation on which to build in the coming years.

MacArthur Elementary School: Effective Inclusive Teaching in an Urban School

MacArthur Elementary School serves a racially and socioeconomically diverse student body. MacArthur is located in Southfield, one of the most integrated communities in the Detroit metropolitan area, with a mix of people of Anglo-European, African, Arabic, and Jewish descent. The area is home to 140 Fortune 500 companies, yet of 480 students, 53% receive free or reduced-price lunches (Peterson, Tamor, Feen, & Silagy, 2002). Less than a mile from the Detroit border, many students live in Detroit but claim local residence for eligibility to attend this school.

Nestled in a forested residential area off a major street, MacArthur has been known for many years as one of the most ground-breaking schools in this small district. In 1990, an innovative principal brought to MacArthur a commitment to inclusive education, presaging the districts ultimate board-level commitment to inclusion in 1996.

As of the 2000 school year, only 12 students at MacArthur were classified as "special education certified students." Whereas students with more severe disabilities continued to attend separate schools in this district, this school intentionally labeled few children. Instead, children simply received assistance and support. As teachers discuss their classes, they often refer to children who "in another building would be labeled." For example, during her tenure, the principal resisted labeling children with behavior challenges and social needs as emotionally impaired. She often told staff, "You go spend time in this child's home and then tell me his problems are just his, and then we will talk."

Change and growth have been promoted in a variety of ways. In 1991, MacArthur had traditional separate special education classes. The principal hired in 1990, however, further helped to install the use of Glasser's (1992) approach to quality schooling—an approach which encourages staff to help meet the human needs of children (survival, love/belonging, fun, freedom, and power). This philosophy provided a values base and practical strategies for dealing with many issues in the school. Many staff participated in training, visited "Glasser schools" in other states, and encouraged multiage teaching by attending workshops and visiting multiage schools. Similarly, a holistic, workshop-based approach to literacy instruction has gradually developed and strengthened, and a professional development consultant hired by the district met with a group of teachers sharing practice and strategies. The move to adopt Whole Schooling as an expanded but consistent framework builds on this work.

Although the needs of the children constantly challenged staff, the school has developed impressive resources to support children and teachers. Support staff work as a team to assist and collaborate with general education teachers. There are two special education teachers, two Title I funded teachers, one additional support teacher (funded through a class-size reduction grant), a reading clinician, and a speech-language pathologist. A social worker and school psychologist also work part time. Finally, a full-time coordinator provides conflict-resolution training and support to children through a grant with a local hospital. These individuals work as a team to develop collaborative schedules for in-class support. Students are heterogeneously placed in rooms across the school, with much collaborative conversation among teachers across grade levels. No special education or pull-out classes exist.

The teaching approaches of staff are highly conducive to inclusive teaching. A culture of open and active learning has gradually developed over the years. Few teachers arrange students' desks in rows. Most use tables, where children work often in groups. In the 2001 school year, every teacher in the school was involved in either a multiage class or "looping," whereby teachers serve the same students for 2 years (i.e., a third-grade teacher might have the same group of children in fourth grade). These two practices provide powerful continuity and a sense of community among children, as well as a context in which multilevel teaching becomes a natural part of the total curriculum. Reading and writing workshops are used in which children work at their own levels, either separately or in pairs or small groups, as teachers conference with individual students. Many teachers use individualized spelling lists drawn from words that certain students misspell in their work.

Project-based learning also is a centerpiece of learning at MacArthur. The school is involved in the Jason Project, a science curriculum using satellite conferences that involve children in data collection and connect them with actual scientists conducting investigations. In addition, students select their best work from various subjects and show parents what they have learned in student-led conferences, which students plan and conduct under the guidance of their teachers. Furthermore, medical residents from the local hospital weekly engage children in authentic, hands-on learning regarding health. Combined with in-class support, these strategies provide many options for students with differing abilities, needs, and challenges.

The Glasser philosophy helps many teachers give students options and support in making effective choices. When conflicts or problems occur with a particular student, the student completes a "success plan" and negotiates with other students and the teachers. Teachers use many other strategies to build community in their classrooms and thereby meet children's social and emotional needs and prevent problems: peer partnerships, cooperative learning, student-led classroom activities, circles of support for some students, and classroom meetings to discuss issues that may arise.

MacArthur is in the midst of change. Although the school effectively includes children with mild to moderate disabilities, it has yet to include children with more severe disabilities. In addition, the demographics of the school district in which it is located (Southfield) continue to change, with increasing numbers of children of differing ethnicities and families with low incomes. Many children have emotional challenges, so the full-scale commitment to inclusive education is an issue with which staff continue to grapple. The school also has faced much pressure to raise standardized test scores, with increased concerns over the use of multiage teaching and workshop and project approaches to teaching. Rather than using trade books and other materials that could help students learn to read at their own levels, the school district adopted a reading basal in 2001. There is a growing emphasis on keeping children at grade level, resulting in pressures to teach at one level. How MacArthur will be able to maintain and build on its exemplary work is yet to be seen (Peterson, Tamor, Feen, & Silagy 2002).

Hillside Elementary School: Collaboration for Inclusive Teaching

Hillside Elementary School is one of the newest schools in Farmington, a suburb of Detroit, and is home to many individuals in higher socioeconomic brackets. Hillside once predominantly served students from families that were Caucasian, Christian, affluent, and long-time U.S. residents. In the 1990s, however, the school saw an influx of students from Middle Eastern countries, particularly Iraq; an increase in African American students who had moved from nearby Detroit or other suburbs; an increase in students whose parents are recent immigrants from all parts of Asia; and a significant number of children from various countries who had been adopted by U.S. families. Hillside staff are being challenged to teach an increasingly diverse population, thus placing the commitment to inclusion of students with disabilities in a broader context.

All students with disabilities who are identified as special education students at Hillside are included in general education classes full time, with support from special education staff, related services personnel, and/or paraprofessionals. Two special education teachers co-teach with several teachers to whom they are assigned. As a result, fewer children are labeled in Hillside than in many other schools in the district. In addition, specialists are available for bilingual education and gifted education. A school psychologist also serves in a dual role as a parent–community facilitator and liaison. She helps develop drug- and violence-prevention programs that include support groups. An early intervention team works in the lower elementary grades to provide intensive services to support students' literacy skill development.

Hillside's school district sends students with moderate to severe disabilities to special education classes that serve as district centers. Thus, some children who would be considered Hillside students based on their residence attend other schools, and Hillside itself hosted two separate special education classes for students with moderate disabilities from throughout the district. Beginning in 2000, however, Hillside's staff engaged in dialogue and formed focus groups to develop next steps toward inclusive schooling, and students from these rooms began spending substantial portions of the school day in general education classes. In Fall 2001, Hillside included these students full time in general education classes, releasing special education teachers to support general education teachers as co-teachers and consultants. At the same time, staff have identified students with more severe disabilities who are attending special education programs elsewhere even though Hillside is their neighborhood school, and the staff anticipate inviting these students to attend Hillside. New models of supporting services to other labeled students (e.g., gifted, at risk, English as a second language) without pull-out programs have also been explored.

Hillside's staff has received training in the multiple intelligences theory, instructional differentiation, bilingual education, cooperative learning, co-teaching, and alternative assessment strategies. Many teachers use multiple approaches to design and implement engaging lessons. School halls are decorated with students' written and drawn representations of their personal lives and the research that they have conducted. Certain students often work in small groups or pairs in the hall outside of the classroom, giving them a place that is quieter to work. Teachers use cooperative learning, inquiry-based projects, activity-based learning, and authentic reading and writing strategies. Many teachers have implemented alternative assessments such as portfolios, and some teachers have begun implementing student-led parent conferences. Hillside offers a unique program of optional special-interest classes in the late afternoons, which aids in providing a range of opportunities for students. In addition, the school has a full art and music program.

Hillside's students participate in the development of classroom rules and learn to be part of a team through cooperative groupings in many classes. Many teachers use multiple strategies to involve students in decision making and in having an active role in the conduct of the class. The student council gives students an opportunity to practice leadership skills. Several monthly community service projects also provide students the chance to practice citizenship skills.

The leadership and staff of Hillside have sought to be an inclusive school. The principal who served at Hillside from 1994 to 2002 gave substantial leadership, constantly providing forums for staff discussion; inviting outside perspectives; asking questions; and promoting dialogue, site visits to other schools, investigations, and the collection of information. Teachers were encouraged to take initiative and to obtain the support and input of the principal. The faculty continues to elect a Teacher-Leader, who serves in a support role in many school projects and as a liaison between the principal and teaching staff. The school is still working to develop strategies for accommodating students with learning challenges. Staff have been trained in collaborative consultation, whereby teachers and support staff jointly consider problems that students have in the classroom and develop instructional modifications. Teachers and administrators report that this process has been very helpful. The school staff are engaging in dialogue and efforts to further multiability teaching and, in turn, to assist in expanding inclusion in the school.

In addition, the principal and other staff have provided leadership toward this direction in the district. The principal chaired the district's committee that developed a 10-year (1994–2004) strategic improvement plan for elementary schools. The plan incorporated numerous innovations: inclusion, multiage grouping, looping, bilingual services, differentiated instruction, social and emotional supports for children, and partnerships with parents. She also chaired the district's Inclusion Forum, a dialogue group across schools that developed out of the strategic planning committee.

In 1998, the school applied to be part of the Whole Schooling Research Project. Participation allowed Hillside to obtain the assistance of an outside group, which asked "different questions" to help the school staff see a broader range of possible strategies and solutions and to clarify its vision of a genuinely inclusive school. Researchers were invited to be part of the school change process and have been involved in individual interactions with teachers, support staff, the principal, and focus and dialogue groups.

Constantly engaged in growth and change, Hillside represents a school that has seen inclusive education as part of its overall mission. As a suburban school near the Detroit city limits, it is experiencing shifts in population that will provide an ongoing experiment in developing an effective inclusive school and engaging in partnerships with other schools. In the 2000–2001 school year, Hillside was named as both a state and national Blue Ribbon School, achieving special recognition for its inclusion work in special education.

PRACTICAL IDEAS FOR MAKING INCLUSION PART OF SCHOOL RENEWAL AND EXEMPLARY TEACHING

Many important lessons have been learned from inclusive efforts in the Detroit metropolitan area. A few are shared in the following subsections.

Make Inclusion Part of a School's Culture

In Beard, MacArthur, and Hillside Elementary Schools, efforts have been made to enable students with meaningful differences to learn together. However, in the Detroit area, segregation persists. For inclusive education to be effective, it must become a part of the total school culture. Every aspect of school life is touched in the process. Rather than being negative, however, addressing the challenges posted by inclusive education can help schools through their struggle with essential issues. For example, when teachers learn how to teach children learning at different levels, academic learning for all increases; as schools commit to building a community of care, thereby helping children with emotional and behavioral challenges learn social skills, discipline referrals and the threat of school violence go down.

What makes inclusion work? Leadership from the principal, supported at other levels within a school system, is critical. In each of the highlighted schools, the principal has been deeply committed to inclusive education. A principal leads school staff in a series of meetings and actions that empower all parties tackling questions abut what the school and individual teachers can do to achieve successful student outcomes and inclusion efforts. Leaders involve parents in this dialogue, and in their classes, teachers help children ask the same questions as they seek to build a learning community. Inclusive education cannot successfully be mandated. It must come from the combined willingness of school administrators and staff to work toward another way of educating children.

Build a Support System Across Schools

A support system beyond individual schools is also needed to link teachers and parents in networks and provide support to principals. This support has occurred in several ways in Beard, MacArthur, and Hillside Elementary Schools. The following strategies are recommended for replicating such support.

Within-District Collaboration

For the three schools described in this chapter, district-level commitment was important. In each case, local school leaders were active in helping to foster district support. This occurred in different ways. In Detroit, the principal of Beard responded to central office requests for students with disabilities to return to the neighborhood school, further insisting that this be done inclusively. At MacArthur, the principal set a model of inclusive education for the district at a time when the school board passed a policy supporting the move toward inclusive education. Hillside's principal was instrumental in chairing a strategic plan for elementary schools, which crafted a commitment to inclusive education and established the districtwide inclusion forum. Thus, principals, involving their staff in multiple ways, took part in *creating* district-level support. School staff—teachers and principals—can help create the necessary leadership and support for inclusive education.

University–School Collaboration

The three schools demonstrated initiative. However, the role of university faculty and staff as critical friends was valued by the schools. This role also took various forms. Faculty spent time in schools—observing in classrooms, getting to know teachers—and sought to assist as needed. This assistance took the following forms: providing consultation and feedback regarding children with serious behavior challenges; helping to establish circles of support for students with behavior challenges; meeting with school staff to discuss issues of concern and interest (e.g., multilevel teaching, behavior challenges); and helping to organize the Michigan Network for Inclusive Schooling. One principal stated that critical friends helped bring new questions that would lead to new answers.

School-to-School, Teacher-to-Teacher Networks

Based on reports by teachers and other school staff, the most valuable strategy has been the connection with staff across schools and across districts. Sharing practice, developing relationships, and building a network of people in various roles committed to inclusive education has been powerful. Teachers in Beard and Hillside are developing strategies to engage their students in collaborative learning activities, thereby linking city and suburb. Another small group of teachers from all three schools meets once per month at a local restaurant to share challenges, successes, and practices and to provide support. Such networking has grown out of the development of the Michigan Network for Inclusive Schooling.

Action Research

Most inclusion efforts in the Detroit area have grown out of involvement in the Whole Schooling Research Project. Researchers saw themselves as participant observers, and in each case were invited to be part of school change. This has been a valued relationship on both sides, providing the opportunity for outsiders who see the school from a different perspective to ask new questions that lead to new answers.

Establish Inclusion as Being Beyond Special Education

For inclusive education to be successful, multiple resources must be used to establish a solid support team and create ways of teaching, thereby developing a caring community that responds to the needs of all children. Special education, Title I, bilingual, gifted, at-risk, and resources, among others, may be configured in a seamless manner to develop a support team for the entire school. In each school discussed in this chapter, the challenge of diversity extended far beyond disability and special education. Segregation and separation are deeply embedded in the Detroit metropolitan area. Yet, gifted students; children with different socioeconomic statuses; and children from different racial, ethnic, and cultural groups require responses directly related to inclusive education of students with academic, socioemotional, and sensory-physical differences.

Consider the Impact of Standardized Testing

In Beard, MacArthur, and Hillside Elementary Schools, the use of a standardized test (the MEAP) has created pressure to raise the scores and move away from practices that support inclusive education. A group of teachers from these schools joined concerned individuals from other schools and communities, sharing at conferences and organizing advocacy work to address this policy issue. Educators and advocates should examine the impact of the relationship between standardized tests and practices that support inclusive education and consider policy advocacy to address these problems.

Implement Inclusive Teaching

Inclusive education is centrally about teaching. On a very practical level, inclusive teaching is not about whether a student with a disability is present in a classroom. Inclusive teaching has to do with teaching style and strategies. It embodies a philosophy and practice of teaching that allows students to work and learn together at different levels of ability in heterogeneous instructional groups. It is reflected in the attitudes of teachers who intentionally seek to include different types of students. To strengthen inclusive education, then, educators and advocates must both seek to include students with disabilities in general education classes and to develop supportive inclusive teaching approaches.

Build Community and Support Children with Behavior Challenges

One of the most important issues in urban schools is dealing with children whose many life challenges may manifest in behaviors that are challenging or sometimes even dangerous. Schools vary dramatically in the degree to which they are willing to grapple in proactive ways with these challenges. For inclusive education to be effective, systematic and intentional effort is needed in this area. When schools seek to build community and a culture of care throughout the building and in classrooms, many socioemotional needs of children are met. In such an environment, teachers have a framework for understanding the needs of children and using positive behavioral support strategies. However, even in schools that support community building, staff must intentionally commit to supporting students with substantive behavior challenges and work together to use systematic procedures of support among children and with one another. Special education teachers can play a critical role in this process.

CONCLUSION

As shown by experience in Detroit at the elementary school level, building inclusive urban schools has many challenges. Yet, inclusion is not a fringe element to be set aside as schools deal with what some consider the larger, more important issues in urban schools. Rather, learning good teaching practices for classrooms of children with different ability levels is at the essence of what must be addressed if urban schools are to be effective for children.

Building inclusive schools is a lifelong journey for all involved. It involves the total culture of a school. Research in which teachers, parents, researchers, and administrators collaborate is critical before connections among practice, schoolwide culture, support systems, and local and state policy changes can enhance efforts to build inclusive schools. Successful inclusive urban schools ensure that all stakeholders are working together on these issues.

REFERENCES

Burnley, K. (2001, April 5). *Letter to staff members of the Detroit Public Schools.* Detroit, MI: Detroit Public Schools.

Chaffets, Z. (1990). *Devil's night: And other true tales of Detroit.* New York: Random House.

Detroit Public Schools. (1994). *Special education strategic plan.* Detroit, MI: Author.

Detroit Public Schools. (2000). *Annual report.* Detroit, MI: Author

Detroit Public Schools. (2001a). *Detroit Public Schools announces unprecedented plan to transform the District.* Detroit, MI: Author.

Detroit Public Schools. (2001b). *Efficiency and effectiveness report.* Detroit, MI: Author.

Farmington Public Schools. (1994). *Elementary study (1994–2004).* Farmington, MI: Author.

Gibson, R. (2000). The theory and practice of constructing hope: The Detroit teachers' strike of 1999. *Cultural Logic, 2*(2). Retrieved from http://eserver.org/clogic/2-2/gibson.html

Gibson, R., & Peterson, M. (2001). Whole schooling: Implementing progressive school reform. In W.E. Ross (Ed.), *The social studies curriculum: Purposes, problems, and possibilities.* Albany: State University of New York Press.

Glasser, W. (1992). *The quality school: Managing students without coercion.* New York: Harper Perennial.

Henrickson, W. (1991). *Detroit perspectives: Crossroads and turning points.* Detroit, MI: Wayne State University Press.

Kohn, A. (1999). *The schools our children deserve: Moving beyond traditional classrooms and "tougher standards."* Boston: Houghton Mifflin.

Kozol, J. (1991). *Savage inequalities.* New York: Harper Perennial.

Mast, R. (1994). (Ed.). *Detroit lives.* Philadelphia: Temple University Press.

Michigan Network for Inclusive Schooling. (2001). *Mission and organization.* Retrieved January 28, 2003 from http://www.coe.wayne.edu/CommunityBuilding/MI-NIS.html

Mirel, J. (1993). *The rise and fall of an urban school system: Detroit, 1907–81.* Ann Arbor: University of Michigan Press.

Nease, R. (1998, January 19). What we found [Electronic version]. *Detroit Free Press.* Retrieved February 12, 2003, from http://www.freep.com/news/meap/index_1.htm

Office of Early Childhood Education. (1999). *Head Start program data*. Detroit, MI: Detroit Public Schools.

Peterson, M. (1997). *Inclusive education in Michigan: A story of educational change*. Detroit, MI: Renaissance Community Press, Wayne State University.

Peterson, M. (2000). *Assessment of strengths and needs: Eastside Detroit Whole Schooling Cluster*. Detroit, MI: Whole Schooling Consortium, Wayne State University.

Peterson, M. (2001). *Key elements in building whole schools*. Detroit, MI: Renaissance Community Press, Wayne State University.

Peterson, M., Beloin, K., & Gibson, R. (1997). *Whole schooling: A framework for quality education for all students*. Stevens Point: Whole Schooling Consortium, University of Wisconsin–Stevens Point.

Peterson, M., Gibson, R., & Feen, H. (1999). *Whole Schooling research in Michigan: Initial analysis*. Unpublished manuscript, Wayne State University, Detroit, MI.

Peterson, M., Tamor, L., Feen, H., & Silagy, M. (2002). Learning well together: Lessons about the connection of inclusive education to whole school reform. In *Whole schooling research project final report*. Detroit, MI: Whole Schooling Consortium, Wayne State University.

U.S. Census Bureau. (2000). Census data retrieved January 2003 from http://www.census.gov

commentary **9**

THE SHAPING OF INCLUSION

Efforts in Detroit and Other Urban Settings

FREDDA BROWN AND CRAIG A. MICHAELS

Peterson's report of inclusive schooling efforts in Detroit metropolitan area schools raises critical issues related to inclusion in general and to urban inclusion more specifically. The purpose of this commentary is to discuss a sample of such issues that we consider important for all educators to reflect on as they move forward in promoting access to quality public education for all learners. These reflections may be particularly critical as we attempt to infuse the principles and practices of effective inclusive education within the urban context. This commentary focuses first on some learning points or patterns that we see evolving as the education field progresses across time. Second, the commentary provides a critical discussion of some elements of this progress. This discussion is not intended to diminish the great strides made in the field—or in Detroit and other urban areas—but, rather, to reflect on the pattern of this progress and discuss the shaping of inclusion.

LEARNING POINTS

The learning points that we address in this commentary are based directly on the inclusion experiences in the Detroit Public Schools and on the thoughts and reflections about urban inclusion that Chapter 9 generated for us. These learning points are broadly categorized into four, nonmutually exclusive areas:

1. Urban inclusion efforts must be embedded in school reform efforts.
2. Urban inclusion efforts must be embedded in diversity efforts in general.
3. Urban inclusion efforts must focus on changing school culture.
4. Urban inclusion efforts must be philosophically *and* pedagogically sound.

A fifth factor or learning point related to urban public education serves as an overriding principle that is alluded to throughout Peterson's chapter. This overriding principle (or fifth learning point) is addressed first in a direct and nonapologetic manner: Schools exist within communities. In general terms, public education—and, more specifically, urban inclusion initiatives—operate within the context of the urban environments in which they exist. As such, many of the societal issues, environmental concerns, economic realities, and racial/ethnic tensions found in urban communities are also found or reflected in the public schools within those communities. The next subsection further discusses this overriding principle and is followed by additional commentary on the four learning points derived from Chapter 9.

Schools Exist within Communities

Critical to urban inclusion efforts and school reform is the realization that inclusive education and school reform efforts are embedded within the broader social context. In other words, the opportunities and the challenges within local communities are reflected in the school. We believe that within the current societal contexts and urban landscape, how educators look at schools and education, and ultimately at inclusive education, changes as a function of a city's economic health and prosperity. Within American public education, a continual tension has always existed as to whether public education exists to reflect and maintain the status quos of the urban landscape or whether public education can serve as an agent for positive change—at both the individual learner and community levels (e.g., see Calderwood, 2000).

It would be nice to envision inclusive urban education as the catalyst for positive change within urban communities. In many urban public schools, however, there are top-down decisions to cut back or eliminate programs, teachers, and services; to privatize the management of at-risk schools; or to close school buildings entirely. These decisions only serve to "inflame conflicting goals and interests. It is much easier to be tolerant of differences when new functions are added than when they [existing or essential functions] are swept away.... [Scarcity and diminishing resources only provoke] competition, conflict, and teacher and administrator burnout" (Tyack & Hansot, 1982, pp. 250–251).

Although the answers or any proposed solutions to ease this ongoing tension may be at the heart of successful urban inclusion efforts, these answers also directly reflect on what purpose public education actually serves in American society. Bowles and Gintis suggested that schools and public education "are constrained to justify and reproduce inequality rather than correct it" (1985, p. 298). In fact, according to Bowles and Gintis, a major purpose of public urban education may be the "legitimation of preexisting economic disparities" (p. 299).

In writing this commentary, we attempt a more optimistic and proactive approach and perspective on public education. Yet, we also believe that addressing this tension may be at the heart of urban inclusion efforts. Beyer and Apple (1998), for instance, described eight levels of tension and complexity that all educators should struggle with in relation to the politics of curriculum and instruction and mobilizing public education to challenge the status quo. These include, for example, what should be learned, who has access to the curriculum, what knowledge is most valuable, and how the control of knowledge is linked to the distribution of power within society.

This tension and complexity is significantly intensified when educators embed the issues of inclusion and consider the individual needs of all learners within urban schools. Inclusion efforts cannot operate within a vacuum in the urban context any more than they can within the more affluent suburban environments in which many of the more publicized successful inclusion efforts are located. If educators believe that education does not have to reflect or perpetuate the status quo, then their decisions about curriculum and instruction must be grounded in teaching tolerance and social justice and in producing future citizens who value and honor diversity. As a result, educators should be willing to struggle with levels of tension related to curriculum and instruction on the epistemological, ideological, technical, aesthetic, economic, political, ethical, and historical levels (Beyer & Apple, 1998).

While taking on the status quo (or perhaps even prior to doing so) and addressing the politics of curriculum and instruction as they relate to the purpose of education, educators must reflect on the most basic levels of human survival and safety, going back to Maslow's (1962) Hierarchy of Needs. Revisiting Maslow's model reveals that urban inclusion may need to be viewed as a developmental process in which issues of belonging and self-esteem can only be addressed when basic existence and safety issues have first been met. Following this argument to its logical conclusion within many urban public education contexts (e.g., Detroit, New York, Los Angeles, Chicago), the basic human (or student) needs for food, shelter, and security must be in place within schools before educators begin to address issues of self-actualization for learners. In fact, if educators truly observe the life experiences of many urban youth, they will find that exclusion (rather than inclusion) is alive and flourishing in many U.S. cities. We all should feel outraged when students in urban communities go to school hungry and malnourished and do not receive even basic medical services or care. The lack of inclusive education within the school community may be only one small component of the education system's collective failure. Narrowly focusing this discussion about inclusion on access to standards or the general education curriculum seems quite decadent. The societal inclusion of urban youth who have been marginalized is one of the major and most basic challenges facing American society—and perhaps it is what makes urban education and urban inclusion efforts unique and most challenging.

Ultimately, many of the learning points that follow can be framed within a top-down perspective, starting with the societal contexts as the broadest context (focusing on things such as the economic health and prosperity of urban communities), then narrowing to urban school reform within general education, followed by special education reform efforts to promote inclusion. However, focusing solely on special education reform efforts might distort the reality of the urban landscape and result in an oversimplification of the work ahead.

Urban Inclusion Efforts Must Be Embedded in School Reform Efforts

Inclusion efforts in Detroit clearly demonstrate that inclusion must be embedded and grounded in the broader context of school reform. Educational reform championed in the 1980s and 1990s focused primarily on raising standards and increased accountability for both teachers and students. Within the context used here, school reform focuses on curricular and instructional reforms to promote collaboration, shared decision making, and meaningful/active learning opportunities for students. School reform efforts include changes in organizational structures to increase the following: school-based and classroom-based autonomy and management; cooperative learning and differentiated instruction; active involvement of stakeholders, including students and families; and participation by community members in the school.

In Chapter 9, Peterson highlights the relationship between inclusion and educational reform designed to make education more meaningful and instructionally sound for all students. For example, he describes how teachers participated in a variety of training opportunities in important areas (e.g., the theory of multiple intelligences, instructional differentiation, bilingual education, cooperative learning) and that they were supported to participate in a variety of best practice strategies (e.g., co-teaching, alternative assessment, cooperative learning, inquiry-based projects, activity-based learning, authentic reading and writing strategies).

Schools engaged in these types of broader-based educational reforms are more likely to provide exciting learning environments for a great diversity of students and their teachers. In fact, a hallmark of these types of educational reforms is a shift in focus away from the diversity of students' abilities within the classroom to a more proactive focus on the diversity of instructional approaches and supports for students. The latter ensures that high expectations are maintained and achieved by all learners. Frequently, although their efforts are not "packaged" as inclusion, these schools address issues related to adapting what is taught, how teachers teach, how students learn, and how students demonstrate or use what they learn. In the schools described by Peterson, educational staff already seem engaged in a process of learning about and seeking to address the particular learning needs of a heterogeneous group of students by 1) varying approaches to curriculum, instruction, and assessment; and 2) maximizing the sharing and coordination of resources to offer a broad range of support services to meet the individual needs of all students. Inclusion is a natural extension of these school reform efforts. Within the context of school reform efforts, educators must ensure that the needs and interests of students of all ability levels are constantly included rather than tacked on as afterthoughts.

Urban Inclusion Efforts
Must Be Embedded in Diversity Efforts in General

Chapter 9 also highlights the notion that within educational inclusion efforts in urban contexts, race and ethnicity may often be hidden exclusion factors that are difficult for public educators to acknowledge and discuss. Similarly, we believe that within urban public education, race and ethnic diversity, when combined with disability, may have multiple (or perhaps exponential) exclusionary effects. In fact, some literature suggests that educators frequently overlook these diversity issues in special education. In turn, Pugach stated that educators

> Lose a significant opportunity for taking full account of how special education research and practice is positioned with respect to issues of race, class, culture, and language. As a result, [educators] delimit the stories of diversity that are told by special education scholars, opting instead for stories of disability alone. (2001, p. 448)

Future research within the urban context should address the relationships among race, ethnicity, poverty, and disability in urban inclusive reform efforts. As educators move forward in urban inclusion efforts, it seems prudent to ensure that these efforts are grounded within school reform efforts and within the broader diversity context as related to public education.

From the diversity perspective, educators must also begin to acknowledge that their ideologies about disabilities may limit the potential futures that they envision for students. These ideologies are also directly communicated to students through educators' thoughts, deeds, and attitudes—if not through their words. Educators must consciously begin by shifting their belief systems about the value of including students with disabilities within the general education classroom. In relation to ethnic and cultural diversity, the education field has at least begun to make this shift. Most school professionals now do believe that ethnic and cultural diversity can make classrooms and schools richer learning communities. However, what is the education field's position on issues of diversity in learning and behavior? This shift also is necessary if educators are going to truly embrace, rather than just merely accept, students with disabilities as full and contributing members of school communities.

Urban Inclusion Efforts Must Focus on Changing School Culture

As Peterson states, "[I]n the Detroit area, segregation persists. For inclusive education to be effective, it must become a part of the total school culture" (p. 225). Although laudable progress has been made within some very challenging urban education environments, we keep asking, "Are our inclusion efforts really becoming part of the culture of schools, or are these efforts instead championed by one or two individuals in positions of power (or through university-school initiatives)?" In other words, are any substantial shifts, or systemic changes, taking place in school culture as a result of the inclusion efforts? If not, then the efforts are likely to be unsustainable once those individuals or special initiatives championing the cause are no longer in place. What must occur to ensure that inclusive education becomes part of the fabric or the culture of urban public schools? Assuming that educators are successful in changing school culture and embedding inclusive educational practices within urban school environments, some additional questions suggested by the Peterson chapter can be asked. For example, will successful inclusion efforts ultimately change the nature and frequency of referrals to special education, especially for students with learning and emotional disabilities? Will changes in referral practices, or inclusion in general, affect the special education resources and staffing available to support inclusion efforts?

Urban Inclusion Efforts
Must Be Philosophically *and* Pedagogically Sound

The Detroit efforts described in Chapter 9 were grounded in the Five Principles of Whole Schooling—empowering citizens in a democracy; including all; using authentic, multilevel teaching for learners of diverse abilities; building community and supporting learning; and partnering with families and communities (see Table 9.1). Peterson acknowledges the challenge of interfacing urban inclusion and school reform efforts within the context of standards-based instruction initiatives. He seems to suggest that to some degree, these may be perceived to be mutually exclusive. Can inclusive education initiatives and standards-based instruction and school accountability coexist? Such questions emerging from the efforts in Detroit have significance for all educators involved in urban inclusion as they move toward standards-based education and greater accountability. Additional questions include the following: What does poor performance of a school on standardized testing really mean? How should educators use this information in terms of school reform, inclusion, and school renewal efforts? What relation should this information have to the allocation of additional resources and staff for school reform and inclusive education initiatives?

We believe there is a danger when so much inclusion rhetoric is focused on philosophy and so little is focused on pedagogy. Peterson warns that as schools face increased pressure to raise the scores on standardized tests, there may be a backlash against values-based reform efforts and the inclusion of students with disabilities. Peterson cautions that initial strides at personalizing instruction and differentiating curriculum may be thrown out the window because "there is a growing emphasis on keeping children at grade level, resulting in pressures to teach at one level" (p. 222).

As resources become further stretched and *accountability standards* and *outcomes* become the watchwords of politicians, educational administrators, business leaders, and parents, educators must continue to demonstrate that inclusion makes good sense both philosophically and instructionally. They must openly acknowledge and collaborate with the standards-based instruction movement rather than run from it. Key to the success of the standards-based instruction movement are many of the pedagogical principles that are the instructional foundations of inclusion. This is especially true within the urban context, in which standards-based instruction must address the diversity of learners within the classroom. These overlapping pedagogical principles include

- Modes of instruction that actively involve students
- Instructional strategies that match the end use of content and students' needs
- Continual gauging of what works and which students may need to work at a more advanced or basic level
- Active attempts to nurture student interests
- Teachers who collaborate with other professionals to make individual and small group contact with each student and thereby ensure high levels of quality (i.e., standards achievement) and mastery

Clearly, special educators must begin to ally with general educators who are truly interested in reforms that focus on differentiating instruction to personalize standards-based instruction for all students. In an article focused on general education administrators, Kluth and Straut (2001) clearly articulated the potential for strong special education and general education collaboration and coordination based on shared goals. For promoting standards-based instruction with diverse learners, Kluth and Straut argued that 1) standards must be both developmental and flexible, 2) standards require a wide range of assessment tools, 3) standards-based instruction must allow for equitable access to meaningful content for all students, 4) it takes a community to implement standards, and 5) standards are often the catalyst for other school reforms (2001).

ANALYSIS OF CURRENT PROGRESS

The previously discussed learning points from Chapter 9 remind us of the great progress made since 1975, when the Education for All Handicapped Children Act was enacted (PL 94-142; now known as the Individuals with Disabilities Act [IDEA] of 1990 [PL 101-476] and its 1997 amendments [PL 105-17]). Reflecting on the state of the special education field at that time, great strides have been made. Consider an early article, co-authored by the first author of this chapter, entitled "Educability: Both Sides of the Issue" (Noonan, Brown, Mulligan, & Rettig, 1982). This article took the brave (for that time) position that those with even the most profound disabilities have a right to and could benefit from an education. This article was motivated in part by Baer's (1981) seminal article "A Hung Jury and a Scottish Verdict," in which he argued that it would be impossible to prove that an individual *could not* benefit from an education. Baer stated that

> [A] child cannot be declared unteachable in fact until teaching has been tried and has failed; teaching is too large a set of procedures (even in its known world) to have been tried and to have failed in its entirety[; and the] cost of truthfully affirming a child to be unteachable is no less than the cost of continuing to attempt teaching the child. (pp. 96–97)

Thus, it must be assumed that *all* people can benefit from education.

Now the arguments have changed. Professionals no longer discuss the educability of people with disabilities, and they no longer have to come up with clever arguments about educating even those with the most significant disabilities. Instead, they discuss the best way that individuals can learn; where they can best learn; what they should learn that will most affect their quality of life; and how they can participate, in self-determined ways, in this process.

With this praise for progress acknowledged, educators must take the step of critically considering the momentum of inclusion and the path of that momentum—especially if educators are not vigilant and valiant in their efforts. Going under the assumption that Detroit is a fair representative of other urban centers, what its inclusion efforts have to teach other educators and what can be predicted about the future of this momentum must now be considered. Two constructs are used to frame this discussion: form versus function and the behavioral concept of shaping.

Form versus Function

Form versus function refers to the inappropriate focus on how something looks (i.e., its topography) versus the value or impact that the thing or act truly has. For example, if a school district has exemplary individualized education program (IEP) documents but little connection actually exists between the goals and objectives identified in those IEPs and the educational programs of students, then one would conclude that the educational team focused on form (the physical display of the IEP documents) instead of function (IEPs that result in meaningful and effective educational programs). The true measures of an excellent IEP are the impact on the educational program for the individual for whom it was specifically designed and the effect of the educational program on the student's quality of life. Whether IEPs written in exemplary form are sufficient to have an impact on a student's life is an empirical question—that is, one can objectively determine if this is the case. In other words, the measurement of socially valid and revealing outcomes is critical to the determination of success. Similarly, when evaluating the impact of inclusion efforts, educators must define what should be measured as a reflection of success. Are measures related to form (or process inputs), or are they related to function (actual educational outcomes)? Unfortunately, it appears that successes are most often measured by engagement in form, not function.

In Peterson's chapter, which may be a microcosm for the larger picture of urban schools, there are many instances of this focus on form rather than function. This statement is not made to deny the excellent and hard work that the Detroit schools, and many other urban schools, are doing. Indeed, the activities described in Chapter 9 are hailed by most as hallmarks of successful inclusion. However, we believe that caution should be taken to be aware of the limitations of such hallmark measures. For example, at one of the schools described, school leadership was "providing forums for staff discussion; inviting outside perspectives; asking questions; and promoting dialogue, site visits to other schools, investigations, and the collection of information" (p. 224). It is also reported that staff members have "received training in the multiple intelligences theory, instructional differentiation, bilingual education, cooperative learning, [and] co-teaching" (p. 223). These "formal" activities should be followed by an important question reflecting "function": What impact do these activities actually have on the inclusion and education of the students in the schools—both students with disabilities and their peers?

Engagement in such "form" however, may be developmentally appropriate from the historical perspective. That is, perhaps such focus is a natural part of the evolution of services—perhaps it is necessary to first "talk the talk." Yet, it also follows that the evolution of the field may be progressing at rates that are terribly frustrating for proponents of inclusion, especially for those families of children who are excluded from whatever momentum exists (e.g., families of children with severe or profound disabilities). The gradual nature of progress is one of the characteristics of the strategy of shaping.

Shaping

Maag defined the behavioral strategy of shaping as the "development of a new behavior by the successive reinforcement of closer approximations and the extinguishing of preceding approximations of the behavior" (1999, p. 553). Shaping is a gradual process, with the initial behaviors that are reinforced sometimes only slightly resembling the terminal behavior. Early in the shaping process, the most primitive or imperfect approximation is prompted and reinforced and then increasingly more sophisticated responses are reinforced (Schloss & Smith, 1998). The key to effectively shaping behavior is the selection of subgoals that are small enough to be easily achieved and, thus, allow access to reinforcement. Gradually, the goals are increased to more closely resemble the desired outcome. The challenge in this strategy is choosing the optimal distance between steps. Schloss and Smith (1998) pointed out that steps that are too small waste valuable time, whereas steps that are too large will frustrate the participants (i.e., result in lack of access to reinforcement).

Applying this concept to the shaping of inclusive education for all children with disabilities, educators must determine the correct size of steps that should be expected in their current progress, (i.e., what should be reinforced and what should no longer be reinforced). How long should educators accept that in many locations across the country the more "primitive" steps toward inclusion continue to be accepted and reinforced? Can they afford to wait another decade for closer approximations of the terminal goal—that is, inclusion of *all* children in their neighborhood schools? In the meantime, what happens to the children, especially those with the most severe disabilities, who typically are not yet part of the identified "approximations" and may not be for many years to come? Is it acceptable for the education field to praise its progress when generations of these students are excluded?

Peterson's description of three Detroit schools reveals such an approximation of which students are to be included in inclusion efforts. As the focus on standards intensifies, Peterson warns that tolerance of the diversity of students to be included will shrink (i.e., increasing numbers of students with disabilities may be excluded from participation in general education). It appears that when schools reflect on the meaning of inclusion and identify their own guiding principles, they invariably acknowledge that "all should mean all" (e.g., the second principle of Whole Schooling model, as described by Peterson in Table 9.1). Yet, in most cases, inclusion is for some, not all. Although progress is clearly being made, students still need to earn the right to be included based on behavioral, social, and/or academic performance approximating that of typical students.

Many inclusion efforts seem to reflect that the education field really means eventually, one day down the road, all will mean all, that it is hoped someday, when society changes and general education is more accepting (and so on), even students with the most severe disabilities will be included. Yet, at what point is the system going to be ready for them? At what point will the dust of the initial inclusion and school reform efforts settle and allow a closer approximation to the ultimate goal of inclusion for all, not some, students? Even for supporters of inclusion who are willing to wait it out, Peterson points out the potential for backlash against inclusion efforts, especially within urban settings, as resources get scarce and standards are increased. Educators must work to ensure that waiting for "one day" is not another example of the "never" that has so often been applied to people with more severe or profound disabilities through other readiness models (e.g., prevocational training used in the context of building readiness for community-based completive employment).

In Detroit, as elsewhere across the United States, such shaping also is applied to preparation and expectations of staff. At what point do administrators and inclusion specialists begin to reinforce teachers for progressing to the next step of quality inclusive teaching and no longer reinforce earlier efforts? Similarly, just as administrators and inclusion specialists within schools may attempt to "shape" teachers, the university community attempts to contribute to shaping schools. We fully support and value the collaboration between higher education and schools, but this effort too often is also based more on form than function and may suffer from the early stages of shaping as well. Certainly, we in the New York City area cannot claim any more successes in this realm than the collaborations seen in Detroit. We, too, have given many in-service trainings to "heighten conversation and thinking" (p. 220). Yet, what are the outcomes? Do these collaborations actually result in more students being effectively included in their neighborhood schools? Is this being measured?

As Peterson points out, Chapter 9 explores "efforts in process." How long is long enough to be "in process?" Peterson suggests that Detroit is a bellwether city in the country. This appears to be true: Most U.S. schools , regardless of the numbers of books, chapters, and articles describing the progress in inclusion, are more accurately "in process" regarding inclusion. Thus, most (certainly not all) urban communities are still in the early steps of shaping, with a goal of only closer approximations to the distant goal of quality inclusive schooling for all children.

CONCLUSION

Inclusive educational reform must be grounded in sound educational practices; personalizing education or differentiating instruction to promote high levels of achievement for all students appears to be one of these practices. Now perhaps more than ever, there is a critical need for less rhetoric and more data-driven decision making if inclusive education is to be a reality within the urban context. Inclusion must be tied to sound pedagogical practice. All members of the field need to talk about implementing and monitoring standards responsibly and taking responsibility for outcomes. Peterson implies that standards may be the enemy of inclusive education. However, we believe that if educators cannot determine how to align a focus on high educational accountability for all with inclusion efforts, then they and (more important) the students they are dedicated to including in local schools, their communities, and society overall, may be left behind—especially within urban areas.

What measures must be taken now to ensure that the field goes from research to practice, from university to school, from form to function? Educators must become more aware of the danger of the "successive approximations" approach to evaluating their progress. Consider how many students will continue to be excluded as inclusion is shaped. Perhaps it is fitting to remember Brown's "Criterion of Ultimate Functioning" (see Brown et al., 1979) and his warnings about the "bottom-up approach"—that is, taking too many years to develop a functional skill. Brown and his colleagues taught the necessity of going directly to the desired outcome. Within the context of this commentary, then, the desired outcome (or challenge) to take on directly is making urban inclusion available to *all* students and for all of us to commit to supporting *all* students in achieving high standards within age-appropriate classrooms and with age-appropriate curricula.

REFERENCES

Baer, D.M. (1981). A hung jury and a Scottish verdict: "Not proven." *Analysis and Intervention in Developmental Disabilities, 1,* 91–98.

Beyer, L.E., & Apple, M.W. (1998). Values and politics in the curriculum. In L.E. Beyer & M.W. Apple (Eds.), *The curriculum: Problems, politics, and possibilities* (2nd ed., pp. 3–21). Albany: State University of New York Press.

Bowles, S., & Gintis, H. (1985). Education, inequality, and the meritocracy. In J.H. Ballantine (Ed.), *Schools and society: A reader in education and sociology* (pp. 298–321). Mountain View, CA: Mayfield Publishing Company.

Brown, L., Branston, M.B., Hamre-Nietupski, A., Pumpian, I., Certo, N., & Gruenwald, L. (1979). A strategy for developing chronological age-appropriate and functional curricular content for severely handicapped adolescents and young adults. *Journal of Special Education, 13,* 81–90.

Calderwood, P. (2000). *Learning community: Finding common ground in difference*. New York: Teachers College Press.

Education for All Handicapped Children Act of 1975, PL 94-142, 20 U.S.C. §§ 1400 *et seq.*

Individuals with Disabilities Education Act (IDEA) Amendments of 1997, PL 105-17, 20 U.S.C. §§ 1400 *et seq.*

Individuals with Disabilities Education Act (IDEA) of 1990, PL 101-476, 20 U.S.C. §§ 1400 *et seq.*

Kluth, P., & Straut, D. (2001). Standards for diverse learners. *Educational Leadership, 59*(1), 43–49.

Maag, J.W. (1999). *Behavior management: From theoretical implications to practical applications*. San Diego: Singular Publishing Group.

Maslow, A. (1962). *Toward a psychology of being*. Princeton, NJ: Van Nostrand.

Noonan, J., Brown, F., Mulligan, M., & Rettig, M. (1982). Educability of severely handicapped persons: Both sides of the issue. *Journal of The Association for the Severely Handicapped, 7*(1), 3–14.

Pugach, M.C. (2001). The stories we choose to tell: Fulfilling the promise of qualitative research for special education. *Exceptional Children, 67*(4), 439–453.

Schloss, P.J., & Smith, M.A. (1998). *Applied behavior analysis in the classroom*. Boston: Allyn & Bacon.

Tyack, D., & Hansot, E. (1982). *Managers of virtue: Public school leadership in America 1820–1980*. New York: Basic Books.

chapter **10**

Systems Change in Los Angeles, the City of Angels

RICHARD A. VILLA, MARY FALVEY, AND JUDY A. SCHRAG

AN IMPORTANT TREND in U.S. school systems since the mid-1980s has been toward providing more inclusive educational opportunities for students eligible for special education. Educators, parents, policy makers, students, advocates, and consumers who have persevered, articulated, and built consensus for their inclusive vision have led the inclusive education movement. The result has been schools and school districts across the country implementing complex systems change initiatives to restructure in ways that welcome, value, empower, and support the diverse academic and social learning of students with disabilities in shared environments and experiences with typically developing peers. These systems change efforts are helping students with disabilities obtain access to the general education curriculum and demonstrate increased knowledge and skills based on state standards for all students through participation in district and state assessment programs (i.e., with or without accommodations or through alternate assessment).

An increasing number of schools have begun the journey toward crafting inclusive schools, albeit amidst tremendous challenges and sometimes as a result of legal action. The challenges to urban school reform include complex governance structures, high turnover rates for administrators, the absence of teaching personnel who "mirror" the students whom they teach, and the recruitment and maintenance of qualified personnel.

Given the challenges of urban school reform; the culture of segregation that has evolved in many urban school districts, including the Los

Angeles Unified School District (LAUSD); and the need to link inclusive education with general education school reform, there is no single identifiable cause for the intractability in urban school restructuring. Frequently cited causes for intractability are 1) inadequate teacher preparation; 2) inappropriate organizational structures, policies, practices, and procedures; 3) lack of attention to the cultural aspects of schooling; and 4) poor leadership (Thousand & Villa, 1995).

Change takes time as well. According to Fullan and Steigelbauer (1991), 2–5 years are needed for systemic change to occur. As Schrag (1994) noted, such time allows people to identify new practices, digest new ideas, talk, and create together. In addition, change must be planned by those who will implement the new actions as well as those who will be affected by the changes, including school staff and parents (Schrag, 1994). Without broad involvement in site-based planning, the vision, directions, and changes to be made will not be owned by the school staff and parents and may not be sustainable once implemented.

There is no simple method to forward change. This chapter describes the *Chanda Smith Full Continuum of Services in the Least Restrictive Environment Implementation Plan* (2001), which was developed by three least restrictive environment (LRE) consultants, the Chanda Smith Consent Decree Administrators, and the LRE subcommittee within the LAUSD.

HISTORY AND PROGRESS TOWARD THE LEAST RESTRICTIVE ENVIRONMENT IN THE LOS ANGELES UNIFIED SCHOOL DISTRICT

The LAUSD is the nation's second-largest school district, serving more than 1% of the nation's school children (i.e., 740,000 students) in more than 900 school buildings. Approximately 80,000 (11%) of the LAUSD students have been identified as eligible for special education. The LAUSD employs approximately 36,000 teachers—4,600 special education teachers and 1,300 administrators, 60 of whom are special education administrators. The LAUSD is organized into 11 sub- or mini-local districts.

History of Noncompliance

For years, the U.S. Department of Education, the U.S. Office for Civil Rights, the California State Department of Education, and the California

Office for Civil Rights have found the LAUSD out of compliance with both federal and state laws. In addition, parents of students with disabilities have often become exasperated and discouraged in their efforts to secure appropriate supports and services for their sons and daughters with disabilities.

Class Action Lawsuit and Consent Decree

In 1995, a class action lawsuit, *Chanda Smith v. Los Angeles Unified School District*, on behalf of all students with disabilities challenged the entire special education system of the school district. As a result of the lawsuit's negotiated settlement, Judge Laughlin Waters ordered the Chanda Smith Consent Decree on April 15, 1996. The Consent Decree was based on *Chanda Smith v. Los Angeles Unified School District Consultant's Report* (1995), a 199-page report prepared by Dr. Louis Barber and Dr. Mary Margaret Kerr. The Consultant's Report found that the LAUSD was out of compliance in 23 areas of the Individuals with Disabilities Education Act (IDEA) of 1990 (PL 101-476). The report concluded, "The District suffers from a pervasive, substantial, and systemic inability to deliver special education services in compliance with special education law" (1995, p. 3). Thirteen committees were formed to develop 31 implementation plans to address the areas of noncompliance. The implementation plans were to be in effect by April 2001.

As of 2002, the majority of implementation plans have been developed and agreed to by the LAUSD school board, the Consent Decree Administrators, and the plaintiffs' attorneys. In addition, the federal court has ordered the implementation of five plans, including the *Chanda Smith Full Continuum of Services in the Least Restrictive Environment Implementation Plan* (2001; hereafter called "the LRE Implementation Plan"). The original Consent Decree called for three consultants in the area of LRE to assist the Consent Decree Administrators in the development of an implementation plan to bring the district into compliance with the LRE requirements of federal and California law. The authors of this chapter are the three LRE Consultants required by the Chanda Smith Consent Decree. The LRE Consultants developed the plan through extensive collaboration with the Consent Decree Administrators and an LRE subcommittee consisting of parents, teachers, administrators, and community members, LAUSD personnel, and legal counsel representing the LAUSD and the plaintiffs. In addition, the three LRE consultants conducted site visitations and record reviews. The LRE consultants held 30 focus-group interviews with more

than 140 participants (i.e., special education, bilingual, and general education teachers; inclusion specialists; related service personnel; paraeducators;
and students with and without disabilities). Numerous sources of data—
including placement patterns by age, disability, and ethnicity—also were
reviewed.

The LAUSD's disproportional placement of students with disabilities
into more restrictive, segregated settings is in violation of federal and state
law. Table 10.1 presents the discrepancy between the proportion of students with disabilities placed in general education classes, resource specialist programs, separate classes, and separate and nonpublic schools within
the LAUSD as compared with the State of California and national placement patterns.

Students with disabilities placed in segregated special classes often
must change schools and clusters to receive supports and services. In addition, the percentage of students in LAUSD with physical/orthopedic disabilities in self-contained classes is excessive and significantly higher than
the national percentages (i.e., 63% of students with physical/orthopedic
disabilities are in self-contained settings in the LAUSD, whereas only
18.5% nationally are in such restrictive settings).

Another important LRE consideration within the LAUSD is the over-
representation of African Americans among students with disabilities
receiving special education services. The percentages of students across
disability categories and ethnic groups are the same in special and general
education within the LAUSD, except for students who are African American. Table 10.2 shows that during the 1998–1999 school year, nearly twice
as many African American students were enrolled in special education than

Table 10.1. Comparison by percentage of federal, state (California), and
Los Angeles Unified School District (LAUSD) placements of students with
disabilities

	Federal 1997–1998	State 1997–1998	LAUSD 2000
General education	46.4	52.4	18.7
Resource	29	21	36.1
Separate class	20	23	35.5
Public separate (special schools)	2	1	5.1
Private separate	1	2	4

Table 10.2. Comparison of African Americans among different educational categories in the Los Angeles Unified School District (LAUSD)

Educational category	Percentage of African American students (1998–1999)
General education population	13.8
Overall special education population	22
Overall special education population classified "severely emotionally disturbed"	40
Overall special education population classified "mentally retarded"	20

in general education (i.e., 22% compared with 13.8%). In addition, 40% of the students labeled as having a severe emotional disturbance and being eligible for special education are African American. Finally, 20% of the special education students labeled as having mental retardation are African American. Students identified with mental retardation or emotional disturbance tend to be placed by the LAUSD in the most restrictive settings (i.e., special day classes, special centers, and nonpublic schools).

These findings raise serious questions about misidentification, misclassification, or inappropriate placement in special education programs and classes. Both stigma and penalty may be attached to this labeling and categorization—all the greater for those categories in which African American students are overrepresented. In addition, the numbers raise issues of racial segregation, as most special education classes are separate from regular classes, particularly for those categories in which African Americans are overrepresented. Substantial research (Gartner & Lipsky, 1998) indicates that these classrooms are characterized by lower expectations and less-demanding curricula and result in negative student outcomes (e.g., on student learning, dropout rates, graduation rates, postsecondary education and employment, and living in the community).

Conceptual Underpinnings of the LRE Plan

Beliefs, knowledge, and values directly affect how federal, state, and local policies are implemented. For example, in a study of implementation of the LRE policies in six states, Hasazi, Johnston, Ligget, and Schattman found that "how leadership at each school site chose to look at LRE was critical to how, or even whether, much would be accomplished beyond the status quo" (1994, p. 506). In addition, teacher commitment was found to be critical to implementation of innovations. However, teacher commitment often emerged at the end of the implementation cycle, after the teachers had gained mastery of professional expertise needed to implement the new innovation (McLaughlin, 1991). In other words, negative or neutral attitudes of teachers at the beginning of an innovation, such as inclusive education, may change over time as a function of experience and the expertise that develops through the process of implementation.

A complex change process is needed for the LAUSD to fully implement federal and state legal requirements.

Contents of the LRE Implementation Plan

The LRE Implementation Plan developed for the LAUSD contains the following five interrelated goals:

1. Policy development

2. Management and resources

3. Accessibility

4. Instructional support

5. Evaluation, accountability, and monitoring

Tables 10.3 through 10.7 briefly describe 15 of the 31 detailed activities from each of the five interrelated goal areas of the LRE Implementation Plan[1]. Table 10.8 clarifies responsibilities across job categories for meeting the needs of students with disabilities in the LRE.

Implementation and Outcomes of the Change Process

A great deal of activity at the federal court level, the district level, and at the school site level has occurred as a result of the LRE Implementation Plan.

---

[1]A complete copy of the *Chanda Smith Full Continuum of Services in the Least Restrictive Environment Implementation Plan* may be obtained by contacting the Chanda Smith Consent Decree Office, Los Angeles Unified School District, 450 North Grand Street, Los Angeles, CA 90012-2100.

Table 10.3. Least Restrictive Environment Implementation Plan policy development activities

Articulate LRE policy	The superintendent will articulate and distribute in the Los Angeles Unified School District the *Special Education Compliance Guide*, a written least restrictive environment (LRE) policy.
Disseminate LRE policy	The LRE policy will be described within the local plan required of all special education local planning areas by the California Department of Education.

Source: Chanda Smith Full Continuum of Services in the Least Restrictive Environment Implementation Plan (2001).

In 2001, the LAUSD requested that the federal court suspend the Chanda Smith Consent Decree, thereby relieving LAUSD of the obligations of the Consent Decree. The court not only dismissed the district's request, but also demanded that the LAUSD implement the five Chanda Smith Consent Decree Implementation Plans that the LAUSD school board had denied. The LRE Implementation Plan was one of the plans that the LAUSD school board had rejected. All activities in the LRE Implementation Plan are scheduled to be implemented by December 31, 2006.

Subsequent to the court-ordered implementation of the LRE Implementation Plan, a new associate superintendent was recruited and hired to provide leadership and vision to the Division of Special Education. The immediate corrective action LRE awareness level training required by the plan has been occurring throughout the LAUSD for teachers, administrators, paraeducators, and related service personnel. New special and general education teachers receive LRE awareness level training as part of their orientation to becoming LAUSD teacher. School teams of special and general educators have been attending training that focuses on the strategies for implementing collaborative models for teaching students with and without disabilities. Other teams of general and special educators, along with parents, have received substantial training on facilitated individualized education program (IEP) meetings, during which all members of the team use respectful communication skills (e.g., active listening, turn taking, encouraging others to participate) to develop IEPs that meet students' needs. Special education schools are making concrete plans and establishing time lines for inclusion so that students without disabilities will be able to attend and receive a high quality education. In addition, many of the elementary, middle, and high schools are beginning to build their capacity by providing

Table 10.4.   Least Restrictive Environment Implementation Plan management and resource activities

1. Use the *Special Education Compliance Guide*	The Los Angeles Unified School District (LAUSD) will incorporate into the *Special Education Compliance Guide* procedures to support the placement of students in the LRE, including but not limited to the following: • Guidelines for determining whether the general education classroom is the least restrictive environment (LRE) • Guidelines for individualized education program (IEP) teams considering other options along the continuum • Procedures for the identification of supplementary aids and services • Guidelines for facilitating student success in the LRE
2. Establish LRE support teams	The LAUSD will establish LRE support teams consisting of four people, with at least one special education teacher and at least one general education teacher. The remaining two positions must be staffed by people knowledgeable about instructional interventions and implementing LRE legal requirements. The LRE support teams will be designed to provide training to local schools sites in their implementation of LRE.
3. Reduce nonpublic school placements	The LAUSD will reduce the reliance upon nonpublic school placements and increase reliance on the LRE in the LAUSD by building its capacity to effectively educate students who attend those schools.
4. Create LRE Site-Level Plan and Budget	Building principals will annually submit to their supervisors a Site-Level LRE Plan and Budget for approval. This plan will be developed collaboratively at the site by the administration, general and special education staff, parents, paraeducators, related service personnel, and students with disabilities, if appropriate. The Site-Level LRE Plan and Budget will address the following: • A description of school procedures to include students with disabilities in the development of high expectations and standards identified for all students • A description of school procedures to ensure student access to extracurricular activities • Assessment and standardized testing procedures, including guidelines for modifications and adaptations • Established procedures for collaborative teams to create less restrictive environment opportunities for students with disabilities

- Planned staff development activities to support access by students with disabilities to the general education classroom and the general education curriculum, as well as the integration of instructional strategies and curriculum adaptations to address diverse learners and to increase interaction with peers without disabilities
- Procedures for involving parents of students with disabilities in educational decision making for their child
- Procedures for reviewing and monitoring IEP progress to support movement of students with disabilities into less restrictive environments and increase their interaction with peers without disabilities
- An inventory to determine the availability of supplemental supports, aids, and services needed within the school
- A description of intervention services utilized to support students who have not yet been identified as having disabilities
- The budget required to implement the Site-Level LRE Plan and Budget
- A review and documentation of the site's success in implementing the prior year's Site-Level LRE Plan and Budget

Source: Chanda Smith Full Continuum of Services in the Least Restrictive Environment Implementation Plan (2001).

training that enables staff to educate students with disabilities on their campuses, including students who have previously attended segregated special education centers.

CONCLUSION

The activities described in the previous section represent a sampling of the kinds of activities, mandated by the Chanda Smith Consent Decree, in which the LAUSD is engaged and will continue to be engaged in through 2006. This chapter emphasizes that moving toward more inclusive educational opportunities for students with disabilities involves complex change, particularly in urban school districts such as the LAUSD. Clearly, a tremendous amount of work remains to be done to bring the LAUSD into compliance with federal and state LRE mandates. The Chanda Smith Implementation Plan provides a path for change in the LAUSD and other

Table 10.5.   Least Restrictive Environment Implementation Plan accessibility activities

1. Establish collaborative consultation models	The Los Angeles Unified School District (LAUSD) will establish collaborative/consultative services (e.g., co-teaching, consultation, methods and materials teachers) for both resource specialists and the special education class service delivery system at every school site.
2. Develop services for students with physical/orthopedic disabilities	The LAUSD will develop and implement a plan to provide programs and services in both special and general education that will adequately support and address the needs of students with physical/orthopedic disabilities. The LAUSD will make available equipment, technology, and other materials needed by students with disabilities across local school districts rather than cluster these items at regional locations.
3. Distribute special education programs and services throughout the LAUSD	By July 2005, 90% of all schools, including the 18 special centers in the LAUSD, will have a natural proportion of their students identified as eligible for special education services (i.e., falling within a range from 4% above to 4% below the mean percentage of LAUSD students identified as eligible for special education).[a]

[a]It should be noted that the implementation benchmarks are intended to assist in the monitoring of least restrictive environment (LRE) implementation within LAUSD schools required by the Chanda Smith Consent Decree and are not intended to supersede the IEP decision-making process. This activity, as well as several others in the LRE Implementation Plan, requires the attainment of certain placement percentages. It should be noted that the Individuals with Disabilities Education Act (IDEA) neither requires nor prohibits certain placement percentages. These placement percentages are required to dramatically shift the LAUSD into compliance with the law.

Source: Chanda Smith Full Continuum of Services in the Least Restrictive Environment Implementation Plan (2001).

Table 10.6.   Least Restrictive Environment Implementation Plan instructional support activities

1. Distribute parent information	The Los Angeles Unified School District (LAUSD) will utilize a variety of formats to inform parents about least restrictive environment (LRE) mandates. The following content must be included in information provided to parents: • LRE legal requirements and definition • Roles and responsibilities in implementing LRE mandates • Supports and services that can be successfully used to facilitate the education of students in the LRE • Case studies and examples of successfully educating students in the LRE • Strategies for addressing and determining LRE in the individualized education program process • Characteristics of school cultures that welcome, value, empower, and support the learning of students with various abilities
2. Institute immediate corrective action awareness level training	The LAUSD will prepare a staff development training plan designed to increase the LRE awareness of LAUSD administrators, teachers, related service personnel, counselors, and paraeducators. In addition to the content provided to parents, the following content will be included in the awareness level training: • History and evolution of special education service delivery models • Rationale for LRE (Villa & Thousand, 2000) • Models for adult collaboration in planning and teaching • Relationship of special education compliance activities to general education school reform initiatives • Strategies for developing a community of learners and providing peer supports (Thousand, Villa, & Nevin, 2002)
3. Develop competency level training for LAUSD staff[a]	The LAUSD will develop competency level training for all LAUSD employees responsible for instruction, program specialists, inclusion teachers, and other school district personnel to implement LRE mandates. *Competency level training* refers to a process in which 1) staff participate in the previously described awareness level training; 2) staff conduct a self-assessment related to the implementation of LRE mandates; 3) each staff person's immediate supervisor assesses the

(continued)

Table 10.6.   *(continued)*

	employee's mastery related to LRE competencies; and 4) if both parties agree that the employee possesses the necessary competencies, additional training will not be required. Otherwise, the employee will participate in activities mutually agreed on by the employee and the supervisor (e.g., workshops, in-service training, visitations, videotape and/or journal article review, course work, Internet/distance learning, mentoring).

[a]The LRE Implementation Plan identifies 30 competencies needed by employee groups to provide students with disabilities access to the general education curriculum in the LRE. In addition, it distinguishes the level of competence (i.e., awareness, knowledge, implementation) needed by various employee groups (e.g., administrators, psychologists, general education teachers, special education teachers).

Source: Chanda Smith Full Continuum of Services in the Least Restrictive Environment Implementation Plan (2001).

Table 10.7.   Least Restrictive Environment Implementation evaluation, accountability, and monitoring activities

1. Data collection and monitoring of data	The Los Angeles Unified School District (LAUSD) will revise its data collection system to obtain information about the percentage of time students with disabilities are enrolled in the general education environments (i.e., 0%–21%, 21%–60%, 60%–80%, or more than 80% of the time). These data will be compared with racial, ethnic, gender, language, cultural, and other demographic factors to ensure the identification of potential over- or underrepresentation as well as the placement in more restrictive environments of students with varying characteristics who are labeled as "disabled" (e.g., African American boys, English language learners).
2. District validation review	The LAUSD's validation review process will determine school compliance with least restrictive environment (LRE) procedures by reviewing each school's LRE Site-Level Plan and Budget to ensure that policies and practices identified in the plan are being implemented at the site. Data will be compiled by disability, and compliance will be considered to be the following in comparison with the national averages of the 2003–2004 school year: • Within 5% of the national average for students served outside the general education classroom for 0%–21% of the day • Within 5% of the national average for students served outside the general education classroom for 21%–60% of the day • Within 5% of the national average for students served outside the general education classroom for 60%–80% of the day

	• Within 5% of the national average for students served outside the general education classroom for more than 80% of the day
	• Within 2% of the national average for students served in a public separate school facility
	• Within 2% of the national average for students served in a private separate school facility
3. Job evaluation procedures	The LAUSD will provide notice to school staff and principals of the evaluation requirements for implementing LRE mandates. Principals will inform their staff that the LRE activities must be taken seriously and that future performance evaluations will assess staff implementation of LRE mandates. The evaluations will include the following components:
	• Evidence of collaboration between general and special education personnel
	• Evidence of the use of adaptation and accommodations specified in individualized education programs
	• Evidence of the use of differentiated instructional strategies and materials matched to students' individual strengths and learning styles
	• Evidence that staff have provided opportunities for students with disabilities to gain access to extracurricular activities
	• Use of a variety of assessment strategies to authentically measure student progress
	• Provision of appropriate assessment accommodations for students with disabilities, if needed

Source: Chanda Smith Full Continuum of Services in the Least Restrictive Environment Implementation Plan (2001).

Table 10.8. Roles and responsibilities of various Los Angeles Unified School District employee groups related to implementation of the least restrictive environment (LRE)

Principals	• Make provisions for teachers to work collaboratively in planning, instructing, and evaluating the performance of students with disabilities.
	• Inform parents of students with disabilities about the LRE mandates and their child's rights.
	• Help school personnel to redefine their roles, if necessary, to implement LRE.
	• Ensure the provision of needed in-service and technical assistance related to LRE for school personnel, parents, and students.
	• Ensure that the school climate is welcoming to students with disabilities and their parents.
	• Observe, supervise, and support special education and related service personnel on campus.

(continued)

Table 10.8. *(continued)*

	• Ensure that all educational reform efforts at the school address the needs of students with disabilities.
	• Ensure the development of transition plans to facilitate students' movement from grade to grade and to a new school.
General education teachers	• Participate in collaborative planning for, the instruction of, and the evaluation of students with disabilities.
	• Help plan for transitions to facilitate students' movement from grade to grade and to a new school.
	• Utilize effective instructional practices—such as cooperative group learning, peer tutoring, and active learning—to support effective LRE implementation.
	• Supervise and facilitate paraprofessionals to provide students with disabilities needed supports.
	• Establish shared expectations for student learning and classroom management with special education teachers, paraeducators, related services personnel, parents, and students.
	• Teach students without disabilities to respect their classmates and school mates with disabilities and to facilitate positive relationships between them.
	• Assume primary responsibility for including students with disabilities assigned to their classes in meaningful ways within instructional activities.
	• Implement specific curricular adaptations and instructional strategies identified as needed by each student with a disability.
	• Participate in the individualized education program (IEP) meetings for students with disabilities who are included in their classes.
	• Assume primary responsibility for assigning grades and other assessment/evaluation for students with disabilities.
	• Communicate with parents on an ongoing basis related to the needs of their child with disabilities.
Special education teachers	• Participate in collaborative planning for, the instruction of, and the evaluation of students with disabilities.
	• Help plan for transitions to facilitate students' movement from grade to grade and to a new school.
	• Utilize effective instructional practices—such as cooperative group learning, peer tutoring, and active learning—to support effective LRE implementation.
	• Supervise and facilitate paraprofessionals to provide needed supports for students with disabilities.
	• Establish shared expectations for student learning and classroom management with general education classroom teachers, paraeducators, related services personnel, parents, and students.
	• Facilitate positive relationships between students with and without disabilities.
	• Facilitate including students with disabilities in the LRE in meaningful ways.

	• Implement specific curricular adaptations and instructional strategies identified as needed for each student with a disability.
	• Participate in the IEP meetings for students with disabilities.
	• Work collaboratively with general education teachers when assigning grades and other assessment/evaluation for students with disabilities.
	• Ensure that students' IEP objectives are addressed in their daily schedules.
	• Communicate with parents on an ongoing basis related to the needs of their children with disabilities.
Paraeducators	• Under the direction and supervision of the classroom teacher, implement specific curricular adaptations and instructional strategies identified as needed for each student with a disability.
	• Facilitate opportunities for natural interactions and friendships between students with and without disabilities.
	• Model respectful interactions with all students.
	• Keep data and anecdotal information on students' progress under the direction of classroom teachers, special education teachers, or related services personnel.
	• Monitor and assist students during directed and independent learning activities.
	• Assist students with personal care/hygiene needs as appropriate.
	• Accept and solicit direction from the classroom teachers and special educators.
	• Establish shared expectations for student learning and classroom management with general education classroom teachers, special education teachers, related services personnel, parents, and students.
Related services personnel	• Participate in collaborative planning for, the instruction of, and the evaluation of students with disabilities.
	• Help plan for transitions to facilitate students' movement from grade to grade and to a new school.
	• Utilize effective instructional practices within the LRE.
	• Establish shared expectations for student learning and classroom management with general education classroom teachers, special education teachers, paraeducators, parents, and students.
	• Facilitate positive relationships between students with and without disabilities.
	• Facilitate the inclusion of students with disabilities in the LRE in meaningful ways.
	• Participate in the IEP meetings for students with disabilities.
	• Work collaboratively with general education teachers when assessing and evaluating students with disabilities.
	• Ensure that students' related services IEP objectives are addressed in their daily schedules.
	• Communicate with parents on an ongoing basis related to the needs of their children with disabilities.

urban school districts. This path for change—combined with new leadership, skill acquisition, resource allocation, accountability, and site-based planning—leave the authors hopeful that this will result in improved programs, services, and outcomes for students and their families. This is, of course, the desired goal within the LAUSD—an urban school district in a city that has been termed "the City of Angels."

REFERENCES

Chanda Smith full continuum of services in the least restrictive environment implementation plan. (2001). Los Angeles: Chanda Smith Consent Decree Office.

Chanda Smith v. Los Angeles Unified School District consultant's report. (1995). Los Angeles: Chanda Smith Consent Decree Office.

Chanda Smith v. Los Angeles Unified School District, No.93-7044-LEW (GHKX) (C.D. Cal. 1996).

Falvey, M.A. (Ed.). (1995). *Inclusive and heterogeneous schooling: Assessment, curriculum, and instruction.* Baltimore: Paul H. Brookes Publishing Co.

Fullan, M., & Steigelbauer, S. (1991). *The new meaning of educational change.* New York: Teachers College Press.

Gartner, A., & Lipsky, D. (1998, September/October). Over-representation of black students in special education: Problem or symptom? *Poverty and Race Research Action Council Newsletter, 7*(5), 3, 4, 8.

Hasazi, S., Johnston, P., Ligget, A., & Schattman, R. (1994). A qualitative policy study of the least restrictive environment provision of the Individuals with Disabilities Education Act. *Exceptional Children, 60*, 491–507.

Individuals with Disabilities Education Act (IDEA) of 1990, PL 101-476, 20 U.S.C. §§ 1400 *et seq.*

Knoster, T.P., Villa, R.A., & Thousand, J.S. (2000). A framework for thinking about systems change. In R.A. Villa & J.S. Thousand (Eds.), *Restructuring for caring and effective education: Piecing the puzzle together* (2nd ed., pp. 93–128). Baltimore: Paul H. Brookes Publishing Co.

McLaughlin, M. (1991). Learning from experience: Lessons from policy implementation. In A. Odden (Ed.), *Education policy implementation* (pp. 185–195). Albany: State University of New York Press.

Schrag, J. (1994). *Organizational, instructional, and curricular strategies to facilitate the implementation of inclusive school practices.* Arlington, VA: Council for Exceptional Children.

Thousand, J.S., & Villa, R.A. (1995). Managing complex change toward inclusive schooling. In R.A. Villa & J.S. Thousand (Eds.), *Creating an inclusive school* (pp. 51–97). Alexandria, VA: Association for Supervision and Curriculum Development.

Thousand, J.S., Villa, R.A., & Nevin, A.I. (Eds.). (2002). *Creativity and collaborative learning: A practical guide to empowering students, teachers, and families* (2nd ed.). Baltimore: Paul H. Brookes Publishing Co.

Villa, R.A., & Thousand, J.S. (Eds.). (2000). *Restructuring for caring and effective education: Piecing the puzzle together* (2nd ed.). Baltimore: Paul H. Brookes Publishing Co.

Villa, R.A., Thousand, J.S., Meyers, H., & Nevin, A. (1996). Teacher and administrator perceptions of heterogeneous education. *Exceptional Children, 63*(1), 29–45.

commentary **10**

Facilitating Sustainable Systemic Change in School Systems

Lessons Learned from Los Angeles

Diane Lea Ryndak

Sustainable systemic change takes massive, long-term effort that incorporates active involvement and earnest attempts to change on the part of every individual involved in a system. Frequently, such efforts fail because individuals in a system do not understand or accept the proposed change, are fearful of the effect of the proposed change either on themselves or on others, lack the skills or resources required to implement the proposed change, or are not committed to sustaining the effort required to complete the activities that lead to the implementation of the proposed change over time (Hall & Hord, 2001; Hord, Rutherford, Huling-Austin, & Hall, 1987; Wiles, 1993). This book describes several urban school district efforts to effect sustainable systemic change. Just initiating systemic change efforts in a large urban district is no small feat, as evidenced in Chapter 10.

In Chapter 10, Villa, Falvey, and Schrag present data that clearly demonstrate the extent to which the Los Angeles Unified School District (LAUSD) had been out of compliance with both state and federal averages related to several issues. For instance, there was disproportionate placement of students with disabilities in nongeneral education settings, disproportionate placement of students with disabilities in nonneighborhood schools or schools of choice, disproportionate placement of students with physical/orthopedic disabilities in self-contained classes, and overrepresentation of African American students with disabilities in special education services. These data raise questions about misidentification, misclassification, and inappropriate placement of students with disabilities. Singularly, each issue could entail an extensive effort to facilitate change; together, they require an effort that is even more extensive, across every aspect of the school system. To make matters even more complex, these issues must be addressed in the second-largest school district in the country, thus multiplying the number of individuals involved both in administrative and instructional services.

Villa and colleagues discuss the lengthy legal proceedings and the Chanda Smith Consent Decree of April 15, 1996, which led to the formation of 13 committees responsible for the development of 31 implementation plans. They describe in depth one of these plans, the Least Restrictive Environment (LRE) Implementation Plan, and how it incorporates interrelated goals that cover 1) policy development; 2) management and resources; 3) accessibility; 4) instructional support; and 5) evaluation, accountability, and monitoring. The implied intent of the LRE Implementation Plan is that after its completion, all students will have access to the general education curriculum and will demonstrate their increased knowledge and skills based on state standards through participation in district and state assessment programs with the use of accommodations and alternate assessment strategies as appropriate. In 2001, the LAUSD was ordered by the court to implement all 31 of the implementation plans, including the plan related to LRE, by 2006.

It is evident that the road to this point in systemic change efforts for the LAUSD and the students and families that it serves has been long, arduous, and fraught with conflict. This situation cannot be avoided when the need for change is identified by individuals or forces that are not perceived as part of the system (Hord et al., 1987). In this case, the need for change in the services provided by the LAUSD was identified by parents, consultants, and the court (see Chapter 10). The degree to which this impetus for change can be shifted to the individuals in the school district is one variable that will determine the extent to which the LAUSD change efforts actually result in sustainable systemic change (Hall & Hord, 2001; Hord et al., 1987).

VARIABLES THAT EVIDENCE SUCCESSFUL SYSTEMIC CHANGE

Wheatley stated,

> I no longer believe that organizations can be changed by imposing a model developed elsewhere. So little transfers to, or even inspires, those trying to work at change in their own organizations. Second . . . there is no objective reality out there waiting to reveal its secrets.

There are no recipes or formulae, no checklists or advice that describe "reality." There is only what we create through our engagement with others and with events. Nothing really transfers; everything is always new and different and unique to each of us. (1994, p. 7)

When considering change in schools, McLeskey and Waldron (2000) concurred. They indicated that there is no blueprint for achieving sustainable systemic change, that there is no one plan that can be implemented across schools or school districts. In fact, every school and every school district has unique characteristics, including—but not limited to—the individuals, leadership style, strengths and weaknesses of instructional practices and organization, and belief system. Because of this uniqueness, each school and school district must determine its own approach to facilitating sustainable systemic change (Halvorsen & Neary, 2001; McLeskey & Waldron, 2000; Ryndak, Stuart, & Pullen, 2001; Villa & Thousand, 1995).

An analysis of the research on sustainable systemic change does, however, offer some suggestions about how to proceed. For instance, it indicates that when efforts at systemic change have been successful, several variables are evident (Clark, 2001). When speaking of schools and school districts, these variables can be described as follows: 1) an internal impetus for the change in educational services; 2) a common vision of what educational services should be; 3) a common understanding of the change process and a willingness to put forth the effort to produce sustainable change; 4) facilitative leadership that can lead the school and/or district to this common vision and common understanding, as well as through the change efforts; and 5) external critical friends, or experts in specific areas who have an ongoing relationship with a school or district that allows the experts to bring a more objective eye to a situation and to offer suggestions for improving services.

To accomplish this, leaders must help build consensus among members of each constituency involved in the change (e.g., parents, general educators, special educators, school and district administrators, related services personnel, paraeducators). Two logistical methods are helpful in building consensus (Clark, 2001). First, facilitative leaders use a forum that allows members of each constituency to discuss key issues related to the proposed change (Reardon, Ryndak, & Benner, 2002). Through this forum, individuals can discuss concerns, issues, and fears, along with approaches and plans to address each of those in a proactive manner. Although such a forum can be open to all individuals, either jointly or in segments, many organizations use this forum to bring together representatives of each constituency. The second method involves the role played by the representatives who participate in the forum (Reardon et al., 2002). Each representative must be willing to become the main communication system between the forum and their constituency members. This role must include 1) voicing the thoughts of their constituency members within the forum as well as the thoughts of the forum to their constituency; and 2) communicating decisions and plans for implementation between their constituency members and the forum. In this way, members of each constituency have a representative who shares their concerns and suggestions with the forum, communicates to them about the decisions that were made during the forum, takes their constituents' reactions back to the forum, and so forth. The use of these two logistical methods in tandem allows an organization to build consensus among members who participate in discussing the issues inherent within a proposed change and in developing plans to address those issues so that efforts to achieve the proposed change will be effective.

Along with an understanding of the use of these two logistical methods that support ongoing open communication across constituencies, it is important to discern how their use can affect the variables that the literature indicates have been evident when school change efforts have been successful. The following subsections discuss each of these variables.

Internal Impetus for the Change

All change is stressful. Because of this, individuals only change when they

- Perceive a problem (e.g., most students with disabilities do not have access to the general education curriculum and contexts)
- Identify what needs to change to solve that problem (e.g., students with disabilities must receive special education services within general education contexts)
- Identify what needs to occur for those changes to happen (e.g., placement procedures must start with presumption of placement in general education contexts; general and special educators must have expertise to collaborate and provide accommodations)
- Identify what needs to happen for those changes to occur (e.g., change placement procedures; provide training for individuals who make placement decisions; provide training for general and special educators)
- Commit themselves to the effort required to implement those changes (Hall & Hord, 2001; Hord et al., 1987)

When considering a school or school district, leaders and change initiators must

- Determine what must occur across all constituencies (e.g., general educators, special educators, parents, administrators, support personnel) to make that change happen both short and long term
- Implement in a systematic way the activities needed for each set of constituents to achieve the change

- Understand the complexity of the change process and how sustainable change occurs
- Verify that a commitment to the efforts exists across constituencies (Halvorsen & Neary, 2001; Ryndak et al., 2001)

Individual schools and school districts begin change efforts because of different catalysts, so they frequently achieve sustainable change with differing levels of success. Through the use of the discussion forum and a representative-based communication system, schools and school districts can build consensus about the need for a proposed change, thus spreading the impetus for change across individuals within the system.

Villa and colleagues describe the impetus for change in the LAUSD as external to the system. To ensure sustainable systemic change in the educational services provided for students with disabilities, the constituencies will need to shift this impetus for change by building consensus about the existence of a problem, the practices and procedures that are causing the problem, the changes needed to fix the problem, and the way to proceed.

Common Vision of Educational Services

If inclusive schools are desired, as implied by Villa and colleagues, then there must be a clear definition of inclusion that is espoused by all constituents in the LAUSD. Although there is much debate in the broader field of special education about what constitutes school inclusion, there is consensus within the area of significant disabilities. When experts in the field of school inclusion for students with significant disabilities were asked to define school inclusion, Ryndak, Jackson, and Billingsley (2000) found that several components were consistently evident in the definitions. Furthermore, they concluded that the combination of these components is essential for a school to provide inclusive services for students with significant disabilities. That is, schools or school districts cannot implement services that reflect some of these components but not others and consider themselves providers of inclusive educational services. These components include the following:

1. Students with disabilities are placed in natural environments (i.e., chronological age-appropriate general education classes in the school that students would attend if they did not have disabilities).

2. The placement of students with disabilities in general education classes occurs for all or most of the school day and occurs on a daily and ongoing basis for both instructional and noninstructional activities.

3. *All* students receive instruction and learn *together* during the same academic and nonacademic general education activities throughout the school community.

4. Individualized education program (IEP) teams consider meaningful outcomes related to the general education curriculum (i.e., content, activities, environments) and to a student's independent functioning and participation in real-life activities, both in and out of school.

5. Supports, services, accommodations, and modifications related to curriculum and instruction occur within general education classes and the school community.

6. Education teams collaboratively plan, implement, and evaluate instruction for *all* students throughout general education activities.

7. A shared sense of ownership exists among team members, and students recognize that *all* of them are equal members of the class and that they belong, are accepted, and are valued.

These components can be represented visually as a puzzle: With any one piece missing, the puzzle is incomplete. The same is true with inclusion: If any component is missing in a school or school district's implementation of services, then inclusive services are not being provided. Figure 10C.1 illustrates inclusion as a complete puzzle when each of the seven components is present.

Whether the LAUSD accepts this definition of school inclusion or another definition, it is essential that it develops a common vision of what educational services should look like for all students to have access to the general education curriculum and to demonstrate increased knowledge and skills based on state standards through participation in district and state assessment programs. The common vision must be developed over time through consensus-building activities and must be espoused by all constituents involved in providing educational services. Without this common vision, the schools in the LAUSD will reflect the findings of Hazasi, Johnston, Ligget, and Schattman that Villa and colleagues discussed in Chapter 10: "How leadership at each school site chose to look at LRE was critical to how, or even whether, much would be accomplished beyond the status quo" (1994, p. 506). Sustainable systemic change demands that those in leadership positions, as well as members of each constituency involved in providing services, share a common vision of effective educational services. Only then can the system as a whole progress toward that vision. As with spreading the impetus for change across individuals in the system, the discussion forum and representative-based communication system can assist schools and school districts in building consensus toward a common vision.

Common Understanding of and
Willingness to Participate in the Change Process

Although having a common vision of effective educational services is essential, it is insufficient for achieving sustainable systemic change (Hord et al., 1987).

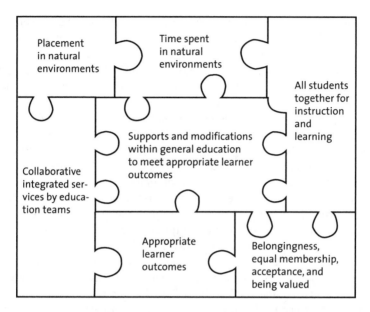

Figure 10C.1. Components of inclusion as a complete puzzle. (*Source:* Ryndak, Stuart, & Pullen, 2001).

Members of each constituency must understand how change occurs and the amount of effort that will be required over an extended period of time to achieve the changes that will lead to the desired educational services. In addition, members of each constituency must be committed to contributing the time and effort required to participate in the full change process. Because of the lack of this understanding and commitment to efforts over time, many innovative educational practices have come and gone, with implementation only in one class or one school. Frequently, the implementation of an innovation is person specific; that is, it is dependent on a person continuing in his or her position. Once that person leaves his or her position, use of the innovative practice often stops. Such implementation of an innovation is not systemic and is not sustainable over time because of the lack of understanding of the change process. Instead, these innovations eventually are seen as "fads," "passing trends," or "another swing of the pendulum."

Although many schools and districts have espoused a common vision, they frequently do not understand how change occurs, especially at a systemic level. Many schools and districts believe that stating the mission behind school services and providing in-service training are sufficient for teachers to use their new knowledge from the in-service training within their classrooms and schools (Reardon et al., 2002). Little or no consideration has been given to the infrastructures that support the *current* educational services, rather than the *desired* educational services (e.g., class or personnel scheduling, placement of students, school or district policies, beliefs and expertise of other personnel). Comprehending the interrelatedness of each component of educational services—as well as the interrelatedness of the beliefs, roles, and expectations of each constituency—leads to a fuller understanding of the complexity of systemic change and the degree of effort over time that is required to achieve it (Reardon et al., 2002). Once this complexity is understood and a commitment is made to change efforts that demonstrate this understanding, a system truly can claim to be engaged in systemic change efforts. This understanding and commitment can be developed across a school or school district through the use of the discussion forum and representative-based communication system.

By supporting the 31 implementation plans submitted by the 13 committees charged with implementing the court mandated changes through the Chandra Smith Consent Decree, the court has begun to acknowledge the level of complexity of the change process required to achieve the desired changes. It is unclear, however, whether LAUSD personnel have a common understanding of the change process and whether they are willing to participate in the level of effort required over time to effect the desired changes. As efforts continue to build consensus about a common vision across constituencies, efforts also must focus on building a common understanding of and commitment to the change process.

Facilitative Leadership

When schools and districts have been successful in facilitating sustainable systemic change, they demonstrate the presence of facilitative leadership that has led the school and/or school district to a common vision and an understanding of the change process, as well as through change efforts over time (Clark, 2001). Facilitative leadership is a style of leading a group of individuals that values each individual and allows his or her active and meaningful participation in the decision-making process. When leaders demonstrate a facilitative leadership style, members of each constituency feel neither caught in a top-down system nor as if the system is rudderless. Rather, constituencies know they are valued contributing members of the system and, as such, partially own the decisions that are made, the policies that are developed, and the services that are provided. The use of a facilitative leadership style encourages consensus building, ownership of the proposed change, and commitment to the change process over time. The discussion forum and representative-based communication system are logistical methods frequently used by facilitative leaders.

If the LAUSD is to be successful in building a common vision of educational services, building a common understanding of the change process, and developing a common commitment to that change process, its leaders should carefully consider 1) what the literature says about the importance of facilitative leadership and 2) the degree to which such leadership is demonstrated in its schools and at the district level. Where leaders already demonstrate a facilitative leadership style, the schools that they serve may become model sites for systems change efforts and the leaders themselves may become model leaders for district activities (e.g., discussion forum participation). Where leaders do not demonstrate a facilitative leadership style, training and technical assistance activities may assist the development of appropriate expertise and interaction styles. Where these efforts fail, however, district leaders may consider personnel moves or replacements—or relinquish hope of facilitating sustainable systemic change.

External Critical Friends

It is interesting to note that when schools or districts have successfully facilitated sustainable systemic change, there is evidence of meaningful and consistent connection to individuals with whom they have developed a long-term relationship and who are 1) external to their system, 2) experts in a pertinent area, and 3) trusted within the system (Clark, 2001; Fisher, Sax, & Jorgensen, 1998). Such external "critical friends" are able to bring a more objective eye to situations, evaluate the services and interactions they observe, and suggest alternate paths that are based on research and their professional experience. Although many school personnel initially are unsure of the role that an external critical friend can play, as a relationship is developed, the input from this critical friend becomes more valued and his or her role becomes more clear. Because of this, potential external critical friends should be selected carefully, and numerous opportunities should be planned so that a meaningful relationship that is built on mutual respect and trust can develop. In addition to many other activities, effective external critical friends participate in the system's discussion forum and assist representatives in their role in the communication system (Reardon et al., 2002). Through this involvement, external critical friends can discern more fully the reality of various constituents, offer objective feedback, and suggest alternate paths to achieve the proposed change.

Although many individuals have been involved in the LAUSD's systemic reform efforts to date, it is unclear whether the LAUSD has identified experts in school inclusion (both for students with mild disabilities and for students with significant disabilities) with whom it has developed long-term, trusted relationships. Because of the size of the district and the multiple levels at which systems change efforts are required, multiple critical friends—each having a clearly defined area of expertise—may be essential.

CONCLUSION

Villa and colleagues state that Chapter 10 provides a path for change in urban school districts. They further state that together with new leadership, skill acquisition, resource allocation, accountability, and site-based planning, this path leaves them hopeful that the LAUSD systems change efforts will result in improved programs, services, and outcomes for students and their families. To support this, Villa and colleagues provide examples of activities that already have been completed, including 1) awareness level training about the concept of LRE for current and newly hired general and special educators; 2) training sessions on strategies for implementing collaborative models for teaching students with and without disabilities in the same environments and during the same activities; 3) training sessions on respectful communication skills and their use when facilitating IEP meetings with parents, general and special educators, and other personnel; 4) development of inclusion plans for segregated special education schools; and 5) the building of capacity for schools that serve students without disabilities to also serve students with disabilities.

Along with the courts, consultants, and numerous committees, the LAUSD should be applauded for its efforts to facilitate systemic change so that students with disabilities can have access to general education in the LRE. Their task is enormous and will take consistent coordinated effort from numerous individuals for many years; however, the task is tenable. Attending to the variables that the literature suggests are evidence of successful systemic change will maximize the extent to which the LAUSD's systemic change is sustainable over time. After all, only when change is sustainable over time and across people—including district administrators, school administrators, and direct services personnel—can the effort taken to create the change truly be worthwhile and appreciated. Only then will *all* of the students and families served by the LAUSD be assured effective educational services in the LRE, including access to general education in the school that students would attend if they did not have disabilities and access to state and district accountability measures with appropriate accommodations and modifications.

REFERENCES

Clark, D. (2001). *Influence of a school task force on school reform efforts to education students with severe disabilities in general education settings.* Gainesville: University Press of Florida.

Fisher, D., Sax, C., & Jorgensen, C.M. (1998). Philosophical foundations of inclusive, restructuring schools. In C.M. Jorgensen, *Restructuring high schools for all students: Taking inclusion to the next level* (pp. 29–47). Baltimore: Paul H. Brookes Publishing Co.

Hall, G.E., & Hord, S.M. (2001). *Implementing change: Patterns, principles, and potholes.* Boston: Allyn & Bacon.

Halvorsen, A.T., & Neary, T. (2001). *Building inclusive schools: Tools and strategies for success.* Boston: Allyn & Bacon.

Hazasi, S., Johnston, P., Ligget, A., & Schattman, R. (1994). A qualitative policy study of the least restrictive environment provision of the Individuals with Disabilities Education Act. *Exceptional Children, 60,* 491–507.

Hord, S.M., Rutherford, W.L., Huling-Austin, L., & Hall, G.E. (1987). *Taking charge of change.* Alexandria, VA: Association for Supervision and Curriculum Development.

McLeskey, J., & Waldron, N.L. (2000). *Inclusive schools in action: Making differences ordinary.* Alexandria, VA: Association for Supervision and Curriculum Development.

Reardon, R., Ryndak, D.L., & Benner, S. (2002, July). *Facilitating systemic change that supports inclusive practices: The Indian River County Schools story.* Paper presented at the Florida Inclusion Conference, Fort Lauderdale.

Ryndak, D.L., Jackson, L., & Billingsley, F. (2000). Defining school inclusion for students with moderate to severe disabilities: What do experts say? *Exceptionality, 8*(2), 101–116.

Ryndak, D.L., Stuart, C., & Pullen, P. (2001). *Developing inclusive schools for all students: Facilitating systemic change.* Unpublished manuscript.

Villa, R., & Thousand, J.S. (Eds.). (1995). *Creating an inclusive school.* Alexandria, VA: Association for Supervision and Curriculum Development.

Wheatley, M. (1994). *Leadership and the new science: Learning about organization from an orderly universe.* San Francisco: Berrett-Koehler Publishers.

Wiles, J.W. (1993). *Promoting change in schools: Ground level practices that work.* New York: Scholastic.

chapter 11

INCLUSIVE URBAN SCHOOLS

A Glass Half Full or Half Empty?

DOROTHY KERZNER LIPSKY AND ALAN GARTNER

THE PREVIOUS CHAPTERS describe important efforts to develop inclusive programs in urban schools. We admire the work of many and share their agony over the length of time it is taking to develop quality inclusive schools, no less districts. Although we are disappointed at the limited gains nationally, we remain encouraged as to the possibilities. Our experience and research in school restructuring general education for students with special education needs support positive outcomes for students with and without disabilities (Lipsky & Gartner, 1997). As Gilhool (1989) said, if a child with a particular set of circumstances (i.e., support needs) can be included in one school (or school system), then there is no reason why her or his "twin" with the same set of circumstances can not be included in another environment. In addition, as Edmonds wrote concerning the gaps in the education of poor and minority students, "[W]e already know how to educate these students, it depends how much we care about the fact that to date we have not done so" (1982, p. 11).

The evidence that "we have not done so" is abundant. The following conclusion, summarizing the findings of a conference of disability leaders convened by the National Council on Disability in 1996, remains all too accurate:

> Despite progress in the last decade in educating students with
> disabilities, current federal and state laws have failed to ensure
> the delivery of a free appropriate public education for too many
> students with disabilities. . . . Lack of accountability, poor en-
> forcement, and systemic barriers have robbed too many stu-

dents of their educational rights and opportunities and have
produced a separate system of education for students with disabilities rather than one unified system that ensures full and
equal physical, programmatic, and communication access for
all students. (p. 53)

The Council's statement moves from the failure to provide individual
students with a free appropriate public education (FAPE) to the broader
issue of establishing a separate system. In effect, the two central features of
the Individuals with Disabilities Education Act (IDEA) Amendments of
1997 (PL 105-17) are combined: FAPE and the least restrictive environment (LRE). The absence of inclusive service delivery systems leaves a serious gap in providing the "appropriate" education required by the law.
Achieving appropriate education and successful outcomes for all students
requires one unified system, not "islands in the mainstream." Serious
improvement of the general education system is the critical first step toward achieving inclusive schooling. The successes and continuing challenges described in *Inclusive Urban Schools* highlight the crucial need to use
the lens of general education as a means for improving the quality of special education.

Unfortunately, inclusion in urban environments is not widespread. Yes,
there are success stories, but too few classrooms, schools, and districts provide quality inclusive education for all students. This lack of progress is not
limited to urban schools. Federal data report that nationally, nearly half of
the students with disabilities spend less than 80% of their school day in
general education classrooms (American Youth Policy Forum, 2002). Even
more troubling, according to the National Longitudinal Transition Study,
students with disabilities in urban schools are twice as likely as those in suburban schools to be in segregated settings (Wagner, Blackorby, Cameo, &
Newman, 1993, cited in Hehir, 2002). Thankfully, this book's contributors
provide readers with information on successful inclusive educational efforts.

COMMON FEATURES OF
SUCCESSFUL INCLUSIVE EDUCATIONAL EFFORTS

Many of the experiences described in this book illustrate key principles in
creating and sustaining successful inclusive education efforts. These experiences suggest a set of common features that can serve as a road map for
other communities as they redefine special education. Each of these is
explored further in the following subsections.

Commitment Is Sustained Over Time

Successful initiators have a powerful ideological commitment and a high degree of perseverance (Fisher, Grove, & Sax, 2000). Data are collected and changes are made to achieve higher levels of success over time. As noted in Chapters 2 and 6 (Boston and San Diego), the initiators can be a school or system administration, a group of teachers or parents, or an outside group—be it advocacy or university.

Partial Approaches or Small Pilots Do Not Grow and Flourish

Although initial efforts may not have building or systemwide support, leadership can make a difference (Villa & Thousand, 2000). Building or systemwide efforts must be large enough to require attention and change by the whole school and, over time, the entire district. For example, in Miami (Chapter 3), whole school change was initiated and supported by a state-level technical assistance provider. The Florida Inclusion Network did not focus on small pilot programs but, rather, on building, district, and statewide change.

A Whole School Approach Is Required

School restructuring must focus on teaching and learning activities and not become mired in organizational, management, and staffing issues (Jorgensen, 1998). Efforts based in Detroit (Chapter 9), such as Whole Schooling, demonstrate that collaboration between and among schools results in creative solutions to the real issues of implementing change and inclusion in urban environments.

Inclusive Education Requires Approaches that Benefit All

Except in very few cases, developing elaborate and separate instructional arrangements for students with disabilities is not required. Inclusive education approaches incorporate concepts of differentiation (Cole et al., 2000; Tomlinson 1999, 2000) and universal design (Center for Applied Special Technology, 2001; Center for Universal Design, 1997; Hitchcock, Meyer, Rose, & Jackson, 2002), both of which benefit all members of the school community. Students with disabilities require the supplemental aids and services noted in their individualized education programs (IEPs). For the most part, however, these should be addressed with natural and common responses—the same ones that teachers use to meet the particular needs of other students in the class. As noted in Chapter 4, Dallas and Houston district administrators recognized that many students in their school system required specialized reading support and designed interventions to include both students with and without disabilities. As the Chapter 4 authors note, the administrators did not create a parallel reading intervention system solely for students with disabilities. Teachers who effectively implement inclusive education programs have said that it is not "rocket science"—in effect, that "good teaching is good teaching."

New Types of Relationships and Forms of Collaboration Are Needed

DeBoer and Fister (1995), Friend (2001), and Snell and Janney (2000) noted that new types of relationships and forms of collaboration are necessary among the adults in the school. Changes in school structure and organization are important but come after the changes in relationships. As demonstrated in Milwaukee (Chapter 5), collaboration and agreement on a mission or vision is essential for inclusion to be successful. The work of inclusion requires many participants: leaders and followers, parents and professionals, advocates and bureaucrats. This is a reflection of the broad political alliances necessary to initiate, sustain, and achieve educational reform. Similarly, for the adults with disabilities who participated in Pathfinders in New York City (Chapter 8), the involvement and subsequent collaboration of many different agencies resulted in community inclusion.

Although collaborative practices facilitate inclusion, it seems that litigation does not. Not meeting legal requirements concerning LRE continues to top the list of compliance failures among the states and school districts. Court cases in the nation's largest cities (e.g., *Chanda Smith v. Los Angeles Unified School District; Corey H. v. Board of Education of the City of Chicago, et al.; Jose P. v. Ambach* in New York) have consumed enormous energy and have diverted hundreds of thousands (if not millions) of dollars from educational activities to litigation expenses, but they have achieved minimal compliance with little "ripple" effect beyond the proximate grievance.[1]

Inclusion and Overall School Success Are Connected

Effective teaching practices benefit all students. Similarly, effective school structures provide opportunities for collaboration, family–school relation-

---

[1]Hehir (2002) presented a somewhat contrary view, especially when plaintiffs join states as defendants. Sandler and Schoenbrod (2003), taking a broader view, challenge the benefits of court intervention.

ships, and a culture of belonging (Fisher, Sax, & Pumpian, 1999). As Henderson writes in Chapter 2, "[I]nclusive practices do not exist apart from the goal of increasing student achievement. Indeed, inclusive practices have been a key component in meeting and exceeding those goals" (p. 11).

COMMON FEATURES OF URBAN EDUCATIONAL REFORM AND INCLUSION

Overall, successful implementation of inclusive programs and school reform (especially in urban areas) share significant features. The goal is to prepare all students to contribute to and participate in a world of increasing interdependence and technological demands. A diverse and heterogeneous student population is the key resource for both urban educators and those engaged in inclusive schooling.

General educators and special educators face a common set of challenges. Seven factors characterize urban schools: 1) unsatisfactory academic achievement, 2) political conflicts, 3) staff shortages and inexperienced teaching staff, 4) low expectations and a lack of a demanding curricula, 5) lack of instructional coherence, 6) disproportionate numbers of students from low socioeconomic households and minority groups, and 7) high student mobility across schools (Snipes, Doolittle, & Herlihy, 2002). These factors also characterize special education programs.

The organizational and strategic approaches necessary to address these factors and to ensure the success of urban schools include the following: 1) a focus on student achievement and specific achievement goals; 2) the alignment of curricula with state standards; 3) the translation of standards into instructional practices; 4) the creation of accountability systems that hold district- and building-level leadership responsible for producing results; 5) a focus on the lowest performing schools; 6) the adoption or development of districtwide curricula and instructional practices (rather than leaving it up to each building to devise its own strategies); 7) support of these districtwide strategies at the central office through professional development and consistent implementation; and 8) the use of data-driven decision making and instruction, providing early and regular data that drive practice and allow for midcourse corrections (Snipes et al., 2002).

The approaches to changing urban schools apply to special education. The data from urban school renewal efforts and inclusive schooling initiatives suggest that whole school approaches are the answer. The next section focuses on the ways in which whole school approaches can be combined to benefit all students.

Table 11.1. Guiding questions for a school self-assessment

Question	Rationale for question
Why have students been referred for special education in the past year?	Referrals generally cluster in three groups: 1) failures in reading and mathematics achievement; 2) issues of student behavior; and 3) matters of student and family life. Referrals often cluster at particular grade levels, frequently at grade 2 or 3, when the curriculum becomes more complex and/or external testing begins. The purpose of the referral analysis is to determine which additional or alternative resources and programs could be established in general education to support students and enable them to remain and succeed in the general education classroom. By understanding the reasons for referral, the school planning group can develop new supports and services for all students.
Who is being referred for special education services, and where are their needs being met?	Too often, African American and Hispanic/Latino students are overrepresented in special education. Nationally, African American students make up 15% of the total student population, but they comprise 20% of those in special education. Within specific special education categories, particularly those that are most stigmatizing, there is an even greater disproportion (e.g., among African American students, 2.2% and 1.3% are labeled as "mentally retarded" or "emotionally disturbed," respectively, whereas only 0.8% and 0.7% of Caucasian students are so labeled) (American Youth Policy Forum, 2002). Students within these categories are often served in the most restrictive settings: separate classes or separate schools.[a] The number of students with special education needs served in general education classrooms or in separate special education classrooms—within the school or elsewhere—needs to be analyzed. By analyzing student demographics and placement information, the school planning group can address institutionalized racism and segregated education.
What is the design of the current special education program?	The school planning group should consider special education classroom personnel and out-of-classroom personnel as it explores the (re)deployment of staff to enable the school to provide needed support for students with disabilities in general education classrooms. The greater the number of personnel staffing separate programs, the greater the resources available to support students in inclusive environments.
Which practices and procedures in general education support or inhibit an inclusive school environment?	Frequently, school and district practices inhibit the development of a unitary system. The school planning group must review the following: student registration procedures, student rosters, procedures for ordering texts or other materials, assignment of evaluators and evaluations of pedagogic personnel, grade-level or department membership, teacher scheduling procedures, reporting lines, lunch room practices, school

transportation practices, length and timing of the school day, practices regarding extracurricular activities (e.g., participation requirements, provision of adaptations), and opportunities for parents to participate and play leadership roles in school organizations. The purpose of this review is to identify practices—whatever their origin or historic rationale—that, in the current period, are inconsistent with the conduct of a unitary system.

Which students presently served in more restrictive settings would benefit from special education services in the general education classroom with needed supplementary aids and services?	Consideration should be based on how an individual student could perform with needed supports in a differentiated classroom. The goal is not simply more seat time in a general education classroom. Rather, it is access to appropriate instructional materials and strategies to enable students with disabilities to meet the academic standards that states and their districts have established for all students. The school planning group should identify students who could immediately move into general education classrooms as well as develop goals and action plans for providing inclusive educational opportunities for all students.
What are the professional development needs of the staff? What is our capacity to provide professional development?	School staff represent an important resource for professional development. Professional development needs will vary by role as well as by prior training and experience. A needs assessment provides teachers the opportunity to identify their professional development requirements without fear of being labeled as incompetent. Some professional development needs will be common across some or all of the schools in the district or among all staff in a particular role. Although district-level professional development activities may be warranted, most professional development will be specific to individual school sites.

[a]For an extensive treatment of the causes, consequences, and strategies to overcome disproportionality, see Losen and Orfield (2002).

A WHOLE SCHOOL APPROACH

The term *whole school approach* is used in IDEA '97 to describe an approach designed to enhance the education of students with disabilities. The term captures the philosophy and practice required to implement a program of inclusive schooling successfully. Whereas special education is designed on a student-by-student basis, as represented in IEPs, the systemic goal is to transform whole districts into unified educational systems that offer special education as a service, not a place.

Between the student and the district is the school, the key building block for reform. The National Center on Educational Restructuring and Inclusion developed a five-step "whole school" planning and implementation process (see Gartner & Lipsky, 2002). Each component of this process is described next.

Establish a School Planning Group

All groups in the school should be represented in the planning process: general and special educators, classroom personnel at the various grade levels and for various subject areas, related services and other support personnel, administrators, and parents. As the changes involved will have consequence for the entire school community, this should not be a special education group. Although the principal does not have to be the group chair or participate in every meeting, it is essential that the school leader is active and supportive.

Conduct a School Self-Assessment

Once a school planning group has been established, the next step toward change requires gathering information about and understanding of the current state of affairs. Table 11.1 provides guiding questions that can be used in a self-assessment.

Develop the School Plan

The plan will provide the basis for the school to move forward in restructuring efforts. The planning group should not be hampered by paralysis of analysis or problem admiration. Several months provide sufficient time to conduct the school self-assessment and to develop a building plan to present to the school staff and parents. The plan should be specific and address the following:

- Students with special education needs who are to be served in general education programs
- Staff to serve students in the new design(s) (e.g., grade level, content area)
- Program model(s) to be used (e.g., full or part time)
- Organizational and scheduling changes, if necessary
- Professional development activities
- Process and methods to evaluate program outcomes
- Timetable for implementation

See the Action Planning Tool in Figure 11.1 for a method to gather this information.

Implement the School Plan

Although it is appropriate to phase in some components of the school plan, a protracted introductory period will neither gain momentum nor attract and sustain attention from building and/or district leadership. As the plan is implemented, the school planning group should provide multiple opportunities for communication among faculty, staff, students, administration, and families. Communication can occur in a number of ways, from brown-bag lunch meetings to student focus groups to family "town-hall" meetings. In this phase, the focus is on processes, not outcomes. The school planning group must monitor the implementation of the plan and be able to respond to any unforeseen circumstances or opportunities that arise.

Evaluate Outcomes and Revise the Plan

An outcome evaluation gives the school planning group an opportunity to address the outcomes for students (both with and without disabilities), the effects for staff, and organizational changes. Experience suggests that outcome evaluations should coincide with natural end points (e.g., semester break, end of the school year, end of a budget cycle). The following items can be reviewed and used for program enhancement or change:

- Student achievement based on established standards
- Number of students previously served in separate settings, within the school building or elsewhere, who are now being served in their home school and in general education classrooms
- Supplemental supports used, successful adaptations, and curricular and instructional approaches
- Enhanced skills of the staff regarding teacher efficacy, changes in organizational practices, (re)deployment of staff, changes in classroom organization, and instructional practices

Numerous models can be used to implement inclusive practices in a school (e.g., Whole Schooling—see Chapter 9). The particular design that a school adopts will vary depending on factors such as the school and district resources, the particular needs of the students, and the experience and skills of the general and special education teachers.

NCLB AND IDEA: A FEDERAL PERSPECTIVE

The No Child Left Behind (NCLB) Act of 2001 (PL 107-110) and IDEA '97, the successor to the Education for All Handicapped Children Act of

Targeted students	People responsible	Program model	Organizational and scheduling changes	Professional development	Evaluation	Timeline

Figure 11.1. Action Planning Tool.

1975 (PL 94-142), address the common issue of educational benefit for all students. The intersection between the two laws is expressed in the reference to NCLB on the first page of the report of the President's Commission on Excellence in Special Education (2002). The report foreshadowed many of the issues being addressed by Congress in developing legislation for the reauthorization of IDEA some time in 2003. Features of the draft legislation are 1) efforts to reduce paperwork; add a provision for early intervention services prior to special education, sometimes called "pre-referral" services; make clearer sanctions with regard to monitoring and enforcement; and make discipline requirements more explicit while maintaining the principle of no cessation of services and 2) several features concerning personnel, including developing personnel standards commensurate with those of NCLB, focusing changes on increasing the quality of personnel, and focusing grants to address the shortage of quality personnel. These proposed changes build on the 1997 amendments, rather than chart a major new direction in the law. Indeed, it may be said that the new direction is to be found in NCLB.

In many ways, NCLB and IDEA '97 are congruent. Both laws emphasize high standards for all students. Whereas NCLB focuses on reading and math, IDEA addresses all subjects. Both laws also require testing of students, with needed modifications[2] so that few are excluded. The results are to be published as part of the school/district's report to parents and to the public. NCLB requires "adequate yearly progress" (AYP) for the school as a whole and for various subgroups, including students with disabilities. Failure to achieve AYP results in a cascade of increasingly onerous sanctions.[3] Likewise, IDEA '97 requires that state plans establish performance goals that address students' progress in achieving general education standards and address the need to reduce dropout rates.[4] However, IDEA does not contain sanctions for failure to achieve these goals.

Teacher qualifications have also been addressed in these laws. IDEA imposes requirements on states for a comprehensive system of personnel development (addressing instructional and support personnel). NCLB requires that all teachers, including those in special education, be "highly qualified" by the end of the 2005–2006 school year. NCLB also requires that all paraprofessionals meet new enhanced standards. The definition of "highly qualified" remains controversial, as do the standards for paraprofessionals.

Furthermore, both laws call for "best practices." IDEA requires that states and local districts acquire and disseminate the results of educational research and adopt promising educational practices. NCLB requires reading and math programs to be "scientifically research-based." What constitutes "best practices" and "scientifically research-based" has generated significant debate.

Finally, both laws encourage flexibility in the use of funds to promote a "whole school" approach. IDEA authorizes the use of "special education"

---

[2]This is explicit in IDEA. According to NCLB, only test results that provide a valid measure of a student's progress are acceptable (i.e., when modifications are provided to ensure that the test measures the student's knowledge and that skills are not masked by the disability).

[3]After 2 consecutive years of failure to demonstrate AYP, either for the school as a whole or for the designated subgroups, students are afforded the opportunity to transfer to another school in the district with transportation provided. After 3 years, students are to have access to "supplementary instructional services" (e.g., tutoring, after-school or summer programs). After 4 years, districts are to undertake "corrective action" plans (e.g., replace staff, adopt new curricula). After 5 years, the school is to be "restructured" (e.g., state takeover, privatization, conversion to a charter school, replacement of all staff).

[4]The former director of the U.S. Department of Education's Office of Special Education Programs affirmed that NCLB reinforces the outcomes-focus of IDEA '97: "[F]ollowing the recently enacted No Child Left Behind Act of 2001, there is no question that students with disabilities must be included in district and state accountability systems" (Hehir, 2002, p. 230).

Table 11.2. Comparison of key features of the Individuals with Disabilities Education Act (IDEA) and the No Child Left Behind Act of 2001 (NCLB)

Feature	Addressed by IDEA	Addressed by NCLB
High expectations and standards	Yes	Yes
Testing for all (with needed modifications) per the standards	Yes	Yes
Progress expected for all	Yes	Yes
Disaggregation of data for the following:		
Outcomes (per major ethnic/racial groups, gender, disability, English language learners)	Yes	Yes
Referral, certification, placement, discipline	Yes	Yes
Individualized education program (IEP) forms the basis of a high quality program prescription	Yes	No
Quality personnel	Yes	Yes
"Best practices"	Yes	Yes
Staff development	Yes	Yes
Flexibility in use of funds	Yes	Yes

funds for services to students without disabilities and professional development activities for general education teachers who serve students with disabilities. NCLB allows school districts to transfer funds among various federal programs (excluding IDEA). Similar flexibility is afforded to state education agencies. (For a detailed analysis of the implications of NCLB for special education, see *No Child Left Behind Act of 2001: Implications for Special Education Policy and Practice*, 2002.) Table 11.2 compares key aspects of IDEA and NCLB.

CONCLUSION

A decade and a half after the passage of the Education for All Handicapped Children Act of 1975, Gilhool described the law's promise for each child with a disability as "an education reasonably calculated to yield real educational benefits" and "the adoption of promising practices and materials" (1989, p. 252). He proposed extending these benefits to all children, in what he called "The Effective Education Act of 1990." In many ways, NCLB is such an act. It focuses on outcomes (what the Education for All Handicapped Children Act called "educational benefits"), which are to be achieved in all schools and for all students; it also requires practices that are "research based" (what the Education for All Handicapped Children Act called "promising practices and materials"), which are to be carried out by teachers who are "highly qualified."

Thus, we have come full circle. The strategies and approaches necessary for the achievement of inclusive schooling are congruent with overall school improvement for students in general while incorporating the whole school approaches encouraged by IDEA '97. A giant step toward the achievement of inclusive education is for school systems to make achievement for all students integral to their school restructuring designs. As seen in many chapters in this book, schools can achieve inclusion and high standards for all students. It need not be one or the other, a zero-sum game.

REFERENCES

American Youth Policy Forum & Center on Education Policy. (2002). *Twenty-five years of educating children with disabilities: The good news and the work ahead.* Washington, DC: Authors.

Center for Applied Special Technology (CAST). (2001). *Universal design for learning.* Peabody, MA: Author.

Center for Universal Design. (1997). *What is universal design?* Raleigh: Center for Universal Design, North Carolina State University.

Chanda Smith v. Los Angeles Unified School District, No.93-7044-LEW (GHKX) (C.D. Cal. 1996).

Cole, S., Horvath, B., Chapman, C., Deschenes, C., Ebeling, D.G., & Sprague, J. (2000). *Adapting curriculum and instruction in the inclusive classroom: A teacher's desk reference* (2nd ed.). Bloomington, IN: The Center for School and Community Integration, Institute for the Study of Developmental Disabilities.

Corey H. v. Board of Education of the City of Chicago, et al. Case No. 92 C 3409.

DeBoer, A., & Fister, S. (1995). *Working together: Tools for collaborative teaching.* Longmont, CO: Sopris West.

Edmonds, R. (1982). Programs of school improvement: An overview. *Educational Leadership, 40*(3), 4–11.

Education for All Handicapped Children Act of 1975, PL 94-142, 20 U.S.C. §§ 1400 *et seq.*

Fisher, D., Grove, K.A., & Sax, C. (2000). The resilience of changes promoting inclusiveness in an urban elementary school. *Elementary School Journal, 100,* 213–227.

Fisher, D., Sax, C., & Pumpian, I. (1999). *Inclusive high schools: Learning from contemporary classrooms.* Baltimore: Paul H. Brookes Publishing Co.

Friend, M. (2001). *Successful co-teaching: Improving the success of your inclusive program.* Bellevue, WA: Bureau of Education and Research.

Gartner, A. & Lipsky, D.K. (2002). *Inclusion: A service, not a place. A whole school approach.* Port Chester, NY: National Professional Resources.

Gilhool, T.K. (1989). The right to an effective education: From *Brown* to PL 94-142 and beyond. In D.K. Lipsky & A. Gartner (Eds.), *Beyond separate education: Quality education for all* (pp. 243–253). Baltimore: Paul H. Brookes Publishing Co.

Guba, E.G., & Lincoln, Y.S. (1989). *Fourth generation evaluation.* Newbury Park, CA: Sage.

Hehir, T. (2002). IDEA and disproportionality: Federal enforcement, effective advocacy, and strategies for change. In D.L. Losen & G. Orfield (Eds.), *Racial inequity in special education* (pp. 219–238). Cambridge, MA: Harvard Education Press.

Hitchcock, C., Meyer, A., Rose, D., & Jackson, R. (2002). Providing new access to the general curriculum: Universal design for learning. *Teaching Exceptional Children, 35*(2), 8–11.

Individuals with Disabilities Education Act (IDEA) Amendments of 1997, PL 105-17, 20 U.S.C. §§ 1400 *et seq.*

Individuals with Disabilities Education Act (IDEA) of 1990, PL 101-476, 20 U.S.C. §§ 1400 *et seq.*

Jorgensen, C.M. (1998). *Restructuring high schools for all students: Taking inclusion to the next level.* Baltimore: Paul H. Brookes Publishing Co.

Jose P. v. Ambach, No. 79 Civ. 270 (E.D.N.Y. January 5, 1982).

Lipsky, D.K. & Gartner, A. (1997). *Inclusion and school reform: Transforming America's classrooms.* Baltimore: Paul H. Brookes Publishing Co.

Losen, D.J., & Orfield, G. (2002). *Racial inequity in special education.* Cambridge, MA: Harvard Education Press.

National Council on Disability. (1996). *Achieving independence: The challenge for the 21st century. A decade of progress in disability: Setting an agenda for the future.* Washington, DC: Author.

No Child Left Behind Act of 2001, PL 107-110, 115 Stat. 1425, 20 U.S.C. §§ 6301 *et seq.*

No Child Left Behind Act of 2001: Implications for special education policy and practice. (2002, September). Arlington, VA: Council for Exceptional Children.

President's Commission on Excellence in Special Education. (2002). *A new era: Revitalizing special education for children and their families.* Washington, DC: U.S. Department of Education.

Sandler, R., & Schoenbrod, D. (2003). *Democracy by decree: What happens when courts run government.* New Haven, CT: Yale University Press.

Snell, M.E., & Janney, R. (2000). *Teachers' guides to inclusive practices: Collaborative teaming.* Baltimore: Paul H. Brookes Publishing Co.

Snipes, J., Doolittle, F., & Herlihy, C. (2002). *Foundations for success: Case studies of how urban school systems improve student achievement.* New York: Manpower Development Research Corporation for the Council of Great City Schools.

Tomlinson, C.A. (1999). *The differentiated classroom: Responding to the needs of all learners.* Alexandria, VA: Association for Supervision and Curriculum Development.

Tomlinson, C.A. (2000). Reconcilable differences? Standards-based teaching and differentiation. *Educational Leadership, 58*(1), 6–11.

Villa, R.A., & Thousand, J.S. (Eds.). (2000). *Restructuring for caring and effective education: Piecing the puzzle together* (2nd ed.). Baltimore: Paul H. Brookes Publishing Co.

Wagner, M. Blackorby, J., Cameo, R., & Newman, L. (1993). *What makes a difference? Influence on post-school outcomes of youth with disabilities.* (Third Comprehensive Report from the National Longitudinal Transition Study of Special Education Students). Washington, DC: U.S. Department of Education.

Index

Page references followed by *t* or *f* indicate tables or figures, respectively.